Heresy and Criticism

Also by Robert M. Grant

Jesus After the Gospels: The Christ of the Second Century
Greek Apologists of the Second Century
Gods and the One God (Library of Early Christianity)

Heresy and Criticism

The Search for Authenticity in Early Christian Literature

Robert M. Grant

Westminster/John Knox Press
Louisville, Kentucky

Book design by Drew Stevens

First edition

This book is printed on acid-free paper that meets the American National Standards Institute Z39.48 standard. ∞

BS
500
.G73
1993

Published by Westminster/John Knox Press
Louisville, Kentucky

PRINTED IN THE UNITED STATES OF AMERICA
9 8 7 6 5 4 3 2 1

Library of Congress Cataloging-in-Publication Data

Grant, Robert McQueen, 1917–
   Heresy and criticism : the search for authenticity in early
Christian literature / Robert M. Grant. — 1st ed.
         p.   cm.
   Includes bibliographical references and index.
   ISBN 0-664-21971-3 (hard : alk. paper)

   1. Bible—Criticism, interpretation, etc.—History—Early church,
ca. 30–600.   2. Classical literature—History and criticism.
3. Heresies, Christian—History—Early church, ca. 30–600.
I. Title.
BS500.G73 1993
273'.1—dc20   92-20017

Contents

Foreword

MUCH OF my writing over the last fifty years has dealt with the correlation of early Christianity with the classical culture (especially Greek) in which it arose. This book is to show that the literary criticism derived from the Hellenistic schools was used first by innovative Christian heretics, then by more famous orthodox leaders. I should express once more my gratitude to the John Simon Guggenheim Memorial Foundation for repeated assistance, to the University of Chicago, and especially to my friend Bernard McGinn.

Preface

THE FIRST extant Christian writings consist of some letters of the apostle Paul. Later on, other letters were preserved and collections of "Gospels" were formed. Church leaders had to develop ideas about who wrote what, especially since an authoritative list was taking shape. At first, it appears, the fact of tradition was expected to guarantee the authenticity of texts or documents, but as the problem of heresy came up, questions about "apostolic" origin and content were raised. Since early Christians did not live in splendid isolation, both heretics and orthodox inevitably employed the Greek literary-critical methods used in dealing with epic and other poetry, and with religious literature, especially in Orphic circles. Authenticity was a matter of concern for students of (for example) Homer, Hesiod, the Orphic literature, and the works of such philosophers as Plato and Aristotle.

The first witness to literary criticism in early Christianity was the heretic Marcion, famous at Rome for his *Antitheses*, contradictions between the Old Testament and the Gospel; his *Gospel*, apparently an edited version of Luke; and his *Apostle*, a collection of ten edited epistles by Paul. It is likely that he edited Luke as he edited Paul and that he did not possess an earlier Gospel, whether authentic or not.

Marcion's presentation of a supposedly "authentic" text was not, of course, the only reinterpretation. Others took Christian texts more or less as they stood and drastically reinterpreted them in the light of their own theologies. Also at Rome, the Valentinian Gnostic Ptolemaeus com-

posed an introductory *Letter to Flora* that looked rational enough to win
Adolf Harnack's admiration but that in fact conceals a complete Gnostic
system, as his other New Testament exegesis shows.

Around the same time, the great physician and author Galen flourished at Rome. He had been trained not only in medicine and philosophy
but also in literary criticism, which proved invaluable to him as he prepared commentaries on the literature traditionally ascribed to Hippocrates. The Hippocratic collection resembled the New Testament
books (with apocryphal additions) in circulation before a canon crystallized. Like the Christians, Galen was searching for authentic writings.
He studied manuscript variants and traditional opinions, and relied on
his own notion of contradictions. He was also guided by his conviction
that he practiced what Hippocrates had preached. He finally wrote commentaries on only fifteen "genuine" treatises. In his medical writings,
Galen criticized the arbitrariness of the Christians' God, while in philosophical writings he explained the use of logic. At Rome some
Adoptionist Christian heretics, said to have revered Galen, argued that
Jesus had been human, not divine, and used syllogisms like Galen's to
prove their point. They also followed him by engaging in textual criticism of sorts.

Also at Rome an ex-disciple of Marcion named Apelles criticized the
Genesis story about the Creator-God as illogical and wrote many books
of *Syllogisms* to prove the point. The logic of the syllogisms sometimes
needs to be restored, but it was evidently difficult to refute them.

By the end of the second century, exegetes who were more orthodox
counterattacked such heretics, using similar criteria of genuineness and
not hesitating to reject not only heretical books but also New Testament
books of doubtful authenticity. The leading bishops and scholars from
the second century through the fourth (notably Origen, Dionysius of
Alexandria, and Jerome) showed that literary criticism could be, and
was, employed for the vigorous defense of Christian positions.

1

Authenticity and Heresy
in Early Christianity

THE CHRISTIAN tradition began with what the apostle Paul called "the gospel," reports of the words and deeds of Jesus. Traditions about what Jesus had said and done surfaced within twenty years in several letters from the apostle Paul to Gentile communities, with specific references to Jesus' teaching about marriage and remarriage, his actions and words at his last supper with the disciples, his resurrection, and his impending return from heaven.[1] Obviously addition and alteration (not to mention subtraction) could take place, and sayings were transmitted in varying forms. Paul wrote that "if anyone thinks that he is a prophet, or a spiritual, he should acknowledge that what I am writing to you is a command of the Lord" (1 Cor. 14:37, RSV). He himself was quite capable of expressing the Lord's mind. "I think that I have the Spirit of God" (7:40, RSV). Some scholars have claimed that, like Paul, early Christian prophets created sayings of Jesus, but as David Aune notes, "The methodology for clearly and convincingly detecting such a process has not yet been formulated."[2] Some oracles by such prophets may have come into the synoptic tradition, but it cannot be proved that prophets freely composed in this way.

Paul claimed that the gospel he preached was true because it had taught him "through a revelation of Jesus Christ" (Gal. 1:11–12, RSV). He liked to call it "the gospel of Christ" or, indeed, "the gospel of God."

Some of his Galatian converts deserted him and turned to "a different gospel," but he insisted they had no independent gospel but merely a perversion of the true one (Gal. 1:6). Similarly he denounces some Corinthians for their lapses: "If anyone comes and preaches another Jesus than the one we preached, . . . or if you accept a different gospel from the one you accepted, you submit to it readily enough" (2 Cor. 11:4, RSV). Windisch complained that we obtain no clear picture of his opponents' preaching.[3] It is more important to recognize that Paul was claiming to possess the only true way of viewing the tradition.

All our Gospels contain anthologies of what Jesus taught, but they have been put together from various points of view. Two endings to the Gospel of John make the point: "Jesus did many other signs . . . not written in this book" (20:30, RSV), and "there are many other things which Jesus did; were every one of them to be written, I suppose that the world itself could not contain the books that would be written" (21:25, RSV). The first verse cited goes on to a theological explanation that "these are written that you may believe that Jesus is the Christ, the Son of God . . . ," while the second leads to a more practical consideration about the sheer volume of the traditions. Only a "historian" like Luke could claim to record "all that Jesus began to do and teach" (Acts 1:1, RSV).

As one Christian generation succeeded another, the small groups that had been personally acquainted with Jesus disappeared, and what had been transmitted orally was finally crystallized in writing. The gospel was expressed in the Gospels. Difficult questions arose when people asked which books were Christian, who had written them, and how early they were. None of the evangelists named himself. The book later ascribed to Mark begins with the words, "The beginning of the gospel of Jesus Christ, the Son of God" (RSV). This may imply that the book was "the Gospel," but its author is not named. What we call the Gospel according to Matthew begins thus: "The book of the genealogy of Jesus Christ, the son of David, the son of Abraham" (RSV), but these words apply only to the first seventeen verses of the book. The anonymous author who addressed Theophilus begins his first volume by referring to his association with eyewitnesses, to his own research, and to his "orderly account" (Luke 1:1–4, RSV). He may not have known that the Gospel-book ascribed to Mark, his principal source, was not from an eyewitness.

At the beginning of his second volume, which deals with the church in Jerusalem and some missions of Paul, he again addresses Theophilus and refers back to his first preface. Presumably his story is complete when he writes that Paul preached and taught "without hindrance" (Acts 28:31, NRSV). At the end of his book John lays emphasis on his own selectivity, as we have already noted. The appendix also testifies to the Gospel itself, for the disciple who bears witness has written the book, "and we" (unidentified) "know that his testimony is true" (21:24, RSV). Such anonymity made it difficult to defend these particular books against others, and "traditions" soon grew up, and/or were recorded, about authorship.[4]

The earliest extant Christian books are not Gospels, however, but the genuine letters of Paul, presumably including 1 Thessalonians, 1 and 2 Corinthians, Galatians, Romans, Philippians, and Philemon; possibly but not certainly, 2 Thessalonians, Colossians, and Ephesians. The apostle did not write the Pastoral Epistles to Timothy and Titus, any more than the anonymous letter to the Hebrews, which ancient literary critics criticized. As the New Testament took shape, however, all fourteen epistles came to be ascribed to Paul, and half as many more supposedly were written by four other apostles. The latter group of "catholic" or "general" epistles includes one from James, two from Peter, three from John (one anonymous, two from "the elder"), and one from Jude "the brother of James." Almost all of Jude is reflected in 2 Peter, which also refers to 1 Peter and to a collection of Pauline letters regarded as "scripture."[5]

Scribes and coauthors are mentioned in several letters. "I Tertius, the writer of this letter, greet you" (Rom. 16:22, RSV). First Corinthians comes not only from Paul but also from "our brother Sosthenes" (1 Cor. 1:1), though Paul writes a greeting with his own hand at the end of the letter (1 Cor. 16:21; cf. Col. 4:18).[6] Second Corinthians, Philippians, Colossians, and Philemon come from Paul and Timothy; 1 and 2 Thessalonians from Paul, Silvanus, and Timothy. First Peter ends with the statement that "By Silvanus, a faithful brother as I regard him, I have written briefly to you" (5:12, RSV). Such statements make it possible that the lieutenants contributed to the ideas found in the letters, just as the generation after Hippocrates was thought to have produced some of the works ascribed to him (chapter 5).

Disagreements, to be sure, had arisen early. Paul was aware that there were divisions among the Corinthians, and he tried to make the best of the situation. "There must be factions (*haireseis*) among you in order that those who are genuine among you may be recognized" (1 Cor. 11:19, RSV). At the beginning of the Christian era, the Greek word *hairesis* did not mean "heresy" but meant no more than "sect" or "school" of philosophy or medicine.[7] When Josephus attempted to present Judaism to Greek readers, he used the term for a sect or party, specifically that of the Sadducees or the Pharisees. The usage of Josephus is what we find in the book of Acts.[8] His *hairesis*, like Luke's or Paul's, is not "heresy" because there is no sense that "heretics" are excluded from the larger group because of their failure to adhere to all its teachings. The Christian bishop Ignatius, on the other hand, assures the Ephesian Christians that they enjoy "good order in God, for all live in accordance with truth and no heresy dwells in you," and he warns the Trallians to abstain from "strange food, which is heresy"—though he does not clearly define what heresy is.[9]

The authenticity of documents had become a matter of practical concern before the first century was over. Paul himself, or an imitator, warned against letters purporting to come from him (2 Thess. 2:2). The Revelation of John warns copyists against interpolations and deletions. "I warn everyone who hears the words of the prophecy of this book: if any one adds to them, God will add to him the plagues described in this book, and if any one takes away from the words of the book of this prophecy, God will take away his share in the tree of life and in the holy city, which are described in this book" (Rev. 22:18–19, RSV). Well into the second century, the author of Second Peter speaks of "we" who are eyewitnesses of Jesus' transfiguration, not followers of myths (1:16–18), claims that this is his second letter (3:1), and speaks of his "beloved brother Paul" and a collection of "all his letters," which presumably agree with 1 and 2 Peter. His opponents "twisted" difficult Pauline passages and "the other scriptures" (3:15–16). Here heretics, destined for a fiery end, are refuted by an incipient canon of scripture including Paul's letters as well as by tradition derived from eyewitnesses.

Inspired Christian and Gnostic Authors

Some Christian authors regarded their own works—and themselves—as "inspired." Such claims do not appear in the New Testament except by inference in the "apostolic decree" of Acts 15:28 (RSV): "It seemed good to the Holy Spirit and to us." However, the "apostolic fathers"—Clement, Ignatius, Barnabas, and Hermas—soon refer to their own inspiration.[10] Such a claim was also made in less orthodox circles. The Christian Gnostic Valentinus asserted that the Logos appeared to him in the form of a child, while Christ came to his disciple Marcus, as well as to the Montanist prophet Priscilla, as a woman.[11] Apelles (chapter 6) had a "Beloved" whose visions inspired his biblical or theological research. Such ideas did not win universal acceptance.

Gnostic Traditions and Books

Gnostics also offered some information about how their tradition had been handed down. The followers of Basilides claimed that he had been taught by a certain Glaucias, while Valentinus had heard Theudas, a disciple of the apostle Paul. The Naassenes claimed that James, the Lord's brother, had delivered their secret traditions to a certain Mariamme.[12] In his *Outlines* the relatively orthodox Clement describes the transmission of secret knowledge (*gnosis*) at Jerusalem. "After the resurrection the Lord delivered the knowledge to James the Just and John and Peter, these gave it to the other apostles and the other apostles to the Seventy, one of whom was Barnabas." This statement recalls the beginning of the Nag Hammadi *Apocryphon of James*: "You asked that I send you a secret book which was revealed to me and Peter by the Lord," or, for that matter, the beginning of the *Gospel of Thomas*: "These are the secret sayings which the living Jesus spoke and which Didymus Judas Thomas wrote down." Obviously it was next to impossible to confirm or refute such claims. They recall the undemonstrable claim of the Gnostic teacher Ptolemaeus to stand in an apostolic succession (chapter 4). As for Clement, we recall that he portrayed an inner circle among the disciples of Jesus, consisting of the future recipients of revelation: Peter, James,

and John. Clement adds the name of Paul and treats all of them as trans-
mitters of tradition to his own teachers.[13] Irenaeus and others took a different line, farther from Gnosticism, when they argued that the church's
successions were publicly known, while a secret succession could not be
substantiated.

Gnostic Use of Christian Literature

Followers of the Gnostic Simon Magus apparently reached Rome before
the end of the first century, though their early history is lost in legend.
According to Irenaeus, these followers claimed that "men are saved by
his grace, not by just works." Evidently they borrowed the expression
from the Epistle to the Ephesians (2:8–9), for there we read that "by
grace you have been saved through faith; and this is not your own doing,
it is the gift of God—not because of works, lest any one should boast."
Certainly Ephesians does not rely on the Simonians, nor is there some
common source, for the passage summarizes Paul's gospel. Evidently,
then, these followers of Simon had some collection of Pauline letters and
perhaps Gospels as well.

Other Gnostics also foisted their own interpretations on Christian
books. At Alexandria the Gnostic Basilides was renowned as an exegete.
A passage from "the 13th book" interprets "the parable of the rich and
poor" (Luke 16:19–31) as referring to a nature without root and place
(presumably the rich man). Clement cites a passage on the sufferings of
martyrs from "the 23rd book of his *Exegetics*." Irenaeus reports
Basilides' opinion that Christ did not suffer on the cross. Instead, Simon
of Cyrene was impressed to carry his cross for him and because of ignorance and error was crucified. Jesus exchanged forms with Simon and
stood by, deriding his opponents. Basilides' account of the crucified
Simon seems based on a severely literal interpretation of Mark 15:21–34,
which, if "twisted," could suggest that Jesus was not crucified, while the
notion that he was derisive seems built on Psalm 2 with its account of
hostile rulers derided by the Lord. On these points the Christian exegete
could only deny the truth of the Gnostic interpretation. When Basilides
went on to cite apocryphal prophets named Bar Kabbas and Bar Koph,
however, the Greek-speaking orthodox could reject revealers with such
barbarian names. They also noted that his son Isidore wrote exegetical

discussions of the prophet Parchor (a variant form of Bar Koph?) while claiming that ancient Greeks had used the prophecy of Cham (Ham, the son of Noah).[14]

Literary heresies tended to flourish in the intellectual environment of Rome, where the dualist Marcion arrived about 137 with an expurgated Gospel and revised Pauline epistles and was able to remain within the church until he was excommunicated seven years later, perhaps by a college of elders.[15] Rome was the setting for his trilogy *Antitheses-Gospel-Apostle* (chapter 3), as well as the antiorthodox syllogisms of the Adoptionists (chapter 5) and Apelles (chapter 6). Valentinus also arrived in the time of Hyginus, flourished under Pius, and finished under Anicetus. His disciples Ptolemaeus (chapter 4) and Heracleon, both Gospel exegetes, also taught in Rome. According to Tertullian, Valentinus hoped to become bishop there; Epiphanius says the same of Marcion.[16] Conceivably they could have shared the hope, though it is hard to imagine either teacher as seeking the episcopate around 155, when the aged Polycarp of Smyrna defended apostolic tradition at Rome for Anicetus and converted many Valentinians and Marcionites.[17] In Anicetus's time, however, a woman named Marcellina arrived at Rome with the teachings ascribed to Carpocrates and "exterminated many" Christians. She and her converts possessed a supposedly contemporary portrait of Jesus and were accustomed to put crowns not only on his image but also on those of Pythagoras, Plato, and Aristotle.[18] Evidently they thought they belonged to the Greek philosophical tradition.

Around 180 Irenaeus of Lyons, who had come to Gaul from Rome, wrote his *Detection and Overthrow of Gnosis Falsely So-Called*, chiefly against the Valentinian teachers Ptolemaeus and Marcus. He tells us that heretical exegetes were breaking up a mosaic portrait of a king and rearranging the stones to depict a dog or fox. Second Peter had already objected that "ignorant and unstable" Christians were "twisting" certain passages in Paul's letters and the other scriptures. Others—to extend Irenaeus's metaphor—simply threw the old mosaic away and introduced new mosaics of their own. In any event the Gnostics employed current methods of literary criticism in their venture, and ultimately more orthodox authors followed them. Heresy and biblical criticism were associated before orthodoxy joined hands with criticism too.[19] The heterodox often—

raised questions about the text, the authorship, and the meaning of biblical books because they wanted to get rid of unattractive doctrines. The
problems they raised made it necessary for churches to create lists of the
books accepted by the churches. Such lists very gradually turned into
canons, or authoritative lists, of the books generally accepted. As late as
the fourth century the church historian Eusebius was still trying to work
out the New Testament canon for himself.[20] With so little fixity, it was
inevitable that problems arose over the authenticity of texts (and translations) and difficulties in interpretation.

What of contradictions or, as Marcion called them, "antitheses"? In
Irenaeus's view the Bible was consistent. The scriptures are perfect
because they were spoken by the Logos of God and the Spirit, and the
apostles were so completely inspired that "they possessed perfect knowledge." He explains some differences on the ground that both the Law and
the new covenant were adapted to their own times and adjusted to human
weakness.[21] Marcion insisted on contradictions in order to stress the nov-
elty of the Christian message.

Irenaeus's contemporary, Claudius Apollinaris of Hierapolis in
Phrygia, faced contemporaries who claimed that Matthew, if not the other
evangelists, believed "the Lord ate the lamb on the fourteenth day [of
Nisan] with his disciples but suffered on the great day of unleavened
bread."[22] It is hard to see how they could make this statement, for
Matthew 26:17 (RSV), explicitly says that Jesus ate the Passover, if not
the lamb, on "the first day of Unleavened Bread."

Evidently Apollinaris assumed that the Gospels were completely consistent. These second-century writers thus shared with Origen the view
that "none of the evangelists made a mistake or spoke falsely" (see
chapter 7).

Christian Traditionalism

Christians obviously needed to circulate information about the origins of
their literature so that they could exclude alien books, such as "apocryphal" gospels, epistles, acts, and apocalypses, from their collections.
Late in the first century or early in the second, Papias of Hierapolis in
Phrygia took an important step in this regard. In his widely read *Exegesis
of the Dominical Oracles*, he discussed his memories about traditions and

even went back to Mark's memories of what Peter taught. Papias considered himself a literary historian, not a literary critic, for he began the *Exegesis* with a rhetorical treatment about traditions. First he made a positive statement about the tradition from the elders. "Whatever I learned well from the *Elders* [all italics added] and remember well, I shall not hesitate to set down for you with the interpretations, confirming their *Truth*." Then he speaks negatively about rival traditions. "For I did not, like the many, delight in those who say much but in those who teach the *Truth*" [noting a contrast with the content of the authentic tradition], nor in those who mention outside commandments, but in those who mention the [inside] commandments given by the Lord to faith, and derived from the *Truth* itself." Thus he continues to contrast his own true tradition with the false tradition of others, before turning to his personal narrative about collecting oral tradition. "If anyone ever came [to Hierapolis] who had followed the *Elders*, I asked about the words of the *Elders*—what Andrew or Peter said; or what Philip, or what Thomas or James, or what John or Matthew, or any other of the Lord's *Disciples*, or what Aristion and the *Elder* John, the Lord's *Disciples*, were saying." Finally he contrasts useless books with the authentic and living tradition. "For I did not suppose that what came from books would help me as much as what was from a living and enduring voice."[23]

In spite of his rhetorically balanced phrases, Papias really tells us nothing about his sources and their value. To judge from the eschatological traditions he said he heard from the "elders who saw John, the Lord's disciple,"[24] he was extremely uncritical and simply recorded tradition, whatever it might be. His "information" would be recognized as useful much later, not in controversy with Gnostics.

It is true that he knew an "elder" (the one already mentioned?) who guided him in matters of literary criticism and gave him information about the Gospels of Mark and Matthew. According to Papias, Mark translated from Peter's teaching (perhaps the elder knew 1 Peter 5:13, with its reference to Mark as Peter's "son"[25]) but apparently got the order of Jesus' sayings and actions wrong when he wrote from memory. He presented Peter's teaching accurately but did not arrange the "dominical oracles" in orderly fashion (*taxei*). He intended not to leave anything out or to put anything in that was false. Matthew "made an ordered arrangement (*synetaxatō*) of the oracles in the Hebrew language and each person translated as he was able." As Schoedel puts it, "what Mark lacks, Matthew has."[26] This does not tell much about either Mark or Matthew, though literary critics raised the question of "order" in regard to some works ascribed to "Hippocrates."[27]

Papias's information from elders is open to considerable doubt, for he relates a vivid legend about the death of Judas and reports some words of Jesus about the fantastic productivity of vines and plants in the age to come. Papias explicitly claimed he had received these words from elders who had seen "John the Lord's disciple."[28] For Papias, as for this John, Jesus was a teacher of Jewish apocalyptic eschatology, much closer to the John who wrote the Apocalypse than to the author of the Fourth Gospel.

Justin on Heresies and Christian Literature

A clearer analysis of the tradition was given by the apologist Justin, acquainted with the history of the Middle Platonic schools from which he acquired many of his terms. According to his own account in the *First Apology,* he composed a *Compend Against All the Heresies That Have Existed*, in which he certainly discussed the heresies of Simon and Menander of Samaria and Marcion from Pontus. (He himself had come to Rome from Samaria via Ephesus.) Marcion, his contemporary at Rome, denied not only the God who made everything heavenly and earthly but also his Son, the Christ foretold by the prophets.[29] In the later *Dialogue with Trypho*, Justin referred to other heresies as well: the Marcianites (or Marcionites), the Valentinians, the Basilidians, and the Satornilians.[30] Presumably he discussed all these when he wrote against heresies. His own standpoint was clearly summed up in the adjective *orthognōmon*, "right thinking," used of himself and the others who maintained, against Gnostic teachers, that there would be a resurrection of the flesh and a millennium in a rebuilt, beautified, and enlarged Jerusalem.[31] In other words, for Justin the ultimate test of orthodoxy is Jewish prophecy, at least at this point. His "tradition" is like that of Papias. Given the presence of Christian credal formulas in his writings, it is obviously not the only test, but it remains important.

Justin was also the first orthodox writer who discussed literary questions, though his answers were not the kind the heretics would find satisfactory. He classified the church's Gospels as *apomnēmoneumata* or "memoirs" of the apostles,[32] a term essentially based on the tradition about how Mark "recalled" or "recorded" Peter's teaching about the words and deeds of Jesus. In addition, he had in mind the literary model of Xenophon's supposedly trustworthy *Memoirs of Socrates*,[33] even though in style and content these are nothing like the Gospels. A title precisely equivalent to Xenophon's would be *Memoirs of* (i.e., about) *Jesus*, not "of the apostles." In Justin's opinion "the memoirs were composed by his [Jesus'] apostles and those who followed them." Perhaps, as E. J. Goodspeed supposed, he was pointing to Matthew and John as apostles, Mark and Luke as followers of apostles,[34] though this is not quite certain. A little farther on in the *Dialogue*, however, Justin stated that two verses from the Gospel of Mark were written by "Peter, one of the apostles, in his *Memoirs*."[35] Like Papias, he must have viewed Peter as Mark's informant.

Traditional information like this was exactly what heretics rejected. Like what Papias provided, it did not come up to the standards set by Hellenistic scholarship and had little more value than hearsay. It was essentially uncritical, while the heretics wanted literary criticism to accompany their critical theologies. While Justin may have known our four Gospels, in controversy he usually used harmonized texts, perhaps in opposition to Marcion,[36] and transposed what Jesus had said eschatologically into antiheretical material. Nevertheless, as Le Boulluec points out, he was quite unable to deal with Marcion's radical criticism of New Testament books. "He remains under the influence of an archaic conception of scripture and of an image of the gospel still very close to that of the apostolic age; this keeps him from perceiving the uniqueness of Marcion's enterprise."[37] The Gnostics were not convinced by his discussions, but his harmonized text paved the way for his disciple Tatian to compose a harmony of the four Gospels, entitled *Diatessaron*.[38]

In addition, in his *Dialogue* he discussed what he imagined were Jewish deletions from the authentic text of the Septuagint, which once had contained very explicit predictions about Christ. He urged that Jewish authorities had deleted mention of the paschal lamb as savior and refuge from 1 Esdras, while from Jeremiah 11:19 they had taken away "I am led as a lamb to the slaughter; they have plotted against me." Justin admitted that in some synagogue copies the words were still preserved, as indeed they are in the Hebrew Bible. In addition, a statement about the Lord's preaching in Hades had been deleted. In his view Psalm 96(97):1 "originally" read "The Lord reigns—from the tree," i.e., the cross. Justin may well have discussed other texts, but the single manuscript of the *Dialogue* has a lacuna just here and the subject changes. He took these texts from a Christian book of "testimonies."[39]

Justin also dealt with the roles of the speakers in the Old Testament. Sometimes the prophetic books simply make predictions ("the law will come forth from Zion and the word of the Lord from Jerusalem"); sometimes they make declarations in the person of God the Master of all ("Israel did not know me"); sometimes they speak in the person of Christ ("I stretched out my hands upon a disobedient people"); and sometimes as from the people replying to the Lord or his Father, for example in Psalm 21 (22).[40]

The classification is aimed at Jewish exegetes, but obviously it could also be used against Gnostics who found Sophia or Achamoth speaking in the scriptures (see chapter 4). In addition, Justin's insistence on the one prophetic Spirit excludes any Gnostic notion that various planetary deities had inspired various Old Testament prophets or, in critical terms, that the Old Testament was interpolated.

Dionysius of Corinth on Interpolations

Dionysius, bishop of Corinth around 160, was an indefatigable letter writer, but he found that his letters were being interpolated by heretics: "When Christians asked me to write letters I wrote them; and the devil's apostles have filled them with tares by leaving out some things and adding others; woe awaits them. It is no wonder if some have undertaken to falsify even the dominical writings when they have plotted against writings that are not such."[41] Dionysius's words about the tares echo the parable in Matthew 13:25, while adding and subtracting recalls Revelation 22:18–19. The formula does not come from Revelation, however, but from Greek discussions concerning legal texts and treaties between city-states.[42] Dionysius implicitly treats his own letter as inspired and reflects an earlier, simpler time when "apostolic fathers" claimed divine inspiration. He is not likely to have used literary criticism in support of his denunciations.

More probably, like orthodox leaders before him, he was content with simple stories about the way traditions had been handed down, recalling the *halakha* and *haggada* of Judaism or the *hadith* of Islamic tradition. Indeed, his concern for tradition shines through the fragments of his letters,[43] while his opposition to Marcion makes it virtually certain that he rejected Marcion's critical method as well as his theology. The times were not yet ripe for literary criticism in the church. Justin had taken a short step toward it; others would have to go farther.

2

Literary Criticism
in Early Christian Times

LITERARY CRITICISM could be serious business.[1] The words "genuine" and "spurious" refer to legitimate sons and bastards in *Iliad* 11.102–104, where a bastard drives the chariot for his "glorious" partner. The invidious distinction was carried over into literary criticism, where it was needed when deletion and forgery were rampant.[2] The Stoic Athenodorus, in charge of the library at Pergamum, was said to have deleted unsuitable passages from the works of Zeno, the founder of his sect, though they were replaced after he was caught.[3] As later Stoics grew closer to conservative Roman politicians, the rationalist ethics of early treatises, often entitled *Republic*, became embarrassing. A Stoic teacher ascribed to Epicurus the letters "commonly attributed" to the Stoic Chrysippus, but when a Stoic forged fifty scandalous letters in Epicurus's name, an Epicurean philosopher killed him.[4]

Grammar-Rhetoric

As for the method of detection involved, Dionysius Thrax defines grammar as "experiential knowledge of most of what was said by poets and prose-writers," so that the student could attain to "the judgment of poems" (and prose), often in matters of authorship. As the London Scholia on Dionysius put it, the student learns to consider what is similar, what not; what fake, what genuine. "There are many forgeries such as the

Antigone of Sophocles, said to be by Iophon son of Sophocles, as well as the *Cypriaca* and *Margites* by Homer, the *Thytica* and *On Birds* by Aratus, and the *Shield* by Hesiod"[5] (no reasons given!).

The rhetorician Dionysius of Halicarnassus (late first century B.C.E.) naturally discussed authenticity when he dealt with the speeches of Lysias, for he had suspicions about many that were "commonly considered genuine." They lacked Lysias's charm and euphony. An important example was the speech *On the Statue of Iphicrates*, for Lysias died seven years before the bill to erect the statue was brought forward. Another speech defending Iphicrates must have been written twenty years after Lysias's death.[6]

Much later, Dionysius devoted most of a study of the orator Dinarchus to the authenticity of his speeches. He discovered that Dinarchus wrote speeches for others for fifteen years after the death of Alexander and then spent fifteen years in exile, returning to Athens as an old man with failing eyesight. Dionysius rather arbitrarily sets the age of 70 for his return and the age of 25/26 for his first speeches, at a time when Demosthenes was especially influential. In consequence of these calculations, Dionysius then rejects some speeches "in circulation before his prime" or from the time he was in exile, and others because of their style. Style was a less reliable criterion than chronology since Dinarchus imitated other orators. In his *First Letter to Ammaeus* Dionysius provides similar chronological calculations to show that Demosthenes did not write in accordance with Aristotle's *Rhetoric*, as a Peripatetic philosopher had claimed he did.

How Many Homers?

The starting point for analysis lay in the inconsistencies, large or small, to be found within one work or more. Such analysis was well known in the Hellenistic world, notably in the study of Homer. The grammarian Aristarchus, himself expert in discovering interpolations in Homer, wrote against what he considered the "paradoxical" or even irrational conclusions of the "dividers," led by Xenon and Hellanicus, who held that *Iliad* and *Odyssey* came from different authors.[7] Others, like the author of *On the Sublime*, argued that Homer wrote the *Iliad* at the peak of his powers, the more "mythical" *Odyssey* only in old age, when his sun was setting or his tide ebbing.[8] The Roman Seneca thought that both these theories were typical of sick Greek minds. In his view, Greeks were the ones who liked to ask how many oarsmen Odysseus had, or which came first, *Iliad* or *Odyssey*, or whether both were by the same author.[9]

Homer and the Epic Cycle

For some centuries *Iliad* and *Odyssey* did not stand alone but were associated with other epic poems about early times. There was even an edition of Homer that included the other poems of the epic cycle. At the end of the *Iliad*, ancient critics noted, lines 804–805 connected the work with the "cyclical" *Aethiopis*.[10]

These poems of the epic cycle were composed in the seventh and sixth centuries, flourished in the fifth and fourth, and gradually disappeared in imperial times. There are fragments from ten poems in cycle with the *Iliad* and the *Odyssey*: These were the *Titanomachy* (War of the Titans), *Oedipodea* (Story of Oedipus), *Thebais*, *Epigoni*, *Cypria*—then came the *Iliad* of Homer—*Aethiopis*, *Ilias Parva* (Little Iliad), *Iliou Persis* (Sack of Ilium), *Nosti* (Returns of the Greeks)—then came the *Odyssey* of Homer—and *Telegonia* (Story of Telegonus and the death of Odysseus). While Homer, as we have seen, was generally regarded as author of *Iliad* and *Odyssey*, the other epic poems were open to doubt and discussion, especially in the early Christian era. Both Philodemus and the third-century essayist Athenaeus use the expression "the author of *The War of the Titans*," though Athenaeus ascribes it once to Eumelus, once to "Eumelus of Corinth or Arctinus."[11] In the second century Pausanias speaks of the author of the *Oedipodea* but hesitates to express a judgment on the author of the *Thebais*, while Apollodorus and Athenaeus simply refer to "the author" of this work.[12] Hardly anyone gave a name to the author of the *Cypria*, for Herodotus denied that Homer had written this poem. It related that Paris brought Helen to Troy "in three days from Sparta, having a fair wind and a smooth sea," while the *Iliad* stated that he wandered off his course and took longer.[13] The great critic Aristotle himself in the *Poetics* had spoken of "the author of the *Cypria* and the Little Iliad*."[14] Sometimes the *Aethiopis* was ascribed to Arctinus, though often it was regarded, like the other poems, as anonymous. The Roman poet Horace differentiated Homer and the beginning of the *Odyssey* from the "ancient cyclical author" who began his poem: "I shall sing Priam's fortune and noble war," and then gave birth to the famous "ridiculous mouse."[15]

Obviously, schoolboys dealing with the epic poems of Homer were exposed to questions about authorship not only of *Iliad* and *Odyssey* but of the whole epic cycle. The so-called *Tabula Iliaca* proposes a particular author for each poem of the cycle.[16] During the imperial period grammarians still discussed these poets, as we plainly see in two "contributions" by Clement of Alexandria, who names five of them,[17] while Eusebius assigns dates to another five in his *Chronicle*. Proclus (possibly the Neoplatonist) provided the summaries that are printed by West. At the same time, many were quite willing to treat the authors as anonymous.

Not everyone accepted the cycle. Seneca ridicules Apion (the target of Josephus's apology) for claiming that Homer, after completing the *Iliad* and the *Odyssey,* composed the epic cycle on the Trojan war.[18] Origen had more sense than to discuss any of the poems, and by the time of Philoponus the cycle was no longer obtainable.[19] The ninth-century Christian bibliographer Photius knew the cycle only from Proclus. That is how we happen to know Proclus's comments.[20] Similarly the "apocryphal" or "pseudepigraphical" writings read by some Christians tended to disappear. They were not read in church, and private reading of them was also discouraged. Generally their authors were unknown or forgotten.

Homer's Other Writings?

Two more poems raised difficulties. Plato ascribed the *Margites* to Homer, the "most divine and most wise poet," while Aristotle compared *Iliad* and *Odyssey* with tragedy, *Margites* with comedy, obviously accepting all as genuine.[21] The Stoic Zeno assigned it to Homer but claimed it was written "when he was rather young and was testing his poetic ability." (Otherwise he held that Homer "has written some things in accord with fancy, some with reality," thus defending him from the charge of inconsistency.[22]) Clement of Alexandria, however, doubted that it was authentic.[23] As for the *Battle of Frogs and Mice,* a Greco-Roman apotheosis of Homer now in the British Museum alludes to the question. The World and Time crown a seated Homer, while above him are Zeus, Apollo, and the Muses. Down beneath his footstool are a frog and a mouse. The low position of these animals must reflect doubts about the quality and/or authenticity of the poem. Plutarch ascribed it to Pigres, about 480 B.C.[24] The first of two lives of Homer wrongly ascribed to Plutarch insists that "he wrote two poems, *Iliad* and *Odyssey*, and—as some untruthfully say—added the *Battle of Frogs and Mice* and the *Margites* for the sake of exercise and instruction."[25]

Editors of Homer?

The Jewish apologist Josephus accepts a current theory about editing when he says Homer "did not leave his poem in writing; it was remembered and later united from the songs; this is why there are so many inconsistencies in it."[26] Other critics named the unifying editor as Pisistratus, tyrant of Athens in the sixth century B.C., or his sons.[27] In the early third century the Christian layman Julius Africanus dabbled in all sorts of studies with considerable success. His study of the *Odyssey*, such as it is, appears in a third-century Oxyrhynchus papyrus (III 412) containing part of Book XVIII.[28] He quotes *Odyssey* 11.34–43 and 48–50 (slightly modified) on Odysseus's meeting with the souls of the dead, then inserts an incantation based on verses from *Iliad* 3.278–280 and epic imitations, along with a faint echo of *Iliad* 6.467. Next he turns to a "magical prayer," with invocations of such non-Greek deities as names like Iaa, Phtah, Phre, Nephtho, Ablanatho, Abraxas, and Phren, not to mention Isis with the Dog Star Sirius, and finally returns to *Odyssey* 11.51, "et cetera."

Africanus ends the book with typical literary-critical questions. "Did the poet himself leave out what was superfluous in this incantation, because of his intention as an author? Or did the Pisistratids remove these verses as alien to the movement of the poem?" Africanus has set them down as "a magnificent product of the epic art." He then discusses his manuscript authorities but makes no judgment on their age or reliability. The whole incantation is preserved "in the archives of our native city, the colony of Aelia Capitolina [= Jerusalem] in Palestine, and at Nysa in Caria[29] and as far as the thirteenth verse[30] at Rome near the baths of Alexander [Severus] in the beautiful library in the Pantheon, which I constructed for the emperor." Nero first built these baths, just northwest of the Pantheon, while Alexander Severus repaired and enlarged them in

227.[31] Perhaps he built the library around the same time, but it has not proved possible to identify any remains.[32]

Homer and Hesiod

Josephus tells us more about grammatical studies when he says that among the Greeks there is no "acknowledged" writing more ancient than the poetry of Homer. By "acknowledged" he means "undisputed" and implies the existence not of universal consent but of vigorous debate. His sentence comes from a grammatical school where it was held that the poetry of Homer is "approved and most ancient, for no poem older than his poetry has come down to us." Josephus does not continue, as Sextus does, by noting that there are people who regard Hesiod, Linus, Orpheus, and Musaeus as older.[33] Like Philo he never mentions Orpheus, and he obviously regards Homer as more ancient than Hesiod.

Opinions often differed on this point. Those who accepted the authenticity of Orpheus were likely to place Hesiod before Homer, probably because of the presumed antiquity of theogonies. This is the case with the fifth-century sophist Hippias, with "Aeschylus" as reported by Aristophanes, and even with Plato, half the time.[34] By the end of the Hellenistic age, however, the priority of Homer to Hesiod was generally accepted although many still revered the poems of Orpheus. Seneca, as we should expect, treats such questions as pointless.[35]

Questions About Hesiod

From the sixth century onward, critics attacked both Homer and Hesiod for telling false stories about the gods. The philosophers Xenophanes and Plato joined the historian Herodotus in criticizing them.[36] The work of Hesiod they had in mind was his *Theogony*, but this was only part of a wider collection that encountered a good deal of criticism in the Hellenistic age.

According to the Roman rhetorician Quintilian, the Alexandrian grammarian Aristophanes was the first to deny that Hesiod wrote the *Admonitions* (= *Works and Days* ?). Later on, questions were raised about the authenticity of his *Catalogue of Women*. A scholiast points out that he treats the Cyclopes as "like the gods" in *Theogony* 142 but in the *Catalogue* says Apollo destroyed them.[37] This contrast explains why

Crates changed "like the gods" to "from immortals, mortal" in that line; he must have wanted to treat the works as both authentic and consistent. Pausanias records doubts but tentatively accepts authenticity. He tells how "the Boeotians around Helicon" think that Hesiod wrote only the *Works and Days* and even regard the introductory lines invoking the Muses as interpolated. Elsewhere he says that "Hesiod in the *Theogony*— for there are some who regard the poem *Theogony* as Hesiod's—speaks of Styx as the daughter of Ocean and the wife of Pallas." He adds that "people say that Linus gives a similar account in his verses, though when I read these they seemed spurious."[38] Athenaeus boldly took *The Marriage of Ceyx* to be "ancient" (and genuine) even though grammarians "divorced" it from Hesiod, but later in his work he claimed that the *Aegimius* was written by "either Hesiod or Cercops of Miletus."[39]

In citing only the major writings *Theogony* and *Works and Days*, Philo of Alexandria is followed by several apologists, and Irenaeus cites Gnostic exegesis of the account of Pandora by Hesiod.[40] Some early Christians refer to the more questionable works as well. Athenagoras cites the *Catalogue of Women*, and Clement of Alexandria, as we should expect, cites the *Melampodia* and the *Idaean Dactyls*, along with five fragments of uncertain location.[41] Origen cites "the poet of Ascra" (probably from an anthology) as author of a fragment with two lines from *Catalogue of Women* that is found more fully in an Oxyrhynchus papyrus. He also ridicules the story of Pandora and her jar, not to be interpreted allegorically unless the story of Eve can be treated allegorically too.[42] His successor, Dionysius of Alexandria, simply notes that "the myth of Hesiod says that Pandora was made by the gods."[43]

Editing the Ancient (?) Poems of Orpheus

From early times the major ancient poets were often considered to be the half-legendary Orpheus and Musaeus, who came before Homer and Hesiod. Plato mentions Hesiod, Homer, Musaeus and his son in the *Republic*; so does Aristophanes in the *Frogs*, as well as the later Stoic Chrysippus.[44] It was Herodotus who said that the Athenian oracle-seller Onomacritus, supposedly a contemporary of Pisistratus, edited the oracles of Musaeus and interpolated them in favor of the Persians.[45] Aristotle held a similar view, holding that while the doctrines came from

Orpheus, the poems had been set in order by Onomacritus; he therefore referred to "the so-called Orphic poems," since "Orpheus was never a poet."[46] Greco-Roman authors often cited "Onomacritus in the poems" or "in the *Orphica*."[47] Ultimately some held that Onomacritus interpolated Homer and Hesiod as well.[48] According to Plutarch he "foisted tragic diction and grandiloquence on the oracles."[49]

Grammar-minded Christians naturally took up the theories about Onomacritus. The Christian sophist Tatian says that "they say" the works attributed to Orpheus were composed by Onomacritus, who lived in the reign of Pisistratus's sons about the fiftieth Olympiad—though he cites a popular tag as by "Orpheus" and treats Musaeus as his disciple.[50] Clement of Alexandria repeats Tatian's information about Onomacritus and adds learnedly that he composed oracles ascribed to Musaeus, while Zopyrus of Heraclea wrote the *Crateres*, Prodicus of Samos the *Descent to Hades*. He knows a pre-Socratic treatise by Epigenes, *On the Poetry of Orpheus*, with learned discussions of authorship: *Descent to Hades* and *Sacred Discourse* were by Cecrops the Pythagorean, while Brontinus wrote the Orphic *Peplus* and *Physics*. Clement also claims that Homer used both Orpheus and Musaeus, and of course he quotes "Orpheus" repeatedly.[51] The apologist Athenagoras names Orpheus before Homer and Hesiod and says that Homer relied on him, but does not discuss editors.[52]

These texts make it impossible to agree with A. Gudeman, who said that "transparent as these forgeries [the pseudo-Orphica] appear to us, they were generally accepted as genuine by the ancients, the Church Fathers in particular treating them as such for obvious reasons."[53] What obvious reasons? Occasionally Christians traced heretical doctrines back to "Musaeus, Linus, and Orpheus," as Hippolytus does for the Sethian Gnostics,[54] but this is unusual. More important was the use by Jewish and Christian apologists of the so-called *Testaments of Orpheus*, which shows how on his deathbed Orpheus abandoned his belief in 365 gods in favor of monotheism. Theophilus, Clement, and Pseudo-Justin refer to the work as his "palinode" or "recantation."[55]

By early imperial times Orpheus and Musaeus had lost authority, however, and grammarians and philosophers dropped their names from the list of ancient poets. Indeed, the papyri listed by Pack do not contain

Orpheus at all, though in recent times a significant commentary of the fourth century B.C. on Orphic and Homeric verses has been found in a papyrus from Derveni.[56] Stoic teachers like Epictetus and Marcus Aurelius do not mention Orpheus; neither do the Christian apologist Justin and the antiheretical bishop Irenaeus. Galen criticizes Chrysippus for filling his books with quotations from Orpheus and other irrelevant sources, and Orpheus himself for writing about poisonous drugs.[57] The Christian scholar and interpreter Origen mentions Orpheus only in replying to a pagan critic. Celsus claimed that Orpheus was like Jesus because he "possessed a pious spirit and also died a violent death," and Origen simply replied that "Orpheus said much worse things about the supposed gods than Homer did."[58] Most of the "fragments," as K. Ziegler noted, have come down through lost commentaries by Neoplatonists who were trying to show how Orpheus agreed with Plato.[59] But Origen never refers to the Orphic poems or the Hermetica or the Sibylline Oracles, and makes no use of other pagan oracles, unlike Christians on a lower level of apologetic writing.

Hermetic Writings

We shall presently turn to the Sibyllines, but here we note (after Nock) that Galen ridiculed the grammarian Pamphilus for quoting from the books, full of myths and magic spells, ascribed to the Egyptian Hermes,[60] while the credulous Iamblichus, as we should expect, defended these tomes on the ground that they had been translated from Eygptian by men "not inexperienced in philosophy."[61] The sixteenth Hermetic tractate, on the other hand, claimed that what was clear and powerful in Egyptian became weak in Greek, especially in Greek philosophy.[62]

Pythagoras Not an Author?

In agreement with the traditions of the Pythagoreans themselves, critics usually recognized that Pythagoras wrote nothing. Plutarch, Galen, Diogenes Laertius, and Porphyry agree on this point.[63] On the other hand, Origen regrettably says that he has read books by Pythagoras, while Diogenes discusses the authorship of books ascribed to him and discusses the "general content" of three treatises on *Education*, *Politics*, and *Nature*.[64] N. Brox draws attention to an Arabic version of Porphyry on eighty books from Pythagoras himself along with two hundred from early Pythagoreans, edited for circulation among Pythagoreans not in Greece but in Italy.[65] This does not sound like what Porphyry would have said.

The Neoplatonists Olympiodorus and Elias cite Pythagoras as an example (with Socrates) of philosophers to whom forged works have been assigned because of book collecting by rulers, the devotion of disciples, and confusion over authors' names.[66] Without explanation Galen refers to moral exhortations "ascribed to Pythagoras," useful though not authentic.[67]

The Sibylline Oracles

Some critics attacked the Hellenistic Jewish and Christian forgeries known as the *Sibylline Oracles*, almost constantly used by early Christian apologists. Celsus said that Christians had interpolated them, and as Henry Chadwick notes, this criticism is "more than justified." Origen never cited the Sibyl.[68] In his time, however, Pseudo-Justin provided historical and archaeological defenses of authenticity. First, he claimed without justification that Plato had mentioned these oracles.[69] Second, he stated that he had visited Cumae in Campania, six milestones from Baiae, where he saw the place in the rock where the Sibyl uttered oracles. His historical information comes from the tourist guides. According to Pseudo-Justin, not all her verses are metrical, for she could not, like a poet, correct her text but spoke at the moment of inspiration.[70] In addition, the copyists were uneducated. In the fourth century both Lactantius and Constantine had to deny the charge that Christians had made them up.[71]

The Bible in Greek

A much more important collection of sacred books used by Jews and Christians was held together in a "canon" of Old Testament scriptures. At the end of the first century Josephus refers to the twenty-two "justly accredited" books of the Jews, which include five books of Moses with the laws and the tradition from the creation to his death. The prophets after Moses wrote thirteen books of contemporary history up to Artaxerxes, king of Persia. Finally, four books contain hymns to God and precepts for human life. Written history exists for the time after

Artaxerxes but is not highly valued "because of the failure of the exact succession of the prophets." No one has ever ventured to add, remove, or alter anything in these writings.[72] More inclusive lists are given by the Christian authors Melito and Origen.[73]

Hellenistic writers sometimes criticized parts of this collection. E. Stein long ago noted the objections, not very incisive, reflected in Philo, as well as traces of Philonic criticism in three anti-Christian authors: Celsus, Porphyry (especially in a critical commentary on Daniel), and the emperor Julian.[74] Such discussions were not related to the philological criticism we have been examining but to history and theology—or, in rhetorical terms, to what is "fitting" in regard to God or God's people.

Since Hellenistic Jews and Christians read the Old Testament in Greek, they had to explain how reliably these Hebrew books had been translated. According to the legend, Ptolemy II or his librarian Demetrius of Phalerum sent to Jerusalem for the Hebrew Bible, which was put into Greek at Alexandria by seventy translators. This story appears in the *Letter of Aristeas*, Philo, Josephus, and Christian authors like Justin, Irenaeus, and Clement.[75] With the passage of time the miraculous element grew, but the names of the important authorities remained. Origen insisted that the traditional Greek version was inspired[76] but did not refer to the legend. As might be expected, however, Pseudo-Justin provided archaeological "proof" for the inspired translation. When he was in Alexandria on the island of the Pharos, he saw the traces of the cells in which the translators lived and heard the story about them from natives.[77]

Stories about the transmission of religious literature were thus fairly common, and we should expect that Christians too would be concerned with the matter.

Minor Philosophers Before and After Socrates

In the Hellenistic world spurious or interpolated works ascribed to philosophers were exceedingly common. Diogenes Laertius, who wrote his *Lives and Opinions of Eminent Philosophers* in the early third century A.D., repeatedly discusses questions of authorship because so many spurious works were in existence. For example, some said Thales wrote nothing, "for the *Nautical Astronomy* attributed to him is said to be by Phocus of Samos." Others said he wrote two treatises, *On the Solstice* and *On the Equinox*, and Lobon of Argos said he wrote two hundred lines. Diogenes next discusses the so-called Seven Sages and ends by quoting Thales' extant letters to Pherecydes and Solon. Both are obvious forgeries. "Some say" that in the *Iliad* after the line "Ajax commands twelve ships from Salamis" (2.557), Solon inserted his own line: "He set them so that they might support the bands of the Athenians." In addition Diogenes quotes four letters attributed to him.[78]

Thus far the information is all traditional, that is to say, presented without the arguments for or against it. On Socrates, however, Diogenes does note an argument mentioned by the second-century sophist Favorinus: "The speech of Polycrates against Socrates is not authentic, for he mentions Conon's rebuilding of the walls, which took place six years after Socrates' death." But then Diogenes goes back to citing authorities. Only two dialogues of the Socratic philosopher Phaedo are genuine, while four are dubious, among them two that are also ascribed to Polyaenus or Aeschines. Nine dialogues of Glaucon are extant in one volume, but there are thirty-two more that are spurious. Some held that Arcesilaus never wrote a book, while others said "he was caught revising some works of Crantor, which according to some he published, according to others he burnt."[79]

Diogenes discusses the Academic philosopher Heraclides Ponticus at length. He was said to have written tragedies under the name of Thespis, or published a plagiarized treatise on Homer and Hesiod as his own. He was so simple that he accepted a forged play as by Sophocles, even when the real author explained just how he had written it.[80] Again, some held that the Cynic Diogenes wrote nothing and ascribed his tragedies to friends who wrote after his death. There were critics who questioned the books said to be by the Cynic Menippus, claiming that the real authors wrote them as a joke and gave them to him so that he could dispose of them.[81]

We have cited enough examples to show how common it was for Diogenes to discuss these literary-critical questions, how infrequently he gave any reasons for the judgments he mentioned, and also how little attention he gave to problems we should consider basic.

Socrates in Plato and Xenophon

Discussions of authenticity were not confined to ancient and/or religious literature, however, but were devoted to more modern philosophical works. Diogenes Laertius is one of our best witnesses, but he paid little attention to the remarkable difference between the Socrates of Xenophon and the Socrates of Plato, dealing only with details and individual books. In antiquity the problem was different because many more "Socratic" dialogues were in circulation. The Stoic teacher Panaetius judged that only those by Plato, Xenophon, Antisthenes, and Aeschines were genuine. He expressed doubts about the dialogues written by Phaedo and Euclid, and rejected all others.[82] According to Diogenes, Xenophon was the first to take notes on what Socrates actually said. Some of this material is echoed in the dialogues of Plato, but the later ones show that the thought is basically Plato's own. Neither Xenophon nor Plato is fully reliable, however. Diogenes claims that Xenophon contradicts himself, for Socrates really discussed physics, as in Xenophon's report of his treatment of providence, even though Xenophon held that he discussed only ethics. Plato, on the other hand, puts everything into Socrates' mouth but treats themes that Socrates rejected. Critics of Plato said that after hearing him read the *Lysis*, Socrates denounced him for reporting what he had never said.[83]

Rivalry and disagreement between Xenophon and Plato is proved by the fact that both wrote a *Symposium*, an *Apology for Socrates*, and "ethical memoirs." Plato's *Republic* deals with general education, but while Xenophon wrote an *Education of Cyrus*, in the *Laws* Plato says Cyrus was not educated at all. Otherwise Plato never refers to Xenophon, and Xenophon refers to Plato only once, in the third book of his *Memoirs*.[84] Plato's own name, however, does not appear in his writings, except for one example in the *Phaedo* and another in the *Apology*. Obviously this "analysis" is based on unanalyzed allegations traded among the various Socratic schools.[85]

Authentic and Inauthentic Works of Plato

The Platonic Academy edited and transmitted the dialogues of Plato along with works not authentic but representing what Plato should have taught. Diogenes Laertius cites Thrasyllus's opinion that fifty-six are genuine, ten spurious;[86] and a third-century papyrus lists the "*Symposium* and twenty dialogues," all genuine.[87] The works were transmitted in "tetralogies" or groups of four and in some manuscripts equipped with "critical marks" (originally used for Homer) to point out editorial corrections, "passages suspected without reason," and "repetitions and proposals for transpositions." The "obelus" marked passages regarded as spurious.[88] (Many of these marks would recur in the *Tetrapla* and *Hexapla* editions of the Old Testament by the Christian scholar Origen.)

In the second century Favorinus thought *Halcyon* was written by "a certain Leon,"[89] while Aelian reflects doubt about the *Hipparchus* and Athenaeus says that "some" call *Alcibiades II* the work of Xenophon.[90] The Christian scholar Clement of Alexandria expressed doubts about the *Demodocus* but quoted *Amatorius* 137B as if it came from that work. He explicitly cites the *Epinomis* and *Alcibiades I*, as well as *Epistles II* ("he says"), *VI* ("in the letter to Erastus and Coriscus"), and *VII* ("in the great letter"), and clearly alludes to the *Minos*.[91]

Diogenes comes close to Thrasyllus when he lists the ten spurious works attributed to Plato. These are *Midon* or *Horsebreeder*, *Eryxias* or *Erasistratus*, *Halcyon*, *Acephali* or *Sisyphus*, *Axiochus*, *Phaeacians*, *Demodocus*, *Chelidon*, *Seventh Day*, and *Epimenides*.[92] The anonymous author of *Prolegomena to the Philosophy of Plato* takes a further step when he reports that the fifth-century Neoplatonist Proclus rejected the *Epinomis* because after the *Laws*, traditionally his last work, Plato would not have had time enough to write it, and because in other dialogues he said the planets moved from right to left but here from left to right. The anonymous author also sets forth the conventional view of authenticity: "Everyone acknowledges that *Sisyphus*, *Demodocus*, *Halcyon*, and *Eryxias*, and the *Definitions* ascribed to Plato's nephew and successor Speusippus are spurious."[93] Such discussions may have had some effect, for in Pack's list of forty-five papyrus fragments of Plato, only three come from non-Platonic works: *On the Just*, *On Virtue*, and *Eryxias* with *Demodocus*.[94]

The Authentic Works of Aristotle

Diogenes Laertius lists "nearly four hundred" of Aristotle's works, apart from those questionably genuine, and says that in all they contain

445,270 lines.[95] Questions were raised about the authorship of many of them, even among the basic rhetorical, metaphysical, and scientific treatises for which he was famous. The sixth-century commentator Ammonius points out that though "ancient libraries" preserved forty books of Aristotle's *Analytics* and contained only two of the *Categories*,[96] "everyone acknowledges that the *Categories* are genuine writings of the philosopher, for he is seen in all his books to be mentioning the theorems found there. Therefore if this is spurious, so are they, and if they are genuine, so is this."[97] Out of just eight papyrus fragments listed by Pack, only one comes from the earlier works (*Exhortation*).[98]

Scholars have thought that the basic scientific works were lost for centuries after Aristotle's death. Evidence for such a loss appears in Strabo's *Geography* and Plutarch's *Life of Sulla*. Strabo tells how Aristotle left his library to his disciple Theophrastus, whose heir, the Socratic philosopher Neleus, took it to Skepsis. Neleus's heirs in turn kept the books locked up, but, on hearing that the kings of Pergamum were searching for books for their library, they hid the books underground, where they were damaged by damp and moths. Finally a collector at Athens bought all the books and incorrectly restored the gaps in them, publishing them full of errors. The Roman general Sulla confiscated the library and took it to Rome, where the grammarian Tyrannion and some booksellers published Aristotle in the first century B.C. Plutarch adds that Tyrannion "arranged" the books, while Andronicus of Rhodes published them with a list.[99] The two authors agree that Peripatetics after Theophrastus were unable to continue the study of Aristotle, and Strabo insists that these early Peripatetics had "only a few of his books, especially the exoteric ones"—that is, the early religious treatises. A rather different story appears in Athenaeus, who tells how Ptolemy Philadelphus bought the library of Theophrastus (including Aristotle) from Neleus and took it to Alexandria.[100] Presumably both accounts are partial.

The early writings, now preserved only in fragments, include the *Gryllus* or *On Rhetoric*, *Eudemus* or *On the Soul*, *On Philosophy*, and the *Protrepticus* or *Exhortation*. Several of these works, doubtless early, imitated Plato's dialogues and shared his concern for religion. Werner Jaeger and others argued that Aristotle wrote them under the spell of Plato and only after his death in 347 B.C. turned away from them to write his major scientific and metaphysical treatises.[101] The theory is jeopardized, however, by Aristotle's very early zoological research between 345 and 343, soon after Plato's death and his departure from the Academy.[102]

It has also been believed that soon after Aristotle's own death his scientific and metaphysical works disappeared, to be recovered in the first century B.C., while the earlier and more religious writings held the field and influenced such authors as Philo and the early Christians—only to be lost in turn. This theory too is not altogether correct since echoes of the metaphysical works appear in the Hellenistic schools. The use of Aristotle's metaphysics by Philo of Alexandria in his treatise *On the Eternity of the World* could point either way.[103] It may be significant that while Clement of Alexandria frequently refers to Aristotle's opinions and indeed paraphrases or simply copies certain texts, he never explicitly cites the texts as from Aristotle. E. A. Clark claims that he once relied directly on the *Nicomachean Ethics*.[104] His silence about Aristotle can be compared with his silence about Musonius Rufus and his infrequent references to either Chrysippus or Philo. Evidently he liked to name sources he did not use and use sources he did not name.[105]

Hippocratic Writings

From the first century of our era comes the glossary of Hippocratic writings dedicated by Erotian to Nero's chief physician Andromachus. Based on the earlier "dogmatic" sequence of the writings, the study is important to us especially because, as Wesley Smith pointed out, it contains the first definite rejection of the authenticity of a Hippocratic treatise. Erotian specifically states that *Prorrhetic II* is not Hippocratic.[106]

In the reign of Hadrian (117–138) came the edition of the Hippocratic books by Artemidorus Capito and his relative Dioscurides.[107] Galen was to complain about the many changes they made in the traditional text of Hippocrates. Indeed, he claims to have turned back to the earliest commentators, who preserved the standard text without the "many novel readings" of the Hadrianic editors.[108]

Critical Method

To questions about authenticity, critics generally relied on the methods of refutation and confirmation taught in the schools of rhetoric. They are discussed, for example, in the *Progymnasmata* of Theon, where we learn how to apply them to myths, narratives, and laws. "Since the mythmaker himself acknowledges that he writes about things that are false and impossible though persuasive and useful, he is refuted by showing that they are unconvincing and unsuitable."[109] Hermogenes' treatment is better. "You will refute from the obscure, the unconvincing, the impossible, the inconsequent and contradictory, the unsuitable, the inconsistent." Examples follow: "'The time when Narcissus lived is obscure.' 'It is unconvincing that Arion would want to sing when in difficulties.' 'It was impossible for Arion to be saved on a dolphin.' 'To save the state was the opposite of desiring to destroy it.' 'It is unsuitable for Apollo, a god, to have intercourse with a mortal woman.' And we say that it is not suitable to hear these things."[110] Dio Chrysostom's eleventh *Oration* gives a good example of the way refutation worked. Assuming the role of a "very aged" Egyptian priest, he "proves" that Homer's tale of Troy is essentially fiction.[111]

When Origen discusses historical fact against Celsus, he too uses the Trojan war as his example. Something is wrong with the narrative because "for some unknown reason" it includes fictitious stories about human beings as children of gods. But everyone (rightly) believes that there really was a Trojan war. So how is one to prove that the war was historical? And what of stories that have the mythical Sphinx "woven in" with real persons? He advocates simply reading the stories without prejudice while keeping from being deceived. The reader must decide what he will accept and will "search out the meaning" of the authors; he will disbelieve what was "written to gratify certain people." But "an attempt to confirm almost any story as historical fact, even if it is true, and to produce complete certainty about it, is one of the most difficult tasks and in some cases it is impossible." Presumably refutation is easier. In any event, some elements in the stories must be recognized as allegorical.[112]

We shall later see that while heretics were probably the first Christians to use criticism on Christian books, it was most effectively employed at Rome by Gaius early in the third century and at Alexandria and Caesarea by Origen somewhat later, reaching a kind of flowering in the work of Dionysius, bishop of Alexandria. These critics were to baptize criticism, so to speak, into Christian use.

Was There a Pagan Canon?

A final question must be raised about the existence of a pagan "canon" of Greek literature as a possible source for the Jewish and Christian canons of scripture. Nearly a century ago classical scholars vigorously discussed the existence of such a "canon" (a modern term, not an ancient one) in the history of Greek literature or, specifically, in the history of schools. The title of O. Kroehnert's book of 1897 ends with a question mark: *Canonesne poetarum, scriptorum, artificum per antiquitatem fuerunt?* Gudeman spoke more definitely about a "Canon Alexandrinus," but H. Rabe was content to write on "the lists of Greek secular writers," while L. Radermacher and H. Oppel preferred not to use the term "canon."[113] In the late second century the Christian author Theophilus of Antioch garbles a rather incomplete list to name Homer, Hesiod, Orpheus, Aratus, Euripides, Sophocles, Menander, Aristophanes, Herodotus, Thucydides, Pythagoras, Diogenes, Epicurus, Empedocles, Socrates, Plato, "et cetera." Since some of these "authors" did not write anything, the list is hardly perfect.[114]

Relying on Pack's *Greek and Latin Literary Texts from Greco-Roman Egypt*, W. H. Willis studied these texts in relation to the "canon" and concluded that the choices were due to "taste and natural selection exercised by the general reading public in the second and third centuries." In other words, lists made by grammarians had little influence on what people read, except in so far as their ideas were shaped by their teachers.[115]

The Christian canon of biblical books was different because it was formal and authoritative. The question of authenticity ("apostolicity") was involved, but the primary basis for acceptance or rejection was conformity with Christian doctrine, not authenticity. Debates over the canon were so vigorous that no church council reached a decision about it before Trent in the sixteenth century, a millennium and a half after Marcion first brought critical method to Rome from Pontus by the Black Sea.

3

Marcion's Criticism
of Gospel and Apostle

Marcion to Rome

AT ROME the literary criticism of Christian books began when the powerful dualist critic Marcion arrived from Pontus, south of the Black Sea, around the year 137. He was opposing Judaism just two years after the violent but unsuccessful Jewish revolt against Hadrian (132–135), and his dualistic doctrine and historical analysis of the Bible won support at Rome during the five or six years before he was expelled from the church, according to Epiphanius, by a group of elders.[1]

Marcion was best known for his trilogy entitled *Antitheses*, *Gospel*, and *Apostle*. The *Antitheses*, with the use of Matthew as well as Luke, explained how Jesus contradicted the teachings of the Old Testament. Indeed, he claimed that when Jesus preached to the dead of Israel, such wicked persons as Cain, the men of Sodom, and the Egyptians came to him and were received into his kingdom. All the righteous, including the patriarchs and the prophets, rejected the gospel, for they supposed that as usual God was testing them and therefore they were not saved.[2]

The *Gospel* set forth the true text of the story of Jesus and his proclamation; and the *Apostle* gave the true text of the genuine letters of Paul. Marcion held that Paul knew the *Gospel*, which was later "interpolated by the defenders of Judaism," as were Paul's own letters.[3]

Whether or not Marcion worked on his theology in Pontus, the church there was fairly old. It must have been founded before 90, for around 110 Pliny investigated Pontic Christians who claimed to have left the church twenty years earlier. At an uncertain date 1 Peter addressed Christians in Bithynia and Pontus who were undergoing persecution. After 132 the violent struggle between Roman troops and Jewish messianists in Palestine produced strong sentiment against Jews throughout the empire, and presumably led Marcion to try to separate the gospel from the Jewish Bible.

Apparently he never discussed the origin of his unique *Gospel.* All his orthodox opponents claimed he had simply taken Luke and "circumcized" it, though they pointed toward inconsistencies in it. Morton Smith commented incisively thus: "Occasional preservation of material inconsistent with an editor's theories is merely evidence of the difficulty of editing a scroll thoroughly. Such inconsistencies are frequent in undoubtedly edited works, e.g., Chronicles and Marcion's edition of Luke."[4] Did he rely on an early document he happened to discover? It seems most unlikely. And even if he discovered such a book, it too could have been the product of editing.

Presumably Marcion did not know Luke as "Luke," any more than its first readers did. A more likely title before the two-volume treatise was divided into Gospel and Acts would have been *To Theophilus I* and *II.* The prefaces of the New Testament Luke and Acts certainly point toward such a title. But Marcion had no use for Acts, and he may have been responsible for the title "Gospel" as applied to Luke. Before his own efforts there is no evidence for Luke as a "Gospel" or indeed for other books as Gospels. Matthew begins with "Book of the generation of Jesus Christ the son of David son of Abraham," and John begins, "In the beginning was the Word." Only Mark's first verse, "Beginning of the gospel of Jesus Christ [the Son of God]," may conceivably point toward "Gospel" as a title. More probably it refers to the content of Mark's work.

Marcion's insistence that both *Gospel* and *Apostle* had been interpolated suggests that he knew current theories about interpolated religious documents, as well as the editorial procedures of the great Hellenistic textual critics.[5] After all, he wrote in a time when scholars were zealously reconstructing the philosophies that supposedly underlay Greek poetry and the authentic ancient myths that underlay current versions of them. They were "demythologizing," using literary analysis to produce theology. Diodorus Siculus, for example, held that the Greeks had distorted ancient theology by introducing "fictitious myths"; thus Orpheus's picture of Hades was really based on Egyptian burial customs combined with his own fictions.[6] At Rome Cornutus explained that a true understanding of nature lay under myths, symbols, and enigmas, for "the ancients were able to understand the nature of the cosmos and they were inclined to philosophize about it through symbols and dark sayings."[7] Plutarch said that "the true devotee of Isis is the one who uses reason in investigating and philosophizing about what is shown and done in the rites related to these gods."[8] Our concept of the divine, said Plutarch, must be framed in accordance with the blessed and imperishable nature, not based on myths.[9] The truths "are always kept away from the ears and eyes of the multitude, being concealed in mystic rites and ceremonies"[10]—presumably by priests.

Marcion's contemporary, Philo of Byblos, analyzed the authenticity of texts and claimed that while the god Taautos = Thoth = Hermes had revealed the ancient Phoenician myths of origins, the first Phoenician hierophant interpolated them with allegories about natural and cosmic matters. The Greeks appropriated much of the result and adorned it further, treating it like tragedy, as in Hesiod and the cyclic poets who wrote theogonies and gigantomachies and titanomachies. Sanchuniathon, in the time of Semiramis, recovered the original doctrines from memoirs in various cities and copies in the temples, but priests in later times made them mythical again.[11] The similarity to Marcion's theory is striking. The priests of Plutarch and Philo of Byblos are Marcion's apostles. Jesus' authentic teaching was interpolated by his Jewish apostles, restored by Paul, then distorted once again. Especially in the case of Philo, the starting point is obvious. It is his own true universal scientific doctrine, as set forth by Euhemerus: the gods were originally human.[12]

Others traced development in the history of religions, notably in Judaism. Strabo held that Moses, himself an Egyptian priest, rejected images and established a pure worship at Jerusalem without images or expensive sacrifices. Unfortunately his successors in the Judean priesthood were first superstitious, then tyrannical. Out of superstition they introduced—interpolated—dietary laws, circumcision, and excision, while from tyrannies came the robbery that subdued other lands and the reign of the Hasmonean priest-kings.[13] Jesus himself contrasted God's purpose in "the beginning of creation" with what Moses later said (Mark 10:5–6), and Paul insisted that the law was added (interpolated) 430 years after the promise, still valid, made to Abraham (Gal. 3:15–19). In recovering the authentic Gospel, Marcion could thus rely on Jewish and Christian precedents as well as contemporary critical approaches.

Marcion's Theological Changes

Marcion sharply differentiated the good God, the Father of Jesus, from the god of the law and justice who was fully anthropomorphic and indeed created evils.[14] Two points should be made about the critical descriptions of the god of the Old Testament. First, many of Marcion's points had already been made by literalists against whom Philo allegorized biblical passages. Second, it was clear that the Pentateuch spoke of God or gods in two contrasting ways. Before the middle of the second century both Philo and the haggadists took *YHWH* (Greek *kyrios*) as representative of God's judging or ruling and *Elohim* (*theos*) of his love and mercy, though later rabbis reversed the interpretation, claiming that *YHWH* referred to God's love and mercy, presumably in the light of Exodus 34:6, while *Elohim* pointed to God's judgment.[15] In fact the biblical terminology is not precise enough for such sharp distinctions, but it gave impetus to theology.

Marcion's criticisms show that he accepted something like the older Jewish view. On this basis he dealt with texts from the Gospel of Luke. Perhaps some of the later rabbis were reacting against his attacks when they reinterpreted the divine names. He also insisted that the Old Testament messiah was to be a warrior who would restore the state of Israel, while "our Christ" treated the kingdom of God as "an eternal and celestial possession."[16] Since the god of the Jews was the creator, devoted to law and administrator of providence, and there was another God above him, unknown to all but Jesus, he omitted Luke 12:6 on God's providential care for sparrows, and probably also verse 7 about the numbered hairs of the head,[17] and at Luke 12:28 deleted "God clothes the chaff," perhaps omitting the whole verse. (Compare Luke 21:18, where he removed "not a hair of your head will perish."[18]) For Marcion God is a god of grace, not of nature.

The one good God, *Elohim*, was the Father of Jesus and Lord of heaven but not of earth. From Luke 10:21, "I thank thee, Father, Lord of heaven and earth," Marcion deleted both "Father" and "and earth," though he continued with "Yea, Father," as Tertullian attests.[19] And while he retained Luke 11:5–13, he ended with "how much more the Father," deleting "from heaven." Marcion viewed angels as messengers of the creator, not the Father. At Luke 12:8, and presumably also at Luke 15:10, he read "before God" (with Codex Sinaiticus and Matthew) instead of "before the angels of God,"[20] though he was willing to refer to angels in the parable about Abraham's bosom, obviously in a Jewish setting (Luke 16:22).[21]

Marcion's version of the Lord's Prayer (Luke 11:2–4) probably began, "Father, let thy Holy Spirit come upon us and cleanse us,"[22] rather than with "hallowed be thy name. Thy kingdom come," for he held that "in the Gospel Christ himself is the kingdom of God,"[23] and therefore did not want Christ to pray for his own coming.

In Luke 18:18–20 Marcion altered Jesus' answer to the "ruler" (deleting "ruler") who addressed him as "Good master." Parallel columns reveal his procedure.

Luke	*Marcion*
Why do you call me good?	*Do not* call me good.
No one is good but the *one God the Father.*[24]	One is the good God.
You know the commandments.	*I* know the commandments.

With these changes we may compare Luke 16:17, where Marcion read "my words" instead of "the law,"[25] and 24:25, where he read "O stupid ones and slow to believe all that *I* spoke to you," not what "the prophets" spoke.[26]

What the Gospel Is

Marcion's *Antitheses* began with an exclamation about the Gospel that recalls the language of Paul in Romans 11:33:

Oh wealth of riches! Folly, power, and ecstasy!

Seeing that there can be nothing to say about it,

or imagine about it, or compare it to!

The Gospel was therefore unique and certainly not fourfold. Indeed, Marcion may have been protesting against the production of apocryphal gospels in his time.

The Beginning of the Gospel

The earliest witnesses to Marcion's work, Irenaeus and Tertullian, describe the beginning of his *Gospel*. Irenaeus says that according to Marcion "Jesus came into Judaea from that Father who is above the world-creating god. He was manifest in the form of a man, in the times of Pontius Pilate the governor, the procurator of Tiberius Caesar. He destroyed the prophets and the law and all the works of that god who made the world." Marcion relied on this doctrine when he "circumcised the Gospel according to Luke and removed everything written about the birth of the Lord as well as much of his teaching, in which he is plainly described as acknowledging the Creator of this universe as his Father."

Tertullian supplied more detail about the work. Marcion "ascribed no author to the *Gospel*" and held that "the title was adulterated."[27] The *Gospel* began with the words: "In the fifteenth year of the principate of Tiberius he came down to Capernaum" (Luke 3:1a, 4:31), and thus lacked any reference to the petty kings and rulers mentioned by Luke. It went on directly to 4:32, which Marcion boldly read thus: "They were astonished at his teaching, *which was against the law and the prophets*."[28] Similarly he modified Luke 23:2 so that the Sanhedrin's charges ran, "We found this man leading the nation astray *and destroying the law and the prophets* and forbidding the payment of taxes *and leading women and children astray* and calling himself Christ a king"[29] (Marcion added the words italicized).

Jesus and His Family

By omitting Luke 1–2 and 3:1c–4:15, Marcion rejected Luke's literary-historical prologue and his stories about Jesus' forerunner, his family, and his birth and infancy. He did not deny that John the Baptist was a witness to Jesus, however, for Luke 7:23, "Blessed is he who is not scandalized in me," referred to John, as did "my messenger" in 7:27.[30] At Luke 16:16 (RSV), "The law and the prophets until John," he modified the text slightly to read not "since then" but "from whom the kingdom of God is proclaimed."[31] As for Jesus' family, at Luke 8:19a, 20a Marcion deleted mention of the mother and brothers but was willing to let people in general (who knew no better) refer to them as "your mother and your brothers." He therefore probably omitted all of verse 19 on the coming of mother and brothers.[32]

Jesus and the Jewish Authorities

We have seen that he refrained from mentioning local rulers at Luke 3:1. He also deleted references to Jewish officials, notably in the Passion predictions, presumably because he thinks of the whole Jewish people as hostile, not just their leaders. At Luke 9:22, "The Son of Man must suffer many things," he omits "and be rejected by the elders and chief priests and scribes" but continues with "and be killed and raised after three days." (He is substituting "after three days" with Mark, Codex Bezae, and the Old Latin version for "on the third day."[33]) At Luke 18:18 he deleted "ruler." Similarly he omitted the whole of the Passion prediction in Luke 18:31–33, presumably because it was repetitious.[34]

Luke 5:14 has Jesus tell a leper, "Go and show yourself to the priest and offer the gift . . . as a testimony to them." Marcion, with Codex Bezae and the Old Latin version, substitutes "that this may be a testimony to *you*," thus diminishing the role of Jewish religious officials. Similarly from Luke 20:19 he removed the mention of scribes, chief priests, and the people because he does not refer to groups within Jewish society. His version of Luke 22:4 has it that Judas "spoke with the generals," omitting "the chief priests and." And from Luke 22:50–51 Marcion deleted Peter's smiting and cutting off the ear of the chief priest's slave, as well as the subsequent healing by Jesus. (Presumably the question, "Lord, shall we smite with the sword?" in Luke 22:49 was also deleted[35] because of Marcion's rejection of force.) In Luke 23:50–53 Marcion omits the description of Joseph (of Arimathea) as related to the Jewish Sanhedrin and simplifies the account generally.

Words of Jesus, Not the Law or the Prophets

Marcion makes minor changes at Luke 10:25. He identified the "certain person" (not "ruler" as in Luke) as a *nomikos* or "lawyer" because he knew the commandments of the Old Testament law. He asked Jesus, "What shall I do to inherit life?"—not "eternal" life but long life as discussed in the Jewish law. But how could Jesus have commended keeping this law? "The Lord answered in accordance with the law, 'You shall love the Lord your God with all your heart and all your soul and all your strength'—since the inquiry was about life under the law." According to Epiphanius, he read thus in Luke 10:26, 28: "He said to the lawyer, 'What is written in the law?' And answering in accordance with the lawyer's reply, he said, 'You said rightly; do this that you may live.'" Marcion thus explains the canonical text[36] but avoids having Jesus require Jewish legal observance. He also replaced "You know the commandments" by "I know the commandments."

In Luke 11:29–32 he removed references to Jonah the prophet and Nineveh and to the queen of the south, for the coming of Jesus was not really anticipated in the Old Testament. Similarly he deleted 11:49–51 because the Wisdom of God is not related to the prophets,[37] as well as the whole section 13:1–9, which suggested that repentant Israel would be saved, and the parable of the Prodigal Son (Luke 15:11–32), which early Christian exegetes referred to Jews and Gentiles.[38]

From Luke 17:10b Marcion deleted "say that we are unprofitable slaves; we have done what we ought to do," for these words implied the duty of obeying the law. In Luke 5:30 and 19:9b he may have considered two tax collectors, Levi and Zacchaeus, as Gentiles, for at the first text Tertullian speaks of "Gentiles and tax collectors" rather than "tax collectors and sinners," perhaps thinking of Levi as a Gentile (*ethnicus*). At the second text he specifically refers to Zacchaeus as a Gentile (*allophylus*).[39]

Marcion probably avoided references to the fulfillment of prophecy by deleting 19:29–46 with its mention of the ass and Bethphage and the city and the temple, whether house of prayer or den of thieves. He also excised the story about the vineyard given to farmers (Luke 20:9–17), as well as the question of what was "the stone which the builders rejected," presumably because of its close connection with Israel, and the verses 20:37–38 because they praised Moses and the patriarchs.

From Luke 21:21–22 Marcion deleted "Then those in Judea should flee to the mountains," etc., because the impending disasters were included in the expression "until everything written is fulfilled," or because after the crucifixion Christians were not concerned with Judea. The expression "Everything written" refers to the Old Testament, and Marcion must have considered it an interpolation. Harnack thought he deleted the whole of verses 21–24 because Tertullian passes from verse 20 to verse 25.[40]

The Passion and the Resurrection

Apparently Marcion cut "many words" from the end of the Gospel (as well as the beginning and the middle),[41] but we do not know exactly what he cut. It is fairly certain that he deleted Luke 22:16 with its reference to eating the paschal meal in the kingdom of God, and probably verses 17–18 as well.[42] "When I sent you out with no purse or bag or sandals, did you lack anything?" (22:35, RSV) was too materialistic for him, and the context may have gone with it because of the reference to the Old Testament in the expression "what is written" (v. 37).[43] In the account of the crucifixion (Luke 23:33–45) he read "And coming to a place called Skull they crucified him," omitting "and the malefactors" (keeping Jesus in the central position) and perhaps verse 34a: "Father, forgive them [the Jews], for they know not what they do."[44] From Luke 23:43 he deleted "Today you will be with me in Paradise" (said to a malefactor) and perhaps the whole of verses 35–43.[45]

As for the resurrection, he read "Those in bright clothing said, 'Why do you seek the living one with the dead?'" omitting "He is not here" (Luke 24:5), perhaps because the risen Christ is everywhere,[46] and continuing, "He has been raised; remember what he said while still with you," omitting "in Galilee" (Luke 24:5–6). The risen Christ says to the disciples, "See my hands and my feet, . . . for a spirit has not [deleting "flesh and"] bones as you see that I have" (24:39, RSV).[47] This is a singular deletion. Did the risen Lord have only a skeleton? Or was Marcion influenced by the important text 1 Corinthians 15:50 (RSV): "Flesh and blood cannot inherit the kingdom of God"?

The Reconstruction of Marcion's Gospel

Much of Harnack's famous reconstruction of Marcion's work had to be tentative, as he himself stated, because most of it is based on what Marcion's opponents said. Tertullian used the *Gospel* simply to show that it confirmed Christian doctrine, while Epiphanius provided a similar discussion but noted thirty-five passages in which (he claimed) Marcion altered the text. Inferences from such testimony are not fully reliable, for both Marcionites and anti-Marcionites altered Marcion's own text. But they are all we have, apart from a few details in the *Dialogue of Adamantius* and minor Syriac witnesses.[48]

D. S. Williams has urged that the most reliable evidence is given by "explicit correlated readings" provided by Tertullian and Epiphanius, though there are only twenty-three of these. In five cases the two authors agree (the difference of word order in two instances is due to the difference between Greek and Latin), and in the remaining eighteen cases the variants are often unimportant, sometimes because of the remarkable variety within the Marcionite text that Williams notes.[49] His article points to the high level of uncertainty about what Marcion wrote.

Marcion and Luke

One might hope that external testimonies to Luke, canonical or not, could illuminate the situation, but Papias's comments, if any, on Luke are not preserved, and the "tradition" cited by Ignatius about the risen Lord may or may not echo Luke 24:36–43.[50] The "traditional" testimony of Irenaeus on Marcion, for example, may not be historical.

New Testament critics have occasionally suggested that Marcion possessed a primitive source of the Gospel of Luke and rejected the church's revised version. Tertullian "explains" why Marcion's *Gospel* contained passages that favored the Catholic position rather than his own. Tertullian claims that by leaving certain contradictions in his book Marcion could argue both that he was not just deleting and that when he did so he was right. Such a psychological and theological claim is convincing only if Marcion was really editing the canonical Luke. It obviously fails if he really used an earlier work. Unfortunately there is no reliable evidence for what his sources and procedure were, though his results may suggest that originally Luke (or the version Marcion used) was not as full as it now is and that the "orthodox" text contains fewer interpolations than he supposed. In other words, the book may not have been composed as systematically as either Marcion or his critics believed.

As for modern studies of Luke's vocabulary and style, Knox claimed that they neither support nor oppose the traditional view, while Cadbury similarly argued that the presence or absence of non-Lucan words cannot be used to prove that Luke was or was not using a source.[51] Such points, along with the failure of Tertullian's claim, suggest that details of Marcion's Gospel can be recovered but not an overall picture. My own argument that the "changes" correspond with Marcion's theology and prove that he was an editor[52] is not convincing because conceivably Marcion relied on his "proto-Luke" and did not create it.

Can we move farther? Conceivably Marcion began his work with the *Antitheses*, first attacking the Judaism with which he was once associated.[53] According to Tertullian, in the *Antitheses* he "tried to destroy the status of the Gospels edited under the names of apostles [Matthew, John] or apostolic men [Mark, Luke]," and therefore must have held that the titles of the books were false, perhaps relying on a theory that involved interpolations. To develop such a theory he needed some source, itself apostolic and based on revelation but critical of the apostles and their followers. The ideal source would consist of letters from the apostle Paul. Some interpolations could be removed from these letters themselves, and a letter—Galatians—opposed to Peter and Judaizers could be placed at the head of the collection. Marcion's Galatians begins with the words: "Paul an apostle not from men or through a man but through Jesus Christ who raised himself from the dead."[54] Marcion could then reject or neglect other epistles such as the Pastorals and Hebrews.

Once he had freed Paul from his interpolators, he could have perceived the full meaning of references to "my gospel," though the Gospel was not Paul's,[55] but really "the only gospel there is."[56] According to Origen, the Marcionites relied on the phrase "according to my gospel in Christ Jesus," presumably finding it in Galatians, in order to attack the notion of a plurality of Gospels.[57]

The patristic testimony doubtless reflects the patristic theory that Marcion worked over the Gospels and did not present an original Luke.

But whereas one can imagine how he moved from his own Paul to his own *Gospel*, it is much harder to see how he could have gone from a primitive Luke as his source to his ideal Paul. There is hardly anything in this Gospel that could start his theological quest, unless the words "Christ Jesus a saving spirit" really come from the beginning of the book[58] and are not a theological interpretation of 1 Corinthians 15:45. One might suppose that he needed an anti-Jewish theology and a spiritual Christ before he could either identify or correct the Gospel. Once more, however, it must be admitted that if he really found a "primitive" version of Luke it might have assisted him in the quest.

He rejected the allegorical method, as Origen noted,[59] since his orthodox opponents could avoid the critical issues by using it. But since he retained Galatians 4:25 in his *Apostle,* he had to admit that it existed in the scriptures.[60] There were nonliteral passages even in the *Gospel*, for example in parables (the banquet in the parable of Luke 14:16–24 was not to be taken literally), and such a saying as "This is my body" in Luke 22:19 did not mean that the bread was literally the body of Jesus.[61] Such nonliteral passages were much less common, however, than those he took literally and used to support his theories.

In addition, in dealing with writings supposed to be interpolated[62] he must have used ordinary methods of literary criticism, commonplace in grammatical-rhetorical teaching. Similarly Origen differentiated Hebrews from the letters of Paul because of diction,[63] and Dionysius of Alexandria, the Apocalypse from the Gospel of John.[64] Presumably Marcion used this critical method, even though there is no record of his doing so. Justin goes so far as to say he provided no proof for his statements,[65] but by "proof" Justin means prediction in prophecy. When Marcion rejected prophecy, he deprived himself of proof. When Irenaeus defended the reliability of Acts, he was arguing against Marcion, though he chose 2 Timothy 4:10–11, "only Luke is with me," which Marcion did not accept, to prove that Luke was inseparable from Paul. Therefore, he said, "we-passages" in the travel narrative of Acts—also not accepted by Marcion—point to Luke (see chapter 7).[66]

There is a heretical Christian parallel to Marcion in the *Clementine Homilies*, which says that interpolated passages in the Old Testament law can be discovered by comparison with the teaching of Jesus. The author starts with the contrast between God's original purpose for marriage and Moses' authorization of divorce. The real grounds for his criticism, however, must lie in rational criticisms of the Old Testament.[67] As summarized in the *Homilies* themselves, in the Old Testament God is described as taking oaths, tempting, lacking foreknowledge, not seeing everything, not good, living in the temple, desiring sacrifices, and wicked.[68] The criticism reappears in the *Letter to Flora* by the Valentinian Gnostic Ptolemaeus (chapter 4).

For the author of the *Clementine Homilies*, the sayings, or certain sayings, of Jesus make it possible to identify uninterpolated teachings. Interpolation obviously occurred when the Mosaic law was being written and rewritten—not by Moses, whose death is described in Deuteronomy 34:5–6, but by someone who transcribed what seventy wise men had transmitted, and later on in the course of transmission.[69] The "true prophet" explains how to tell true from false.[70]

But we do not need to visit heretical Jewish Christianity to see what Marcion was doing. We can appeal to the famous Galen, even though he was obviously later than Marcion, and his work on the *Aphorisms* ascribed to Hippocrates.[71] Jones insisted that "the ancient testimony in favour of the Hippocratic authorship of *Aphorisms* is overwhelming."[72] Galen did not fully agree. He thought it came from Hippocrates but had been interpolated toward the end. The first 112 sayings were genuine, while few of the next 272 were not; but he rejected 19 of the last 22— relying not on textual criticism but on "the language, the thought, and the teaching of Hippocrates."[73] Presumably Marcion worked along similar lines. When Epiphanius says that he cut much from the end of the Gospel, this means in Marcion's terms that the end was heavily interpolated.

Marcion on the Apostle

We know that Marcion created a corpus of ten authentic Pauline letters, beginning with Galatians—presumably because it was Paul's declaration of independence—and continuing through 1 and 2 Corinthians (left virtually intact), Romans, 1 and 2 Thessalonians, "Laodiceans" (Ephesians), Colossians, Philippians, and Philemon. Unfortunately there is no record of the way in which he defended his selection, his sequence, or his text, but we infer that he used the conventional critical methods of the Greco-Roman schools.

Latin "Marcionite prologues" to the major epistles summarize their contents in a rather one-sided manner, beginning with Galatians and stating that "Galatians are Greeks. These first accepted the word of truth from the apostle, but after his departure were tempted by false apostles to turn to the law and circumcision. The apostle recalls them to faith in the truth, writing to them from Ephesus." The second describes the Corinthians "in similar fashion," and closely parallel notices appear for Romans, Thessalonians, Ephesians (Laodiceans), Colossians, and Philippians, with a brief note on Philemon.[74] All of them lay emphasis on Paul as the only true apostle, who rescued Christians from the false apostles who tried to lead them astray.

Conclusion

It has become conventional for modern scholars to reject the unanimous consensus of early patristic writers that Marcion edited the Gospel of Luke. One wonders how such certainty could have arisen. Both the Fathers and Marcion himself lived in the world of Greco-Roman literary scholarship, and there is nothing irrational about either the editorial process or the patristic claim.

Certainly the reaction to such attempts by Marcion or predecessors was merely traditional. The pseudonymous First Epistle to Timothy (6:20) urges its recipient to guard what has been entrusted to him, avoiding "the godless chatter and contradictions (*antitheseis*) of what is falsely called knowledge." This may or may not be an allusion to Marcion's book, but the whole topic was to be shunned. Polycarp, bishop of Smyrna, similarly denounced anyone who "perverts the sayings of the Lord for his own lusts, and says there is neither resurrection nor judgment." Such a heretic is "the first-born of Satan." Obviously Polycarp was not trying to discuss or argue, any more than when he used the expression to Marcion's face. Polycarp simply appealed to the authority of "the wisdom of the blessed and glorious Paul," among whose letters he included the Pastoral Epistles.[75] Critical discussions could arise only when orthodox Christians gained greater skill and self-confidence. Even in Irenaeus's time heretical exegetes were still more sophisticated than the orthodox. And even though not all of them used literary criticism, their theological results were often similar. In effect, the Gnostic Ptolemaeus described the Bible as interpolated by agents of the inferior creator-god.

4

The Hidden Agenda
of Ptolemaeus

PTOLEMAEUS'S MASTER, the great Gnostic teacher Valentinus, came to Rome around the same time as Marcion. According to Tertullian, he was eminently qualified to become bishop, perhaps at Rome, but left the church when another candidate was selected "by the prerogative of martyrdom." Other sources relate that his disciple Ptolemaeus developed the "Western," presumably Roman, branch of Valentinianism.[1] To confirm his "Westernness," we have the fact that most of the description of Valentinian doctrine by Irenaeus, bishop of Lyons in Gaul, is based on Ptolemaeus's views. Tertullian says he located "outside God" the aeons that his master had set inside but gives no explanation for the change.[2]

Because of his style, logic, and exegetical skill, Ptolemaeus was well prepared to present Valentinian doctrine to the "psychic" members of the church. By "psychic" he meant those who were neither "spiritual" nor "material," but between the two, possessed of free will and choice. Ptolemaeus insists that Valentinian Christians "confess and believe" in "the apostolic tradition which we *too* [italics mine] have received from a succession together with the regulation of all our words by the Savior's teaching." His group has the same origins and standards as the orthodox, though a different idea of succession, back through a certain Theodas to the apostle Paul.[3]

The Letter to Flora

Though Ptolemaeus's exegesis, addressed both to "psychics" and to the "perfect" Valentinians, was based not on critical methods but on allegorization, it took account of points made by the critics. Perhaps his first work was his "open letter" to his "sister Flora," which differentiates the law of God, which forbids divorce, from the law of Moses, which allows it. (He claims, however, that divorce might be the lesser of two evils if the couple should turn to acts of injustice and wickedness, resulting in complete moral ruin.[4]) Could Flora have been the whole Roman church? According to Johannes Lydus, Flora was the "hieratic" name of Rome, "known to all."[5] In the letter Ptolemaeus reads a highly esoteric doctrine into the biblical books, using an exegetical method supposedly based on the teaching of Jesus.[6] Could one call it hieratic? Could a Gnostic teacher have thought of "Flora" as existing on two levels, one psychic, the other spiritual?

At first glance the letter seems to contain rational analysis, especially since much of it is plainly related to the Gospels. (This is why Harnack gave it excessive praise.[7]) For both Ptolemaeus and Flora the prime authorities were the words of the Savior, the disciples of Jesus, and the apostle John and the apostle Paul. Ptolemaeus cites the Savior's words exclusively from Matthew, without naming him, though in one instance he seems to combine Matthew 12:25 with Mark 3:25. Obviously Matthew was a "disciple of Jesus," while other disciples informed the authors of the other Synoptic Gospels, Mark and Luke. Valentinians insisted that an apostle, specifically John, wrote the words, "Everything was made through him and apart from him nothing was made" (John 1:3), and that the apostle Paul, who was not one of the disciples of Jesus, spoke of Christ as "our paschal lamb" (1 Cor. 5:7) and referred to the law in two contradictory senses (Eph. 2:15, Rom. 7:12).[8] What John and Paul meant, however, was not quite what they said.

In Ptolemaeus's view the Mosaic law, not ordained by either the supreme God the Father or by the devil, comes from the Demiurge, who is just. It has three parts: (1) legislation from God himself (the Demiurge), (2) legislation from Moses, speaking on his own, and (3) interpolations by the elders of the people. Verses from Matthew prove the point. Again, the first part of the law that came from God himself consists of three parts: (a) the pure legislation from God himself (the Demiurge), the Decalogue, which the Savior cited as from God according to Matthew 15:4 (from Moses according to Mark 7:10): "God said, 'He who curses father or mother shall surely die"; (b) a part mixed with wrong, which the Savior abrogated because of its injustice, for a death leads to a second murder (cf. Matt. 5:38–42); and (c) a typical and symbolical part (sacrifices, circumcision, Sabbath, fasting, paschal lamb, unleavened bread, etc.), which the Savior deepened in their spiritual meaning.

Ptolemaeus gives examples to prove his points. He adds that Flora ought to learn about the origin of things, how from the one good beginning arose both evil and the mediating righteousness. Ptolemaeus is explaining why, according to Matthew, Jesus insisted so strongly on the way to perfection through law-observance while stating that Moses made concessions because of the hardness of hearts. Theophilus of Antioch was to say that the Sermon on the Mount was Moses rewritten to be "more rigorous." Both are upholding Jewish-Christian teaching against Marcion's radical Paulinism. At the same time, Ptolemaeus is leading Flora down the garden path toward Gnostic cosmology.

In his time the orthodox apologist Justin insisted on the importance of Jesus' commandments, especially in the Sermon on the Mount, and similarly divided the Mosaic law into three parts, relying on the teaching of Jesus. The law consisted of commandments instituted (1) for piety and just actions, or (2) in regard to the mystery of Christ, or (3) because of the hard-heartedness of the people.[9] Nominally he shared this division with Ptolemaeus, though his intention was quite different. Justin's division was based on purpose, Ptolemaeus's on origins. Ptolemaeus thus goes farther and speaks explicitly of "interpolations" into the Pentateuch—and possibly into the words of the Savior as well, as Quispel suggests, though Irenaeus may have Marcion in mind.[10] In the *Letter* Ptolemaeus never refers to Jesus or Christ but always speaks of "the Savior" and his words, while in Irenaeus's account he differentiated the impassible Savior from the Christ who suffered.[11]

Ptolemaeus's exegesis of the Savior's teaching appears in Irenaeus's first book *Against Heresies*, which tells how he distorted texts from the

Lord's parables, the oracles of the prophets, and the words of apostles. He insisted that the thirty Aeons of the Pleroma above were to be found in the Savior's first thirty years of private life (Luke 3:23) and in his parable of the Laborers in the Vineyard who were hired at the hours 1+3+6+9+11 (Matt. 20:1–7).[12] Claiming that the Savior came to reveal the passion that the twelfth Aeon experienced in the Pleroma, Ptolemaeus found that the twelve-year-old daughter of the chief of the synagogue, raised from the dead by the Lord (Luke 8:41–42, 49–56), was this twelfth Aeon, Achamoth (whose mysterious name comes from the Hebrew word for Wisdom). A faint trace of justification for this exegesis might be found in the fact that the daughter's age has nothing to do with the story, any more than in the parallel version in Mark 5:42: "the girl immediately arose and walked about, *for* she was twelve years old," but Irenaeus does not say that Ptolemaeus mentioned the point in his quest for twelves.[13]

The Savior appeared to Achamoth when she was outside the Pleroma, for Paul speaks not of himself but in the person of her shapeless offspring when he says, "Last of all he appeared to me as to an abortion" (1 Cor. 15:8). Again, it is clear that when the Savior came to Achamoth he was escorted by his companions, as Paul reveals in the same letter: "The woman must have a veil on her head because of the angels" (1 Cor. 11:10). The same veiling is indicated by Moses' wearing a veil (2 Cor. 3:13). These mysterious statements in Corinthians are only loosely connected with their contexts, and Gnostics could therefore treat them as secret messages.

Like Paul, Jesus could speak in the role of Achamoth, or rather, Achamoth could speak through Jesus. He manifested her passions when he cried out on the cross, "My God, my God, why have you abandoned me?" (Matt. 27:46) He revealed her grief: "How sad is my soul" (Matt. 26:38); her fear: "Father, if it be possible, let this cup pass from me" (Matt. 26:39, RSV); and her anguish: "I do not know what I shall say" (John 12:27). In other words, the various aspects of his Passion, described in the Gospels as merely historical, really reflected aspects of her primary and original passion.

Again, mysterious sayings of Jesus, especially about various kinds of disciples, clearly pointed toward the Valentinian doctrine of the three races of men. The basic text was Matthew 8:19–22 (par. Luke 9:57–62), where the first man Jesus encounters says, "I will follow you wherever you go." Jesus replies, "Foxes have holes and the birds of the air have nests; but the Son of man has nowhere to lay his head." Ptolemaeus took this to refer to the lowest, "hylic," or material race, comparable to foxes or birds, not the Son of man. Another man implies that he will follow, but asks permission to say goodbye to those of his house. He is a psychic person, endowed with soul (*psychē*); he belongs to the intermediate group and though he chose to follow (since he possessed free will), he lacked stability and then chose not to follow. The Lord therefore replied, "Whoever has put his hand to the plow but looks back is not fit for the kingdom of heaven" (Luke 9:61–62). (The psychic race is also represented by the man who confessed he had performed the many duties of "justice" but refused to follow the Savior because of his wealth, which kept him from becoming "perfect" [Matt. 19:16–22].) Finally, the Lord pointed to the spiritual race when he told a man who wanted to bury his father before following, "Let the dead bury the dead, but *you* go and proclaim the kingdom of God" (Matt. 8:22 = Luke 9:60), and also when he said to Zacchaeus the tax collector, "Hasten to come down, for today I must stay in your house," and Zacchaeus received him with joy (Luke 19:5–6).

All three races can also be found in the parable of the leaven that the woman hid in three measures of meal (Matt. 13:33 = Luke 13:20–21). The woman is the heavenly Sophia (Wisdom); the three measures are the three races—spiritual, psychic, earthly; the meal itself is the Savior. The Gospel speaks allegorically, but Paul spoke literally or precisely about "earthy" (= hylic or material), "psychics," and "spirituals." He refers to the first group when he says, "As was the earthy, so also the earthy ones" (1 Cor. 15:48). The reference to the psychic person is more subtle. Paul's words—"The psychic man does not receive the things of the Spirit" (1 Cor. 2:14)—are a generalization about psychics but specifically show that the Demiurge, who is psychic, knows neither the spiritual Mother nor her seed nor the Aeons of the Pleroma. The situation of the spirituals is plainly stated in the very next verse: "The spiritual examines all" (1 Cor. 2:15). Romans 11:16 is a little more obscure: "If the firstfruits are holy, the whole is holy too." This means that the Savior put on the "firstfruits" (the spiritual element) of "the whole," or what he was going to save, that is, the psychic church.

Even more speculatively, Ptolemaeus relates the words of Christ and stories about him to cosmic events in the world above. After Achamoth fell from the Pleroma, Christ (the merely psychic) shaped Achamoth and the Savior looked for her. This is expressed in his declaration that he came to "the lost sheep" (Matt. 18:12–13; Luke 15:4–7), their Mother, from whom the church here below was sown. The sheep got lost in her stay outside the Pleroma, experiencing all the passions from which matter was made. The woman who cleans house and finds a lost drachma (Luke 15:8–10) is the Sophia (Wisdom) Above, who is looking for her lost Enthymesis or Desire. Later, when everything has been purified by the coming of the Savior, she finds it, for this Enthymesis must be restored within the Pleroma.

Simeon, who took the Christ in his arms and thanked God, saying, "Now let your servant depart in peace, according to your word" (Luke 2:29), is equivalent to the Demiurge who, at the Savior's coming, learned of his change of place and gave thanks to Bythos (the Aeon named "Depth"), learning everything from the Savior and joining him with his whole army. He is therefore represented by the centurion in the Gospel who said, "I too have soldiers and servants under my power and they do everything I command" (Matt. 8:9; Luke 7:8). The Gospel tells how the prophet Anna lived seven years with her husband and spent the rest of her life as a widow. Since she saw the Lord, recognized him, and spoke of him to all (Luke 2:36–38), she obviously signifies Achamoth, who saw the Lord with his companions for a moment and then remained in the middle for the whole later period, waiting for him to come and establish her in her syzygy or pair of Aeons. The Savior pointed to her name in his enigmatic statement, "Sophia is justified by all her children" (Luke 7:35, RSV), as did Paul in these words, "We speak of Sophia among the perfect" (1 Cor. 2:6). Paul also spoke of the syzygies within the Pleroma when he spoke plainly about one such syzygy: "This mystery is great, but I speak of Christ and Church" (Eph. 5:32).[14]

The greatness of the mystery could be found especially in the more enigmatic sayings of Jesus in the Gospels. Indeed, Irenaeus complained of the Gnostics that they began with enigmatic sayings rather than clear ones and adapted ambiguous expressions to their fictitious creation. You cannot explain one ambiguity through another, he insisted.[15] He suggested ironically that the Gnostics rightly reserved their exegesis for those able to pay for it since it had cost them an immense effort to produce.[16]

Ptolemaeus on John

In addition, Ptolemaeus provided detailed exegesis of the prologue which "John, the Lord's disciple" (i.e., not just an apostle) had written in order to "point to the Ogdoad or group of eight Aeons." Since this reference is by no means obvious, Ptolemaeus had to reinterpret every verse and nearly every word to fit Valentinian doctrine. He began with definitions and glosses.

In the Beginning (the first principle also called Son and God Only-Begotten) *was* (God the Father, who emitted) *the Logos* (and in him the whole substance of the Aeons, which the Logos subsequently formed). "Since John speaks of the first genesis," writes Ptolemaeus, "he rightly begins his teaching with the Beginning (the Son) and the Logos." For him Beginning is not temporal but locative.

Next he analyzes prepositional relationships (my italics for emphasis). "*In* the Beginning was the Logos, and the Logos was *with* God, and the Logos was God; this Logos was *in* the Beginning and *with* God."[17] John first differentiates three terms: God, Beginning, and Logos, then unites them—in order to show (a) the emission of the Son and the Logos and (b) the unity between them and with the Father. For *in* the Father and *from* the Father is the Beginning, while *in* the Beginning and *from* the Beginning is the Logos. John therefore expressed it rightly when he said, "In the Beginning was the Logos," for the Logos was *in* the Son. "And the Logos was *with* God"—and so was the Beginning. "And the Logos was God" since what is born *of* God is God. "This was *in* the Beginning, *with* God": the phrase reveals the sequence of the emission. "Everything was made *through* him, and *apart from* him nothing was made": for to all the Aeons that came after him, the Logos was the cause of formation and birth. In other words, as Quispel notes, the creation was brought about by Christ (the Son-Logos) and by the Demiurge, the Old Testament God.[18]

John continues: "What was made *in* him was Life," thus indicating a syzygy or "pair." For he says that everything was made *through* him, but Life was *in* him. Life, made *in* him, is closer to him than what was made *through* him. It is *with* him and bears fruit *through* him. Such exegesis, emphasizing the use of various prepositions, is well paralleled in Colossians 1:16–20. "*In* him all things were created, . . . *through* him and *for* him. He is *before* all things, and *in* him all things hold together. . . ." Ptolemaeus's emphasis is similar, but his cast of characters is more extensive.

He continues: "And the Life was the Light of Men." When he says "Men," he signifies "Church" under the same name in order to show through one term the communion of the syzygy; for from Logos and Life come Man and Church. He calls Life "the Light of Men" because they have been illuminated by it, i.e., formed and manifested. This is also what Paul says: "All that is manifested is Light" (Eph. 5:13). So since the Life manifested and generated Man and Church, it is called their Light. Thus John clearly manifested the Second Tetrad: Logos and Life, Man and Church.

But he also pointed to the First Tetrad, for speaking of the Savior and teaching that whatever is outside the Pleroma was formed *through* him, he also says that the Savior is the fruit *within* the Pleroma. For he calls him that Light which "shines in darknesses and is not comprehended by them," because, while harmonizing everything that was made from the passion, he remained ignored by them. John called this Savior Son, Truth, Life, and incarnate Logos. He says that we have seen his glory, and his glory was that such as Only-Begotten has, glory given by the Father to him, filled with Grace and Truth. He speaks thus: "And the Logos became flesh and dwelt among us and we beheld his glory, glory like what Only-Begotten has from the Father, filled with Grace and Truth." So he exactly describes the First Tetrad: Father and Grace, Only-Begotten and Truth. And thus John speaks of the first Ogdoad, Mother of all the Aeons, for he named Father and Grace and Only-Begotten and Truth and Logos and Life and Man and Church—not the incarnation of the Logos.

Gnostic Ideas About Inspiration

Irenaeus tells us that the disciples of Valentinus and the other falsely named Gnostics claim that some things in the scriptures were spoken by the Supreme Power for the seed that came forth from it, others by the Intermediary through the Mother Prunica, but most of them by the Demiurge, by whom the prophets were sent.[19]

In Ptolemaeus's view the Old Testament law belongs to the third category. It was not given by "the perfect God who is the Father" but contains commands from the Demiurge, his prophet Moses, and various elders of the people. Elsewhere he differentiates three sources of the prophetic writings: from the Mother who spoke of things above, from the spiritual seed (souls that had received Wisdom), and from the Demiurge and the souls he made. Similarly the words of Jesus come from the Savior, the Mother, and the Demiurge. The Demiurge was ignorant of these divisions and himself attributed the words of the prophets to the prophetic spirit or the ideal man or a combination of the two.[20] Obviously Ptolemaeus relied on seeming contradictions among his sources in order to establish such groups of three.

Other Gnostics, on a lower philosophical level, applied their modest acquaintance with Hebrew to analysis of inspiration. In their view each of the seven planetary angels with the Hebrew names of God chose his own herald to glorify him. One would expect, therefore, some correlation with such names. According to these Gnostics, (1) the chief angel was Ialdabaoth, the creator, redeemer, and legislator who inspired Moses, Joshua, Amos, and Habakkuk. (2) It was Iao who inspired Samuel, Nathan, Jonah, and Micah; the only real proof for this view is that, according to Jonah, Gentiles speak of Elohim but the prophet knows the name Yahweh. (3) The name Sabaoth does not occur from Genesis to Judges, but Elijah occasionally refers to Yahweh Sabaoth (1 Kings 18:15, 19:10, 14), Sabaoth is named in Joel 2:2–11, 3:14, and Yahweh Sabaoth especially in Zechariah 1 and 14. (4) Adonai appears in the major prophets, notably at Isaiah 6:1, Jeremiah 1:6, Ezekiel 2:4, and Daniel 1:2. (5) Eloeus (Eloa) occurs in Job but not in Tobias and Haggai, named in the Gnostic list. (6) Horeus for Micah and Nahum does not make sense, and neither does (7) Astaphaeus for Esdras and Zephaniah.[21] There are many noncorrespondences because of the ineptitude of either Gnostic or anti-Gnostic writers, but there are enough correlations to show that the idea had a semirational base.

Irenaeus describes Ptolemaeus's exegesis before attacking it as internally inconsistent. The order of the emissions is illogical, he says, and there is no mention of the Valentinian Aeon Church. In addition the exegesis is obviously contrary to what John taught about Jesus Christ as the incarnate Logos.[22] He sets the debate in a literary-critical context when he compares Valentinian exegesis to the so-called *Homerocentones*, poems created by stringing together isolated verses from various parts of Homer to tell a story quite different from Homer's. Ten lines out of context could show how Eurystheus sent Heracles to Cerberus, the dog of Hades. "Anyone who knows the Homeric poems will recognize the verses but not the sequence, knowing that one verse is said of Odysseus, another of Heracles, another of Priam, another of Menelaus and Agamemnon. If he takes the verses and restores each to its original book, he will make the supposed sequence disappear."[23] The telling comparison implies that the Gospels existed before the Gnostic exegesis of them. In any event, the evangelists and apostles did not have Gnostic mythology in mind as they wrote.

Mid-century literary criticism among Christians had reached a stalemate. Marcion had failed to convince the leaders of the churches that he could detect and delete interpolations from *Gospel* and *Apostle*. Ptolemaeus's exegesis was correlated with his ingenious theology and forced his opponents to pay close attention to the smallest details. His allegorizations therefore rested on a severely literalistic base but remained incomprehensible to most Christians. The problems of authenticity had not been solved, and it could only be hoped that sensible literary criticism could deal with them. There would be a fresh emphasis on traditions about the apostolic age, but it could be combined with a critical approach.

Meanwhile at Rome the famous Roman physician and author Galen of Pergamum was engaging in critical analysis of the Hippocratic collection as he commented on it. His approach to criticism and logic was to influence Christians both heretical and orthodox.

5

Galen's Literary
and Logical Criticism

THE GREEK anthologist Athenaeus, who made his collection of materials
at Rome within a decade or so after Galen's death, said that he "published more works on philosophy and medicine than all his predecessors,
and in the exposition of his art was as capable as any of the ancients." He
was an intellectual leader in medicine, philosophy, and literary criticism,
especially in his commentaries on "Hippocrates." Athenaeus himself had
heard of the kind of critical questions Galen discussed. When he dealt
with a word that "Hippocrates" used in his *Barley-Gruel*, he noted that
this particular work was "half spurious, some say entirely so."[1]

Galen had begun studying philosophy at Pergamum in 143 when he
was fourteen. He went on to anatomy three years later, and a year or so
later, after his father's death, proceeded to study medicine at Smyrna,
Corinth, and Alexandria. He became physician to the gladiatorial school
at Pergamum in 157 but after four years left Pergamum for Rome, where
he began his forty-year career as author and ultimately court physician to
Marcus Aurelius, Commodus, and Septimius Severus. During the plague
in Italy that broke out in 166, he withdrew to Pergamum, but in 168
Marcus Aurelius summoned him to Aquileia for the German expedition.
After the sudden death of the co-emperor Verus the next year, Galen
returned to Rome as physician to the boy Caesar Commodus and within a
few years wrote some of his major treatises and practiced medicine. After

his last major treatise, *Therapeutic Method*, he catalogued his own works and may have died in 199.[2]

Obviously Galen moved in "high society" at Rome. He was also acquainted with Christianity and probably with Christians, mentioning their irrational insistence on divine power as well as their contempt of death, abstinence in sex and diet, and pursuit of justice. Marcus Aurelius too had noted their "readiness for death," but without enthusiasm. Under Commodus persecution was unusual, and around 190 his concubine Marcia was able to obtain the release of Christian prisoners on Sardinia.[3] Indeed, as Galen busied himself with antidotes to the poisons Septimius Severus might ingest, the emperor was protecting Christians of senatorial rank from the mob.[4] There were links between the society of Galen and the Roman church, favoring the transmission of his critical ideas.

Galen was aware that both Jews and Christians were concerned with literature as well as tradition, though he did not discuss their literary criticism—if any existed. He referred to what Moses "wrote" or "says" and spoke of "the followers of Moses and Christ."[5] Since he connects the two groups with each other, he may reflect contact with Jewish Christians, probably Adoptionists. In turn, he was to exercise strong influence on the Jewish-Christian heretics who were concerned with logic, biblical criticism, and theology.

His emphasis on critical method is conspicuous in the series of commentaries on "Hippocrates" that he began around 175. These medical treatises, ascribed to the fifth-century physician Hippocrates of Cos but apparently assembled around 300 B.C., were entangled with much contradictory lore. Later physicians had tried to disentangle the true "Hippocratic" treatises, or parts of treatises, from inauthentic materials. Galen, trained in literary criticism and relying on good sources, would become the most famous analyst of Hippocrates. Like commentators on Plato and Aristotle and the Bible, he was dealing with a collection of writings composed over a long period of time and put together by members of schools whose criteria of selection were by no means obvious. Galen made decisions about the "real" Hippocrates, just as Marcion portrayed the Jesus who proclaimed the real revelation that had been distorted by those who did not accept Marcion's criteria. There was little objective evidence to support decisions about either Hippocrates or Jesus, as the history of scholarship ancient and modern shows. For instance, Edelstein vigorously claimed that "it seems likely that none of the books preserved under the name of Hippocrates is genuine," and Lloyd agreed that "the radical scepticism of the Wilamowitz of 1901 and of Edelstein does not seem misplaced."[6]

The Hippocratic collection, with its mixture of genuine and spurious materials, was like the incipient New Testament. It has been claimed for the New Testament that "attribution [of authorship] in the pseudonymous . . . epistles must be regarded primarily as an assertion of authoritative tradition, not of literary origins,"[7] and inevitably authorship was related to the authority of the Hippocratic tradition. Christians and physicians had to face similar problems of method, even though the Christians were concerned with the traditions that formed and informed a whole church, physicians with the ideas of smaller groups. When Marcion tried to preserve only the true teaching of Jesus, he had to differentiate what was authentic from what had been interpolated and what was spurious.

The Hippocratic corpus was assembled at Alexandria during the early years of the Ptolemies and was first given scholarly treatment by a certain Bacchius, who wrote a glossary of the rare words in at least seventeen Hippocratic treatises. Under Nero, Erotian produced his own glossary using thirty-seven Hippocratic works, not including *Prorrhetic II*, which he explicitly denied to Hippocrates. The Hippocratic critical question, of which Galen would make so much, was thus opened.[8] Galen's most important guides were the editions of Hippocrates created in the reign of Hadrian by Dioscurides and Artemidorus Capito, though these critics said little about authorship. Dioscurides attributed part of *Nature of Man* and *Diseases* to a Hippocrates who was son of Thessalus, and he imagined that Thessalus added an "indecorous passage" in *Epidemics VI*.[9] In addition,"a consistent series of stylistic judgments and attributions of works" in Galen's commentaries probably "go back to the work of Dioscurides or 'those about Dioscurides.'"[10]

Galen on Hippocratic Writings

Galen's comments on authorship begin just before his Hippocratic commentaries. In the *Faculties of Food*, he mentioned that the Hippocratic *Regimen* was ascribed variously to Hippocrates, Philistion, Ariston,

Euryphon, or Philetas, "all ancients."[11] This question would remain open throughout the commentaries. Evidently he took his information from older commentators. Around the same time he said that *Epidemics II, IV,* and *VI* were composed by Hippocrates or his son Thessalus, and insisted that *Aphorisms* was by one author, *Prorrhetic* by another.[12] Once more the comments come from the medical tradition.

He went into more detail in *Abnormal Breathing,* where he stated not only that *Epidemics I* and *III* are "recognized by all as from the great Hippocrates" but that "the best judges say *I* and *III* are by Hippocrates." *Epidemics II* and *V,* however, were composed respectively by Hippocrates' sons Thessalus and Dracon, while *IV* is unworthy of the mind of Hippocrates. At another point in the same work Galen could state that "some more accurately assign *V* to Thessalus, *II* to the great Hippocrates; they are entitled 'books' in the little Pinax" (not otherwise identified), while "all agree that *Epidemics VII* is obviously spurious, recent, and interpolated; it is not worthy of the genuine mind of Hippocrates." Outside these books, *Aphorisms* and *Prognostic* are "not unreasonably" considered writings of Hippocrates.[13] Once more, he is relying on the studies of earlier critics.

In a larger precommentary treatise on *The Doctrines of Hippocrates and Plato,* Galen discusses authorship only once, stating that "the four pairs of veins said to descend from the head are obvious falsifications interpolated into the writings that carry Hippocrates' name." He mentions that they were discussed in an "obviously spurious" book and claims that they were inserted at the end of *Nature of Man.* "Others before us," says Galen, "have demonstrated that the anatomy of the above-mentioned veins is not the authentic view of Hippocrates or [his son-in-law] Polybus." He hopes to write a treatise on the genuine works of Hippocrates.[14]

At this point he began the commentaries on the Hippocratic corpus. He started with the "most genuine and most useful works" by Hippocrates, his *Fractures* and *Joints, Ulcers* and *Head Wounds.*[15] He introduced *Fractures* by defining exegesis as explanation, not argument. *Joints* reveals some of the grounds on which he could reject a treatise. While Hippocrates did refer to his own lost book on *Glands,* the extant booklet with this title was composed by some more recent physician who called it *Hippocrates On Glands.* It is inferior in both style and understanding and is not genuine. There is no previous medical commentary on it, and it is not named on lists.[16] These last criteria show how much Galen relied on his predecessors.

Next Galen commented on *Regimen in Acute Diseases*, up as far as the discussion of baths [cc. 65–68] because friends asked him to do so. This was the most authentic part of the book, with many observations in accordance with "the mind of Hippocrates." Ultimately Galen wrote four books on this *Regimen* and said it was a work of Hippocrates "acknowl-eged" to be authentic.[17] His discussion includes an unusual defense of its authenticity. More sceptical critics claimed that the word *chondros* ("spelt groats"), not known in Hippocrates' time, proved the work was a forgery. Using word studies, Galen replied that the word was used by poets of the Old Comedy, and that even if the book was not by Hippocrates, it must come from a medical writer of his time or earlier. He obviously relies on earlier discussions with examples of the use of this word by old comic poets.[18]

Between 176 and 179 Galen composed his commentary on *Epidemics I*, later claiming that it would really need fifty books of commentaries, while the other books needed only two apiece, or even one. As usual, Galen held that the editor Thessalus kept *I* and *III* as Hippocrates left them but interpolated the other volumes of the work.[19]

In some of Galen's last commentaries, he makes clear and detailed statements almost for the first time. For instance, in commenting on *Epidemics II* he repeats his earlier off-hand statement about *II*, *IV*, and *VI*: they were composed by Hippocrates or Thessalus or by Thessalus alone.[20] In this commentary he, therefore, said at first that it makes no difference whether the book was written by Hippocrates or his son Thessalus. Later, however, he went into more detail, obviously relying on earlier sources. "Thessalus son of Hippocrates edited what Hippocrates had written on parchment and paper, and some say he added many inter-polations." Galen agrees with the "some" and adds that Hippocrates wrote only *Epidemics I* and *III* for the general public. The point is proved by the form of expression, which is the same in *I* as in *III*.

At this point he proposes a radical rearrangement of the *Epidemics*: "III" is the wrong title, for "III" is really II, and "II" is III, and so "VI" should be IV. The present "IV" and "V" do not belong to the writings of

Hippocrates, according to *those who have separated genuine from spurious* [my italics], but were assembled from isolated notes as "II" and "VI" were. "II" and "VI" (better numbered III and IV) should be called "the first and second books of the memoranda of Hippocrates," or perhaps "miscellaneous" or "dubious expressions." They are not really part of the *Epidemics.*[21] Much later in the commentary he lists authentic works by Hippocrates. These include *Fractures, Joints, Aphorisms, Regimen in Acute Diseases, Prognosis,* "and other genuine books."[22] At this point he shows how easily works can be forged or interpolated by telling an amusing story about Lucian (presumably the satirist), who created a book full of "dark sayings" and ascribed it to Heraclitus. A philosopher and some grammarians commented on it at length—and to no purpose.[23]

Around the same time, in commenting on the Hippocratic *Seven-months' Children,*[24] Galen provides another analysis of questions about authorship. He sets the stage by recalling that "many exegetes say all the books [in the Hippocratic corpus] are by Hippocrates" and then proceeds to alternatives. "Many say they are not from one author. Four persons bear this name: the son of Gnosidicus, the son of Heraclides, the son of Thessalus, and the son of Dracon. There are writings from all of them. *On the Eight-months' Child* is by Polybus,[25] while *Nutriment* is from Thessalus. Another exegete says that the content of *Epidemics II* is from Thessalus, while others say it was forged by someone else." Now he is ready to explain who Thessalus and Polybus were. "Thessalus was the son of Hippocrates II, the son of Heraclides, who followed the son of Gnosidicus. Polybus was the pupil of Hippocrates who took over the instruction of his pupils, since he lived in the city of Astypelaia [?]. Thessalus traveled most of his life, since he was an associate of King Archelaus of Macedonia."[26]

According to Galen, many think that *On Nutriment* is not from Thessalus but from the circle of Herophilus, and many of them think that the author is unknown. Further, they say of the expressions in parts of *Epidemics* that they are not genuine. Forgery is especially common in *II* and *VI,* which were not composed for reading like *I* and *III.* The son Thessalus collected what Hippocrates had left as notes on papers and leaves. He put in some of his own ideas and another person also made interpolations. (Origen will later speak thus about Hebrews.)

About 180 Galen wrote his commentary on *Prorrhetic I*. Because this work is much inferior to Hippocrates, some ascribed it to Dracon, others to Thessalus. Did the author die before publication? It makes no difference.[27] Galen definitely rejects *Setting Joints by Leverage*, for it contains "not a few examples of bad Greek" that "lead to the reasonable suspicion that it is not by Hippocrates."[28]

About 186 he turned to *Epidemics III* and reiterated his opinion that "accurately following the mind of Hippocrates, Thessalus collected his manuscripts in books *II* and *VI* with some interpolations" and also interpolated the last parts of *Aphorisms*.[29] Three years later he reached *Epidemics VI* and explained its composition all over again, not once but several times.[30]

Among Galen's last commentaries are those on *Nature of Man* in two books and on *Regimen in Health*. He marvels at those who are led astray by the interpolated passages in *Nature of Man* and think it is not among the genuine works of Hippocrates but "spurious," then quotes from his own (or someone else's) *Essay on the Genuine and Spurious Treatises of Hippocrates*.[31] The first 240 lines of the book are genuine but heterogeneous, followed by about 360 lines that are partly interpolated, partly not. The very first part "is entirely in accord with Hippocratic science." After he finished the commentary on *Nature of Man*, he heard doubts about its authenticity and replied in a work now lost, entitled *That Hippocrates Presents the Same Opinion in Nature of Man as in His Other Writings*.[32]

Galen noted that *Regimen*, ascribed to various "ancient" authors, began thus according to some manuscripts: "One must know the power of each kind of food and drink by nature and by art [*Regimen* 2.39]"; in others, thus: "One must know the setting and nature of each kind of place [*Regimen* 2.37]." In the manuscripts it is combined with *Nature of Man*, and Galen observed that "when the whole, consisting of three parts, is found undivided, it is entitled *Nature of Man and Regimen*, but when this part circulates by itself it is entitled *Regimen* and is the second part of the whole divided into three. The second part, dealing with cereals, one might reasonably consider worthy of Hippocrates, but the first is very different from Hippocrates' mind."[33] "Some reject the *Regimen in Health* ascribed to Hippocrates," Galen says, "and assign it to Philistion or Ariston or Pherecydes. Is it from the period of Erasistratus?"[34] More definitely, he insists that "it should be ascribed to Polybus, as it seemed to many."[35] He is relying on authorities, not his own research.

Galen's Literary Criticism

Smith convincingly argued that Galen's critical methods leave much to be desired, even for his time. There is a basic flaw in his ascriptions of authorship. When he assigns various works to the sons Thessalus and Dracon, and the son-in-law Polybus, he neglects his own axiom that these successors maintained Hippocrates' teaching intact.[36] And if this is so, it is obviously impossible to differentiate their works from those of Hippocrates himself.

Such a difficulty helps explain the fluctuations in Galen's own ideas. He can say that *Epidemics V* was composed by Dracon—or more accurately by Thessalus. Again, he can ascribe *Prorrhetic* to either Thessalus or Dracon. And he assigns many works to Hippocrates or Polybus, or to Polybus alone. Beyond such ascriptions, Galen can claim that *Epidemics VII* is universally rejected because obviously spurious, recent, and interpolated; it is not worthy of the genuine mind of Hippocrates. Equally obviously, Galen's judgment is firmly based on traditional opinions.

An unusually substantive argument favors *The Sacred Disease.* Galen says the ancients called epilepsy "great disease" and "affliction of children," as Hippocrates does in his *Waters, Airs, and Places;* some think the wrath of gods causes disease, but Hippocrates never thought so, as is shown by *Regimen in Acute Diseases,* which is among those acknowledged as genuine.[37] In Galen's view the "theology" of epilepsy is based not on reason but on anecdotes; neither epilepsy nor eros is inflicted by the gods. A gloss found in Hippocratic manuscripts tells why Galen rejected *The Sacred Disease.* "It is not a genuine work of Hippocrates, according to Galen, [but of?] a man noteworthy for interpretation and understanding. There is nothing of Hippocrates in it, either as to the manner of interpretation or the accuracy of understanding."[38] Here is a rather convincing argument that we might call theological, or at least convincing.[39]

Lloyd puts it thus in his study of Galen's motives for studying Hippocrates: "If Hippocrates had not existed, Galen would have had to invent him. But then, in a sense, he did."[40] We cannot claim more for him, or for the critics whose work he used without acknowledgment, than that they recognized some of the problems in the Hippocratic tradition. Christian scholars too would be able to identify such problems in their own collections of books, though not yet in Galen's lifetime, as far as we know.

Galen and Logic

On the other hand, Galen soon influenced Christian biblical critics concerned with logical proof of their statements. He himself had looked for proofs of propositions at an early age but had found little of value among the famous Stoics and Peripatetics. Indeed, he would have fallen into skeptical doubt had he not held fast to the propositional geometry to which his father introduced him. Indeed, he refers precisely to a "proof" given by Euclid in the second theorem of the eleventh book of his *Elements* and says that "one must learn proof from Euclid."[41] After reviewing the method, he wrote fifteen books *On Proof*, three *On Aristotle's Hermeneutic*, and eight on syllogistic proof.[42] He praised the works on proof by "the ancient philosophers Theophrastus and Aristotle," but denounced Chrysippus as verbose and unscientific.[43] He also criticized Moses sharply for writing without providing any proofs and supposing that anything was possible for God. In his view the followers of both Moses and Christ taught "undemonstrated laws" and ordered pupils to "accept everything on faith."[44]

Though Galen's books *On Proof* are lost,[45] he naturally discussed logical questions in his *Instruction in Logic* (*Institutio logica*) when he treated conditional and disjunctive syllogisms and alluded to Euclid and Theophrastus, just as the Adoptionists did. He explained that "the Stoics call continuous hypothetical protases 'conditional propositions,' and they call discontinuous hypothetical protases 'disjunctions'; they agree that there are two syllogisms for the conditional proposition and two for the disjunction."[46] Basically the conditional syllogism began with "if," whereas the disjunctive contained "either . . . or."[47] Something like this treatise, with similar sources, was in the hands of Galen's Christian Adoptionist admirers at Rome.

Adoptionism and Orthodoxy

Toward the end of Galen's life these heretical Christians at Rome took pride in using syllogistic and critical methods and explicitly praised him as their model.[48] Their heresy lay in the view that Christ was not God but a human being adopted by God as his Son. Like more orthodox Christians such as Irenaeus, they appealed to the consensus of church tradition but held a very different view of what it was. Using historical analysis of a sort, they claimed that all Christians from the apostles through Victor, recently bishop of Rome, had held their doctrine, although it was "counterfeited" under his successor Zephyrinus. This last bishop was a convenient target for criticism because he was reputed to be "stupid, illiterate, and without experience of the church's rules," as well as "an avaricious bribe-taker."[49] Zephyrinus's basic dogma—the "counterfeited" one—was said to be this: "I know one God, Christ Jesus, and apart from him no other, created and subject to suffering;" though sometimes he added paradoxically, "The Father did not die, but the Son did."[50] Such teaching did not commend itself either to Adoptionists or to more orthodox opponents. The idea that the truth was "counterfeited" under him recalls what Galen said about proof in general. What people usually provide as proof, he said, is like a counterfeit coin.[51]

The church historian Eusebius quotes from an anonymous orthodox critic of the Adoptionists.[52] He argued that their view was opposed to the scriptures and that Christian apologists and antiheretical authors well before Victor treated Christ as God[53] or God and man.[54] Psalms and hymns written "from the beginning" also refer to Christ as Logos and treat him as God—here "beginning," "Logos," and "God" probably point to the prologue to the Fourth Gospel, viewed as a hymn. Presumably the Adoptionists countered by discussing the history of theology, just as Galen had discussed the history of medicine when he attributed Hippocratic works to various authors, but we have no trace of the way they argued.

Adoptionist Logic

The Adoptionists wanted to sort out texts and, like moneychangers, discover the genuine ancient ones, discarding the false.[55] They rejected the analogical exegesis commonly used by Christians in favor of logical methods for explaining the scriptures. Some of them, says the anonymous critic, studied the geometry of Euclid and marveled at Aristotle and his disciple Theophrastus. Above all, Galen, who lived and taught at

Rome in their time, "may be worshiped by some of them"—unlike Jesus, whom they obviously did not worship. (Oddly enough, Galen himself complained that there were those who marveled at the earlier physician Erasistratus "as a god" and thought that everything he said was true.[56]) "If anyone brings forward a text of divine scripture, they determine whether it can be put in the form of a conditional or disjunctive syllogism."[57] The critic supplies no example, but both conditional and disjunctive syllogisms were important in second-century logic, and it was sometimes claimed that Homer himself used syllogistic arguments.[58] The Adoptionists' admiration of Euclid, Aristotle, and Theophrastus is just like that of Galen.[59] He himself must have been the Adoptionists' primary authority, perhaps the only one. They admired the philosophers he cited and joined him in using Stoic, not Peripatetic, terms for syllogisms. Few Roman Christians before their time could deal with their logic (obviously Bishop Zephyrinus did not use syllogisms), though syllogistic arguments had been used at Athens by the apologist Athenagoras and would be used at Alexandria by Clement and Origen, after the Jewish apologist Philo. And as we shall see (chapter 6), the Marcionite Apelles wrote his book of syllogisms at Rome.[60]

Adoptionist Textual Criticism

The critic adds that the Adoptionists "lay hands on the divine scriptures and say that they have corrected them" by comparing manuscripts. He claims that they are highly inconsistent. "The copies of Asclepiades do not agree with those of Theodotus, and it is possible to obtain many of them because their disciples have diligently written out copies, corrected as they say, but really corrupted by each of them. Again the copies of Hermophilus do not agree with these, while those of Apolloniades do not even agree among themselves, for the copies first prepared by them can be compared with those later altered, and much disagreement will be found."[61] What he treats as a fault reflects the kind of situation that critics like Galen and Origen tended to bypass. Galen found "virtually complete agreement among the copies of the text and the [old] commentaries" and was, therefore, "amazed at the recklessness of those who wrote commentaries in recent times."[62]

Adoptionist Fragments

Epiphanius, the fourth-century writer against heresies, provides eight examples of rather simple Adoptionist exegesis, four of them with texts that refer to Jesus as a man. One or two are related to textual variants, while some rely on syllogisms, apparently disjunctive.

One text proving Jesus to be a man comes from the Gospel of John (in spite of its Logos-doctrine), two from the Old Testament prophets, one from the Acts of the Apostles, and one from a Pastoral Epistle. (It may be significant that all these writings were rejected by Marcion.)

  a. "Christ said, 'Now you seek to kill me, a *man* who spoke the truth to you' (John 8:40). You see he is a man."
  b. "Also Jeremiah (17:9, LXX) said of him, 'He is a *man* and who will know him?'"
  c. "And Isaiah (53:3, 7-8) said of him that he is a man: 'A *man* acquainted with grief, knowing how to bear suffering, and we saw him suffering blows and harm, and he was dishonored and not regarded.'"
  d. "The apostles said he was 'a *man* demonstrated to *us* [so the first hand of Codex Bezae] by signs and wonders' (Acts 2:22); they did not say, 'a god demonstrated.'"
  e. "The Apostle said of him that he is 'mediator between God and men, the *man* Christ Jesus'" (1 Tim. 2:5).[63]

The biblical passages obviously depict Christ as human. No orthodox interpreter would have disagreed with this point. Irenaeus, for example, cited four of the five verses (not the one from John) to illustrate apostolic doctrine about the Christ who became human,[64] but he certainly did not agree that he was a "mere man." Thus only a fairly crude syllogism ("if man, not God; man, therefore not God") could have made the Adoptionists' point.

Another piece of exegesis is more complicated. "He who denies Christ [Matt. 10:33 = Luke 12:9] does not sin, for Christ said, [a] '*Every* blasphemy will be forgiven to men' [Matt. 12:31], and [b] 'He who says a word against the Son of man, it will be forgiven to him, but [c] to him who blasphemes against the Holy Spirit, it will not be forgiven' [Matt. 12:32 = Luke 12:10].[65]

The problem was clearly posed by Luke's rigorist version of sayings about denial and blasphemy (Luke 12:9–10, RSV). "[a] He who denies me before men will be denied before the angels of God. And [b] every one who speaks a word against the Son of man will be forgiven; but [c] he who blasphemes against the Holy Spirit will not be forgiven." "Denies" is equivalent to "speaks a word against" and "blasphemes." Thus [a] is congruent with [c] though contradicted by [b].

How to avoid the force of [a]? The Adoptionists appealed to the parallel in Matthew 12:31–32 for their exegetical key. "[a] Every sin and blasphemy will be forgiven men, but [b] the blasphemy against the Spirit will not be forgiven. [a] And whoever says a word against the Son of man will be forgiven, but [b] whoever speaks against the Holy Spirit will not be forgiven, either in this age or in the age to come." The general rule is stated in [a], and [b] is the only exception.

Another attempt to avoid rigorism appears in a fragment of the Valentinian Heracleon, who differentiated basic confession of Christ by faith and life from merely verbal confession. He noted that in Matthew 10:32–33 (Luke 12:8–9) Christ speaks first of "everyone who confesses 'in' me" and then of "whoever denies me." To confess "in him" is to lead a Christian life and to be "in Christ."[66]

Another key Christological text came from Deuteronomy through Acts 7:37. "The Lord your God will raise up (*egerei*, not the biblical *anastēsei*) for you a prophet like me [Moses] from among you, from your bretheren—him you shall heed" (Deut. 18:15). Theodotus argued that "Moses was a *man* and the Christ raised up by God was not God but *man*, since he was from them [men], as was Moses, a *man*."[67]

The proof depends on the New Testament statements that Moses wrote about Christ (Luke 24:27; John 5:46) and that in so doing he was describing a man, as John 1:45 (RSV) indicates: "We have found him of whom Moses in the law and also the prophets wrote, Jesus of Nazareth, the son of Joseph." More than a century later the emperor Julian echoed the Adoptionist complaint: "Moses says the prophet will be like him and not like God, a prophet like himself and born of men, not of a god."[68]

The Adoptionists also provided textual and theological exegesis of an important verse in Luke:

Luke 1:35	*Adoptionists*
The angel (*angelos*)	The gospel (*euangelion*)
said to Mary,	itself said to Mary,
The *Holy Spirit*	The *Spirit of the Lord*
will come upon you. . . .	will come upon you. . . .
	And it did not say,
	The Spirit of the Lord
	will come to be in you.
Wherefore	It did not say Wherefore
	but said,
what is to be born will be	What is to be born will be
called holy, the Son of God.	called holy, the Son of God.[69]

Our passage combines significant textual alterations with logical arguments. First, it was not an angel but "the gospel" that addressed Mary, though the change might be due simply to a scribal error. Second, "the Spirit of the Lord" (a term from Isaiah 61:1 in the sermon at Nazareth, Luke 4:18) is substituted for "Holy Spirit," and as in Luke the Spirit is predicted as coming "upon" Mary, not "in" her. The conditional syllogistic fragment, "if 'upon,' not 'in,'" supports the Adoptionist doctrine that the Spirit entered into Jesus at baptism, not into Mary (cf. eis, "into," at the baptism in Mark 1:10 as well as Luke 3:22 according to Codex Bezae). In addition, the Adoptionists read "what is to be born will be called holy, the Son of God," as do the best manuscripts of Luke 1:35. The result is an ordinary human birth and a prediction not closely related to it. Once more, Jesus is a man. Presumably the Adoptionists supposed that their text antedated the orthodox texts of their time.

The Adoptionist Theodotus therefore held that Jesus was a man born of a virgin by the will of the Father. He lived like all others but was more pious. At his baptism in the Jordan he received the Christ from above that came down in the form of a dove. For this reason he did not work miracles before the time when the Spirit that came down, the Christ, was shown to be in him.[70] Luke may have provided a starting point for this doctrine when he described Jesus as "full of the Holy Spirit" only after his baptism (Luke 4:1)—though John the Baptist was to be "filled with the Holy Spirit" (1:15), like his mother (1:41) and father (1:67).

A Gnostic Alternative

Naturally the Adoptionists were not alone in interpreting this verse. The Valentinian Gnostic Theodotus held that the "incarnation" took place when Jesus "assumed" spiritual and psychic elements. "The words 'Holy Spirit will come upon you' express the spiritual origin of the Lord's body, while 'The power of the Most High will overshadow you' (Luke 1:35) refers to the psychic formation given by the Demiurge, imprinted on this body in the Virgin's womb." Theodotus concludes thus: "Jesus himself was different from the elements he assumed; this is clear from what he declared: 'I am the Life,' 'I am the Truth' (John 14:6), 'I and the Father are one' (10:30). But he expressed the spiritual element he assumed and the psychic thus: 'The infant grew and progressed in Wisdom' (Luke 2:40, 52); for what is spiritual needs Wisdom, while what is psychic needs only size." On the other hand the authentic, spiritual Jesus had to be differentiated from the Son of Man. "When he says, 'The Son of Man must be rejected, insulted, crucified' (Mark 8:31; Luke 18:32, 24:7), he is seen to be speaking about someone else, obviously the one mingled with passions," in other words, the "psychic Christ."[71]

The Valentinians thus found at least two kinds of sayings about Jesus in the Gospels, referring to either the spiritual or the psychic Jesus Christ. In this way they could explain some of the more notable inconsistencies and avoid Adoptionist understandings.

6

The Syllogistic Exegesis
of Apelles

Typological Traditions

From the earliest times, Christian exegetes of the Old Testament found "types" (examples or prefigurations) in the stories about Adam and Eve in Paradise, Noah and the Deluge, the Sacrifice of Isaac, Moses and the Exodus, and the Joshua cycle. They found the gospel in the ancient Hebrew books.

This approach appears in Paul's discussion of Sarah and Hagar in Galatians 4:21–31, along with the word *allēgoroumena* ("meant allegorically"). He provides a rational justification for the method in 1 Corinthians 9:9–10, where he insists that Deuteronomy 25:4 ("you shall not muzzle an ox when it treads out the grain," RSV) refers to Christians because God is not concerned with oxen. His contemporary Philo implied at one point that the verse was allegorical: "The law is concerned not with irrational animals but with those who possess mind and reason."[1] However, when Philo was arguing that the Mosaic law aided irrational animals,[2] he specifically described the "kindly and benevolent injunction on behalf of the oxen," and Josephus claimed that the command was based on justice toward fellow workers.[3] Paul thus agreed with the old Stoics, who argued that human beings and irrational animals had no ties based on justice.[4] The exegetical results depend on a prior decision about the nature of God.

Naturally Adam and Eve presented Jewish and Christian exegetes with many opportunities for symbolical interpretation. Philo had led the way, but the most thoroughgoing allegorizer was the Christian Origen, sometimes willing to deny the literal truth of the creation story as a whole.[5]

> Who is stupid enough to suppose that like a farmer God planted a garden in Eden to the east and in the garden made a tree of life, visible and sense-perceptible, of such a kind that he who ate its fruit with his physical teeth would receive life? And again, that anyone would participate in good and evil by having eaten fruit taken from this tree? [These points reflect some of Apelles' criticisms.] If God is represented as walking at evening in the garden and Adam as hiding under the tree, one cannot doubt, I believe, that everything was expressed in a historical narrative that seems to have taken place but did not take place corporeally, and that it signifies certain mysteries.[6]

Origen was obviously attacking literalists like Apelles and other Gnostic exegetes who took the Old Testament literally in order to attack its veracity.[7]

The Ex-Marcionite Apelles

Apelles was a prominent heretic at Rome in the later second century, famous for his syllogistic attacks on the early chapters of the book of Genesis as well as for the revelations of his female companion "Beloved." Tertullian claims that though he was once a disciple of Marcion, he abandoned not only his teacher's theology but also his strict morality—"under the very eyes of his most holy master," presumably at Rome. After a stay at Alexandria he returned. "He was no better," writes Tertullian, "except that now he was not a Marcionite, and applied himself to another woman, 'Beloved,' at the time a virgin but later a prostitute. Taken in by her activity, he wrote the *Manifestations* that he learned from her."[8]

Eusebius, following Apelles' contemporary Rhodo, takes more interest in his theology. "Apelles acknowledges one first principle but says the prophecies come from a hostile spirit; he himself was convinced by the declarations of an inspired virgin named Beloved.'"9 Finally, Epiphanius quotes Apelles' discussion of his single principle.

> One is the good God [Marcion's text], and one the first principle, and one the nameless power; this one God and single principle is not concerned with what happens here in this world. But that same holy and good God above made one other god, and the other god created everything, heaven and earth and everything in the world. He was not good, and what he made was not well made, but the things made by him were created in accordance with his evil intelligence.10

If this account is correct, Apelles' *Syllogisms* showed that Genesis referred to the evil creator. Obviously this was his theological starting point, not the critical method as such. In addition, Tertullian's claim that he was an ex-Marcionite neglects the obvious resemblance of the *Syllogisms* to Marcion's *Antitheses*. Apparently Apelles simply developed Marcion's objections in a strikingly logical fashion.

As for Beloved, perhaps she influenced Apelles' defense of Eve and criticism of Adam, as set forth below. Tertullian disliked both Eve and Beloved. He called Eve the door of the devil and insisted that she led Adam astray.11 Apparently he knew at least a little more about the prophetess.

> He [Apelles] said that Beloved was a young woman divinely inspired to foretell the future, and he ascribed to her the dreams and movements of his spirit when secretly and alone he would be forewarned by her divinations or forebodings. The same phantom appeared to Beloved dressed as a boy and sometimes stated he was Christ, sometimes Paul, and she would tell her audience what the phantom said. She was also accustomed to work miracles; the most significant was that she put a large piece of bread into a glass jar with a very narrow neck and then took it out undamaged with her fingertips. She was content with this food alone, as if it were divinely given to her.12

Beloved's critic does not say whether she was interested in logic or not.

Junod relied on a notice by Origen about Apelles' "incomplete denial that the law and the prophets are of God"13 to argue that the *Manifestations* come from a stage of Apelles' thought different from (and later than) the simpler, rationalistic *Syllogisms*.[14] It is more likely, however, that he wrote the book late in life "to prove that everything Moses wrote about God is not true but false,"[15] for that was his view in old age when he argued with Rhodo (see below). The *Syllogisms* continued to trouble Christians, for Origen replied to one of them in his *Homilies on Genesis,* and Ambrose noticed more of them (from the thirty-eighth book!) when he wrote *On Paradise*.[16] The syllogisms he quotes are not always complete, but the minor gaps can be due either to Ambrose's failure to follow them or, as is also possible, to the nature of rhetoric as contrasted with dialectic. Aristotle mentioned that the "enthymeme" in rhetoric is "a kind of syllogism, and deduced from a few principles, often from fewer than the regular syllogism."[17]

The Asian Rhodo had once been a pupil of Tatian at Rome and then actively debated with heretics and wrote *Solutions* to Tatian's *Problems* [18] as well as a treatise *On the Hexaemeron*, doubtless directed against the *Syllogisms* of Apelles.[19] Rhodo claimed that Apelles insisted on his views about the Old Testament but refused to use an equally rigorous logic in theology.

> He used to say that one should by no means investigate the doctrine, but each should remain with his own belief: those who set their hope on the Crucified would be saved, but only if they were found in good works. I said to him, "From what do you give a proof, or how can you say there is one first principle?" He replied that the prophecies refute one another because they spoke nothing true at all; they are inconsistent and false and contradict one another.[20] As to how there is one first principle, he said he did not "know" it but was merely "moved" thus.[21] When I adjured him to speak truthfully he said he did not "know" how there is one uncreated god but "believed" it. I laughed at him and condemned him because he called himself a teacher but did not know how to establish what he taught.[22]

Evidently Apelles differentiated the "movement"—perhaps "assent," as in Clement of Alexandria[23]—of faith from the true knowledge based on "demonstration."

Rhodo's criticism itself is not very logical, for logicians were usually aware that at the beginning of a chain of reasonings there were "unprovable" axioms.[24] Clement of Alexandria, following Aristotle, states clearly that "the philosophers admit that the first principles of all things are indemonstrable" and that "all demonstration is traced back to indemonstrable faith."[25] But apparently Rhodo was urging Apelles to apply the same logic in theology as in criticism.

Rhodo's insistence on logical "proof" might well have appealed to his contemporary Galen, who attacked the schools of Moses and Christ for starting with "undemonstrated laws" and criticized pagan philosophers and scientists who were unable to provide logical demonstrations. According to Galen, the Stoic teacher Chrysippus had filled his books with rhetoric rather than logic and used laymen's testimony, poetry, etymology and "other things of that sort" that prove nothing and waste the reader's time.[26] We do not know, however, that Rhodo was acquainted with Galen or his works.

On the other hand, Apelles himself could easily have found some support in what Galen had to say about Moses and the cosmogony. We have already noted that during his first stay in Rome Galen criticized Moses for writing without offering proofs of his statements, and a few years later he contrasted Moses' opinion with "ours." For Moses, it was enough to say that God willed the creation, and it was arranged as a cosmos, for he thought that God could do anything, even making a man out of stone. Galen also attacked the followers of both Moses and Christ for relying on "undemonstrated laws."[27] Apelles went on to show that Moses is inconsistent and self-contradictory. His syllogisms can be viewed as examples of the ordinary rhetorical method of "refutation," which we discussed earlier. Indeed, his conclusions are close to those set forth in the Gnostic *Apocryphon of John*, where we read that various events described in Genesis took place "not as Moses said." The spirit or the Mother did not move to and fro above the waters (Gen. 1:2); the chief archon (creator) did not bring sleep over Adam or take the rib-bone from him (2:21); Noah and his companions did not hide themselves in an ark (7:7).[28] Apelles too, as the fragments show, criticized all such stories. What Moses wrote was not true but false.

Syllogisms on Adam

Several syllogisms have to do with the way in which God created Adam and God's failure to achieve perfection. The first is this: "How does the tree of life (Gen. 2:9) seem to effect more for life than God's breathing (Gen. 2:7)?"[29] And again,"if God did not make man perfect, but each one by effort acquires perfect virtue, does not man seem to acquire more for himself than if God provided it?"[30] Apparently Theophilus rejects this exegesis when he treats Adam's life in Eden as potentially leading to progress, perfection, and even deification (becoming as gods, Gen. 3:5, 22).[31] Finally, God made Adam no more immortal than perfect: "If God had made him immortal from the beginning, he would have made him a god; again, if he had made him mortal, it would seem that God was the cause of his death. Therefore he made him neither immortal nor mortal." (I infer the existence of this syllogism from Theophilus's "answer."[32]) These three syllogisms raise the question of how a perfect God could have made an imperfect human being. (Irenaeus replies that created beings are necessarily inferior to their Creator.)

Why did God forbid this creature to find out about good and evil, and why did the creature disobey? Apelles developed his attack on this picture of the seemingly arbitrary Creator:

> It is not always wrong to disobey a precept, for if the precept is good, obedience is right, but if the precept is wrong, it is right not to obey. Therefore it is not always wrong not to obey a precept, but it is wrong not to obey a good precept. The tree that effects the knowledge of good and evil is good, since God knows good and evil; for he says, "Behold, Adam has become as one of us [knowing good and evil]" (Gen. 3:22). If it is good to have knowledge of good and evil—and the knowledge God has is good—it seems that he who forbids it to man does not rightly forbid.[33]

This syllogism resembles part of a Stoic example cited by Aulus Gellius.[34] (1) Everything a father commands must be obeyed. But what of treason or matricide? (2) Some commands are to be obeyed, others not. (3) "A father's command is either right or wrong. (a) If it is right, it is not to be obeyed because it is his order but because it is right for it to be done. (b) If it is wrong, what ought not to be done should never be done."

This could be taken to mean that a father's command *as such* is never to be obeyed. The Stoics therefore restated the beginning of the last section thus: "A father's command is right or wrong or neither right nor wrong." This made the discussion into a "sound and regular disjunctive proposition" by including commands about "neutral" or "indifferent" matters. In Apelles' analysis, Genesis wrongly ascribes bad commands to God, and therefore some of God's commands are to be obeyed, others not.

"He who does not know good and evil is no different from an infant," according to Apelles. "Before a just judge an infant is not guilty. A just creator of the world would never have accused an infant, for he did not know good and evil; an infant cannot be accused of lying and guilt."[35]

Here Adam is viewed as an infant, just as he is by Theophilus and Irenaeus,[36] but in addition, the creator-god is neither good nor just. Junod suspects that Apelles is attacking his former teacher Marcion.[37] On the other hand, the *Clementine Homilies* state that Adam "was not ignorant and did not need to partake of a tree, that he might know what is good and what is evil."[38] On this basis, Apelles' argument would have been untenable.

"He who does not know good and evil does not even know it is evil not to keep a command, nor does he know it is good to obey a command. And therefore, because he did not know, he who did not obey deserved pardon, not condemnation."[39] Similarly the emperor Julian claimed it was blasphemous to say that God refused to give the knowledge of good and evil.[40]

Apelles also attacked the whole picture of the tree of the knowledge of good and evil. "And if man had not tasted death, then he could not know what he had not tasted; and if he had not tasted, he did not know; if he did not know, he could not fear. Therefore God pointlessly threatened him with death (Gen. 2:17), which men did not fear."[41] How could death have arisen out of eating from this tree?

> Did death affect Adam from the nature of a tree of this sort, or from God? If we ascribe this to the nature of the tree, it seems that the fruit of this tree was more important than the life-giving breath of God (Gen. 2:7), if indeed the fruit of the tree brought to death the one whom the breathing had made live. Or if we call God the agent of death we accuse him on a double charge: either he is so harsh that he would not ignore when he could have ignored or, if he could not ignore, he seems to be weak.[42]

Apelles' argument resembles one found in Sextus Empiricus. If God has the will but not the power to forethink all, he is weak; if he has the power but not the will, he is malignant. Either conclusion is impious. Such an argument was set forth by Epicureans or Academics or both.[43] As a Marcionite, Apelles was likely to criticize the "weakness" of the Old Testament god.[44]

The same objection can be made to the picture of God's foreknowledge:

> Did God know Adam would transgress his commandments or did he not? If he did not know, there is no assertion of divine power. But if he did know and yet gave orders that inevitably were neglected, it is not godlike to give a superfluous precept. But he gave an order to that first-formed Adam which he knew he would in no way keep. God does nothing superfluous; therefore the writing is not of God.[45]

Jerome ascribes the same "syllogism" to "Marcion and all the dogs of heretics." "Either God knew that the man set in paradise would transgress his commandment or he did not know. If he knew, the one who could not avoid God's foreknowledge is not at fault, but he who created him such that he could not avoid the knowledge of God. If he did not know, you deprive of divinity the one whose foreknowledge you take away."[46] Indeed, other Gnostics did share this criticism with Apelles. The Nag Hammadi *Testimony of Truth* claims that "God does not have foreknowledge; (otherwise) would he not know from the beginning?"[47]

Further criticisms deal with divine foreknowledge and

> Did he who created man and impressed these opinions about good and evil on him know he would sin, or not? If you say he did not know, your thought is alien to the majesty of God. But if you say that God, knowing man would sin, impressed on him the common opinions about good and evil, with the result that because of the admixture of evils he could not preserve his eternal life: in the first case he [God] could not foresee the future and in the second you seem to indicate that God is not good. Therefore the creation of man is not of God, for God does not make evil; but man accepted the idea of evil when he was told to abstain from evil actions [cf. Rom. 7:7].[48] . . . How is God good when he not only allowed evil to come into this world but allowed the world to come into such great confusion?[49]

Syllogisms on Eve

"God made Eve out of Adam's rib (Gen. 2:21) because he was unable to make the woman by herself." Again I infer this criticism from Theophilus's rejection of it: God made Eve from Adam to show that they were not made by two gods.[50] Similarly Justin mentions someone who asks, "Could not God immediately make a multitude of human beings?" The earlier works of Philo show that such criticisms were fairly common. Justin's theological answer does not seem to meet the point. He says that God made both angels and human beings with free will for just deeds.[51]

A lengthy fragment preserved under Irenaeus's name attacks various aspects of the criticism of Eve in Genesis.[52] Conceivably there was some confusion between Irenaeus's title, *Examination (elenchos) and Refutation (anatropē) Knowledge Falsely So-Called*, and what Eusebius called Apelles' zeal for the "examination (*elenchos*) and refutation (*anatropē*)" of the Bible.[53]

> How can the serpent, created voiceless and mindless in nature by God, speak reasonably and vocally? For if of itself it had the ability to reason and judge and reply to the words spoken by the woman, then no serpent would be hindered from doing this. . . . It was impossible for the evil demon, mute and irrational in nature, to be given a voice out of the nonexistent into existence; otherwise it would not have stopped conversing with men[54] and deceiving them through serpents and animals and birds. But if they say it addressed her with a human voice in accordance with God's will, they will make God the cause of sin.[55] And how did an animal hear the precept that was originally given privately by God only to man, without even the woman learning of it (Gen. 3:1–2)? Why did it not attack the man rather than the woman? And if you say that it assaulted the weaker one,[56] on the contrary she was the stronger, the helper of man (Gen. 2:18), as she was shown to be in the transgression of the precept. For she alone resisted the serpent, and only after she was tricked by rebellion and craft did she eat of the tree. On the other hand, Adam did not wholly struggle or reply but took the fruit offered by the woman (Gen. 3:6), the greatest proof of weakness and an unmanly mind. The woman, overcome by the demon, deserves pardon; but Adam, inferior to a woman, does not, since he personally had received the precept from God (Gen. 2:16–17). The woman

heard the precept from Adam but thought little of it, or considered it
unworthy for God to speak through it, or doubted it; she probably suspected that Adam had given her the precept on his own.

This fragment is not found in Ambrose but is confirmed by his comments: "Many think that the sin belonged not to the woman but to
Adam. . . . We know that Adam, not Eve, received the commandment
from God; for the woman had not yet been formed. . . . We understand
that the commandment was transmitted through the man to the woman."
Presumably Ambrose ("we") is disagreeing with Apelles ("many").[57] We
were told earlier that Adam deserved pardon because of his ignorance,
but here ignorance is no excuse.

Did the serpent see Eve when she was eating or not eating?

The serpent found her when she was alone, so that it could speak to her
privately. [The serpent saw her either when she was eating or when she
was not eating.[58]] When the serpent saw her eating from the trees
(Gen. 3:2) it advised her to eat from the tree of knowledge, from which she
had not eaten. If she was eating, it is clear that she was [already] in a perishable body, for "whatever goes into the mouth passes into the drain"
(Matt. 15:17).[59] If she was perishable, then evidently also mortal. If
[already] mortal, there was no longer a curse nor was that an answer which
the voice of God spoke to the man: "You are earth and to earth you will
return" (Gen. 3:19).

On the other hand, if the serpent did not see the woman eating, how did
it induce her to eat when she had never eaten before? And who showed
this murderous and criminal serpent that the answer of God to them about
death, "The day when you eat you will surely die" (Gen. 2:17), would not
bring a result ["You will not die" (Gen. 3:4)]?

Not only that, but that with observation their eyes were opened
(Gen. 3:7), which did not see before? With this so-called "opening" they
made an opening for death.[60]

Was the Serpent Literal?

The serpent in Genesis 3 presented early exegetes with rather severe
problems. Philo gave a literal paraphrase of the story before stating that it

did not consist of "mythical fictions" but required allegorical exegesis.[61] Early Christian authors said little about the serpent, usually emphasizing the weakness of Eve. Paul insists that she was deceived by the serpent (2 Cor. 11:3), while 1 Timothy 2:14 (RSV) claims that "Adam was not deceived, but the woman was deceived and became a transgressor."[62] On the other hand, a "Jewish-Gnostic" amulet discussed by Erwin Goodenough suggests that no blame attached to either one.[63]

And at one extreme Gnostics often regarded the serpent as the emissary of Wisdom against the evil creator-god.

In his *Dialogue with Trypho,* Justin mentions an early critic who asked, "Could not God have cursed the serpent into non-existence?"[64] It was Apelles' work, however, that provided a fresh impetus to exegesis. Theophilus argues against many of his points, as we have seen. He repeats Philo's literalist claim when he says that "facts prove the truth of the statements" about the curses laid on the serpent and Eve. Women do suffer in childbirth and the hateful serpent does "creep on its belly and eat dirt," thus "proving to us the truth of what has been said."[65]

Noah's Ark: Cargo and Size

Another section of Apelles' discussion dealt with some logical problems in the story of Noah's ark. "It was impossible that in so short a time [a week in Gen. 7:4] so many kinds of animals, and their food for a whole year, could be taken aboard [Noah's ark]."[66] Obviously calculations underlie these statements. "So many kinds" involves the total number of species, along with an estimate of their food supply for a year. Aristotle knew of 581 kinds of animals and identified 550 of them.[67]

> And when two by two the unclean animals, i.e. two males and two females of each (that is what the repeated statement [Gen. 6:19, 7:9, 15] means), and seven by seven (7:1–3) the clean animals, i.e. seven pairs, are described as led into the ark, how could the space described[68] be made big enough to hold even four elephants? It is clear that the story is false; but if so, it is clear that this writing is not from God.[69]

Again calculations are involved, with an estimate of the size of each animal and the space required. It is hard to see why Apelles thought four elephants needed 150,000 cubic cubits (506,250 cubic feet), even though the ancients agreed that the elephant was the largest land animal and Pliny thought the largest Indian elephants were twenty cubits (thirty feet) high.[70] Of course the estimate included their food supply for a year. But we still have no idea how much space the animals in the ark took or how much they ate.

Apelles' lack of enthusiasm for the story was shared by more typical Gnostics. The *Apocryphon of John* agrees with him that the ark never existed; instead, there was a "cloud of light."[71] *The Hypostasis of the Archons* is also literal-minded and tells how Seth's sister Norea set fire to the ark because she was not allowed on board.[72]

Critics of Homer had raised similar questions about the wooden horse into which Greek soldiers entered outside Troy.[73] The Greek tradition, unlike the story of Noah, gave rather exact numbers—fifty men according to Apollodorus, three thousand in the epic *Little Iliad*.[74] Dio Chrysostom refers to the horse as a "very large structure" but ridicules the notion that an army could be hidden in a horse without any of the Trojans noticing it or even suspecting it, even though a true prophet (Cassandra) was among them.[75] Some gave historical explanations. Palaephatus held that the wooden horse was empty but too large to be brought through the gates of Troy. After the Trojans broke down their wall to take it in, the Greeks entered the city.[76] Pausanias says it was a siege engine, as "is well known to everyone who does not attribute utter silliness to the Phrygians." It is mere legend that a wooden horse "contained the most valiant of the Greeks."[77] For Clement, the horse is metaphor: mankind embraces in one body an army of different spirits.[78] (Of course, not everyone criticized the story. Augustine says that as a boy he hated arithmetic but loved stories about "a wooden horse full of armed men" and the burning of Troy.[79])

To defend the ark from Apelles, Origen proposed to square the number of cubits noted in Genesis. He was following "a learned Jew" who had observed the word "square" in the Septuagint version of Genesis 6:14: "Make for yourself an ark out of squared (*tetragonon*) wood."[80] (The learned Jew was not Philo, for Philo did not square the numbers but pointed out that they contained squares and cubes; Clement followed him, though at some distance.[81]) Origen's theory seemed reasonable to him because Moses, who wrote the story, was "instructed in all the wisdom of the Egyptians" and they were especially famous for geometry! It is unlikely, however, that such an ark could have been built, even in the "hundred years" Origen mentions (subtracting Noah's 500 years in Genesis 5:32 from his 600 in 7:6), and with a volume of 675 billion cubic cubits it could not have sailed. A rabbinic exegete was more sensible when he claimed only that "the Torah teaches you practical knowledge, that if a man builds a ship which is to stand upright in harbor, he must make its breadth a sixth [of its length] and its height a tenth."[82] Origen's venture into the art of shipbuilding was not a success.

Rufinus's Latin version of this "geometrical" exegesis improved it when he multiplied the dimensions by only six. His translation runs thus: "Among students of geometry, in accordance with what they call a 'power (*virtus*),' one out of a solid or a square is generally counted as six, or in special cases as three hundred."[83] *Virtus* obviously stands for *dynamis*, but unfortunately *dynamis* usually means "square" in mathematical writings.[84] The Greek word *stereos* (underlying *solidus*) means either "solid" or, specifically with "cubit," "standard." Origen-Rufinus is saying that a unit is counted either as six (generally) or as three hundred (in special cases). Three hundred would involve squaring the number of cubits in the ark's length (the idea expressed in the Greek fragment on Genesis and *Against Celsus*); Origen-Rufinus prefers six at this point. Could it be that Rufinus did not understand whatever Origen's point may have been? Or was he correcting it? Would 14,400,000 cubic cubits have been enough? Augustine found the notion in Rufinus's version, thought the sentence about geometrical theory was hard to understand, and simply referred to "geometric cubits."[85] (He later explained that since a thousand is the cube of ten, the millennium of Revelation 20 means the totality of human history.[86])

Augustine agreed with Origen that a large enough ark was analogous to an enormous city and, after all, it took a hundred years to build. He added that "if stones can be cemented together by lime alone to form a circular wall many miles long, is it not possible that wood can be joined by tenons, pegs, nails, and pitch-glue to build an ark which would extend not in curving but in straight lines throughout its length and breadth?"[87] The answer, of course, is that it *is* possible.

Beyond criticism of the story lies criticism of the God who changed his mind about the human race and was determined to destroy all but Noah, his family, and some animals. This kind of moral criticism was common among Marcionites and others. Apelles' fame, such as it was, was due to his special rationalistic approach.

Allegorizers and the Ark

Philo states that God's plan was to purify the earth by water and purify the soul as well. The ark means "the body, the vessel that contains the soul," while the seven clean beasts are the five senses plus the faculties of speech and generation.[88] In his exegesis of Genesis, Ambrose too took refuge in allegory and immediately claimed after Philo that the measurements symbolize the proportions of the human body.[89] (Jerome noted how extensive his use of Philo was.[90]) He could not answer the syllogistic arguments set forth in what he says was Apelles' thirty–eighth book, for he was not skilled in "dialectical disputation" and indeed claimed that "God was not pleased to save his people by dialectic."[91] Savon suggests that Ambrose acquired his Philonic-allegorical response to Apelles through Origen,[92] but more probably it was transmitted through Tertullian, who wrote *Against the Followers of Apelles*, now lost.[93] After all, when Origen answered Apelles on Noah's ark, he did not begin with allegorization, though in his homilies on Genesis he was happy to move from history to spiritual edification, including biblical numerology.

Apelles' attack on Genesis and the responses to it recall what Heraclitus, author of *Homeric Problems*, says at the beginning of his book. Homer's entire work would be impiety if he had not written allegorically. Apelles agreed: Genesis is to be taken literally, and it is an impious book. When Origen wrote as a historical critic, he did not agree: the story is to be taken literally, but it does not mean what Apelles thinks it does. Allegorizers tended to share Heraclitus's opinion.

7

The Orthodox Counterattack

FROM THE second century onward, canon, authorship, and exegesis were lively topics of discussion for heretics and orthodox alike. Did a book deserve to belong to whatever canon there might be? Who wrote it? And how was it to be interpreted? Such questions were reflected in the last New Testament book, 2 Peter, as we have already seen. Here we sum up the points implied. The pseudonymous author, supposedly on the verge of death, reminds his readers in general (doubtless including the evangelist "Mark") that he was a witness of the Transfiguration—which was not an "artfully devised myth"—and has already written one letter to them (1 Peter). He is a "brother" of Paul, who also wrote to them (whoever they are), as in all his letters making some difficult statements that uneducated and unstable readers twist to their own destruction. This presumed origin and setting makes the letter apostolic, catholic, traditional, and orthodox. Few later Christian authors would feel able to make such inclusive claims.

Tatian and Literary Criticism

The apologist—and heretic—Tatian is the first Christian we know who insisted on the extent of his literary studies and illustrated his acquaintance with the materials of literary history. He wrote learnedly about Homer's poetry, origin, and date (c. 31), the date of the Trojan War and the date of other seers and sages (36–41). "People say that the works attributed to Orpheus were compiled by Onomacritus the Athenian in the reign of Pisistratus, about the 50th Olympiad" (41).

This shows that he was acquainted with the history, as well as the practice, of editing. It was he who compiled the first Gospel harmony, revised from Justin's combinations with other materials added.[1] In addition, he rejected some of Paul's letters but believed that the Epistle to Titus was certainly by the apostle. He gave "little weight to the assertion [or neglect] of Marcion and the others who agree with him on this."[2] Presumably he gave reasons for the rejections and acceptance, but we do not know what they were. In any case, he fully accepted the grammatical-critical method, at least for pagan literature, and Clement of Alexandria used the passage about Onomacritus, along with much else, in his *Miscellanies*.[3] Clement himself tells us that "some" (Marcion or Tatian?) reject 1 and 2 Timothy because 1 Timothy 6:20–21 speaks of "Gnosis falsely so-called," while Origen says that 2 Timothy is rejected by some because it refers to the apocryphal book of "Jannes and Jambres" (3:8). He calls these people inconsistent because they keep 1 Corinthians, with its allusion to an apocryphal book.[4]

Theophilus, Interpolations, and Syntheses

Around 181 Theophilus, bishop of Antioch, known as an opponent of Marcion, boldly rewrote the Decalogue as he produced an apologetic book with "syntheses" of the Law, the prophets, and the Gospels against Marcion's *Antitheses*. The essential law of God, transmitted through Moses, dealt with piety, well-doing, and justice. It had ten chapters or headings—but not the ten listed in Exodus or Deuteronomy. Instead, Theophilus retained only commandments 1–2 and 5–10, adding to these several "judgments" from Exodus 23:6–9.[5]

Obviously some justification was needed for leaving out the third and fourth commandments, and if we look back to the Pseudo-Clementine theory (chapter 4), we find that Theophilus is omitting two commandments from the Decalogue because Jesus himself set them aside. He had ratified the commandments that Theophilus includes (Matt. 19:18), and had forbidden fraud as well (Mark 10:19), but he was accused of violating the two on blasphemy and Sabbath observance. This point is especially clear in the Gospel according to John, the one evangelist whom Theophilus calls inspired,[6] though other Gospels contain similar statements. John says that Jesus was accused of blasphemy (John 10:33, 36) and did not observe the Sabbath (John 5:18; 9:16).[7] Theophilus is careful to retain some of the content of the deleted commandments, but he definitely removes them from the Decalogue.

By 181, then, relatively orthodox Christian leaders were using the critical weapons of their opponents. About a century later the Syriac *Didascalia Apostolorum* insists that the true Old Testament law consists only of the Decalogue and the "judgments" expressed in Exodus 21–23.[8]

In another book Theophilus had correlated the law against coveting one's neighbor's wife (Exod. 20:17) with what the prophet Solomon said about looking straight ahead and letting eyelids incline justly (Prov. 4:25). In the third he again cites verses from the "king and prophet" Solomon and claims that the "Gospel voice" simply provides "a stricter teaching" on purity (Matt. 5:28).[9] This is defensive exegesis of the Bible, directed against Marcion.

Irenaeus and Literary Criticism/History

A little later, Irenaeus of Lyons occasionally ventured into literary criticism for the sake of biblical exegesis. He touched on textual criticism when he noted a variant reading in the manuscripts of Revelation 13:18, where all the ancient and genuine manuscripts, he said, give "666" as the number of the Beast, though some supply "616."[10] Using literary analysis, he could claim that when Paul said that "the god of this age has blinded the minds of the unbelievers" (2 Cor. 4:4), he was employing *hyperbaton* (inverted order of words) and really referring to "the unbelievers of this age." (This implies no criticism of Paul, for the most famous user of *hyperbata* was Thucydides.) But the comments do not go far toward genuine critical understanding.

Like Dionysius of Corinth, Irenaeus was aware of the prevalence of forgery, and swore by the Lord Jesus Christ that his scribe must "diligently compare what you transcribe and correct it by this copy from which you are transcribing, and similarly transcribe this oath and put it in the copy."[11] He was trying to avoid the situation he found among Gnostics, who have "an immeasurable mass of secret and spurious writings which they have forged." They "smuggle them in to astound those who are ignorant and do not know letters."[12] In addition, he says, they follow a false principle of exegesis when they explain what is obscure by what is more obscure. He insists on the sound rhetorical principle that "intelligent people do not resolve an obscurity by another obscurity, nor an ambiguity through another ambiguity, nor an enigma through another greater enigma; but such things gain solutions from what is clear, consistent, and evident."[13]

Unfortunately Gnostics "when convicted out of the scriptures turn to accusations against the scriptures themselves, [claiming that] they are neither correct nor authoritative, their language is ambiguous, and the truth cannot be found from them unless one knows the tradition." After all, they say, "the truth was not transmitted in writings but through the living voice."[14] Here Irenaeus agrees in part. He was well aware of the multitudes of barbarians who were converted to tradition rather than scripture, "having salvation written in their hearts through the Spirit, without papyrus and ink," and he must have known that the "ancient" Papias preferred the "living voice."[15]

Irenaeus's Roman New Testament

Irenaeus's basic collection of Christian books reflects its Roman (and Asian) origin.[16] He insists that in Gaul he is far from literary culture, but he is well acquainted with a collection of Christian books that excludes Gnostic texts and apocryphal gospels.[17] For him there are four and only four Gospels, composed by Matthew in Hebrew or Aramaic at the time when Peter and Paul were preaching the gospel at Rome and founding the church; Mark, disciple and interpreter of Peter, who recorded Peter's preaching; Luke, who followed Paul and recorded the gospel he preached; and finally John, the Lord's disciple, who reclined on his bosom (John 13:25, 21:20) and published the Gospel when living at Ephesus in Asia. Luke was also the author of Acts.[18]

Paul wrote either twelve or thirteen epistles. Irenaeus never cites the little epistle to Philemon but probably had no reason to do so. There are no real traces of Hebrews in his works, and according to Stephanus Gobarus both Hippolytus and Irenaeus denied its authenticity.[19] Echoes of James, Jude, and 2 Peter are virtually nonexistent. On the other hand, he definitely cites 1 Peter and 1 and 2 John. He knows Revelation, written by John in the reign of Domitian.

Probably outside this collection he knows letters from Clement, who wrote from the Roman church to the Corinthians with tradition from the

apostles, and Polycarp, appointed bishop by the apostles, author of a letter to the Philippians and a visitor to Rome under Anicetus. He refers to
the first *Mandate* of the Roman Hermas, perhaps as scripture. He has also
read what "one of us," Ignatius of Antioch, wrote in his letter to the
Romans.[20] In addition, Irenaeus knows writings from the Roman apologist Justin and his pupil Tatian, once at Rome though later a heretic perhaps at Antioch, and he uses the first two books of Theophilus of Antioch
To Autolycus without naming him. His collection of orthodox writings
has been filtered through Rome, though Polycarp came from Asia,
Ignatius (Tatian) and Theophilus from Syria.

Irenaeus's collection of books, whether scriptural or not, is thus obviously centered on Rome and may well reflect what the Roman church
was reading. His omission of Hebrews agrees with the criticism made by
Gaius of Rome a few years later, though he obviously would not have
rejected the Johannine literature as Gaius did.

His rather simple traditionalist comments on Gospel origins are directed against Gnostics and lead up to a defense of Luke-Acts against
Marcionites, confirming that Luke wrote Acts. The author of Acts was a
companion of Paul, as "we-passages" in Acts show (examples in chapters
16, 20–23, and 25–28). He was with Paul because he knows places,
cities, and periods of time up to Paul's arrival in Rome, and therefore he
was present up to the end of the book. Who was he? Irenaeus relies on
2 Timothy 4:10–11 (RSV): "Demas . . . has deserted me and gone to
Thessalonica; Crescens has gone to Galatia, Titus to Dalmatia. Luke
alone is with me." And Colossians 4:14: "Luke the beloved physician
and Demas greet you" (Irenaeus drops the reference to Demas). Luke
simply transmitted what he had heard from eyewitnesses (Luke 1:2).[21]
This is the "confirmation" of Lucan authorship.

Irenaeus shows how much Marcion had stimulated detailed study of
the Synoptic Gospels, especially Luke. The basic gospel, he claims,
exists in passages found only in that Gospel.[22] These include stories
about Jesus' birth and childhood, as well as the age at which the Lord
was baptized and the fifteenth year of Tiberius Caesar. Farther on in the
Gospel, Luke alone reports woes against the rich and those who are full
and laugh.[23] Many of the Lord's actions, too, are found only in Luke,
including such miracles as the great catch of fish by Peter and his

companions, the woman who had suffered for eighteen years, and the man with dropsy cured on the Sabbath.[24] In Luke alone Jesus taught his disciples not to seek the first places and to invite the poor and the sick who have nothing to pay back, and told about the man who comes to knock at night to get bread and gets it because of his importunity.[25] Luke alone reports his words about the rich and the tax collectors. He tells how he was at table with a Pharisee and a sinner kissed his feet and anointed them with perfume. It is Luke who reports what Jesus said to Simon about the two debtors; the parable of the rich man who stored up the products of his lands but was asked, "Whose will be what you have prepared?" the parable of the rich man clad in purple and the poor Lazarus; Jesus' reply to his disciples when they asked, "Increase our faith"; his conversation with the tax collector Zacchaeus; and the story of the Pharisee and the tax collector who prayed together in the temple.[26] Other passages speak of the universal demand of the gospel. Jesus cleansed ten lepers all together on the road, gave orders to go by roads and byways and gather the lame and the blind for a wedding, and told parables about a judge who was forced to do justice by a widow's importunity and about a fig tree saved to see if it would bear fruit. Marcion and Valentinus use many other items reported only by Luke, says Irenaeus. Finally he refers to the words of the Savior to his disciples along the road after his resurrection, and the way they knew him in the breaking of the bread.[27]

Apart from the reference to the fifteenth year of Tiberius Caesar, which Marcion kept but used to date the descent of the Savior from heaven to Capernaum, only one of these passages can be viewed as one of Marcion's alterations or omissions, and it is not certain that he made the change. It is more important that Irenaeus testifies to what Marcion's Gospel contained that was the same as in his own Luke. He argues that the heretics must either accept the rest of the Gospel or reject the passages already noted. They cannot accept some words of Luke as expressing the truth and reject the others as if he did not know the truth. In other words, Irenaeus assumes the truth of what he is defending, that the Gospel of Luke has not been interpolated. And he runs together objections to Marcion and to Valentinus (whose ideas were quite different), presumably in order to confuse the issue and claim that both groups must either reject the whole, leaving Marcion's disciples without a Gospel, or accept the whole, which would show the disciples of Valentinus how wrong they are. His argument is quite irrelevant if aimed at Valentinus and makes some sense only against Marcion.

Irenaeus's list provides considerable confirmation for the other basic evidence about Marcion's Gospel, for Tertullian and Epiphanius mention only one of these passages (except for chapters 1 and 2) as altered by Marcion. Indeed, when Irenaeus says that Luke mentions the fifteenth year of Tiberius, this was exactly the year that Marcion chose for the descent of Jesus (from heaven?) to Capernaum.[28] But his analysis does not really lead to disproof of heretical contentions. In addition, as A. LeBoulluec notes in a carefully balanced statement, he often reflects the substance of the rhetorical method of "refutation," but he seems not to have had technical training.[29]

Clement's Peculiar Traditions about Mark

Clement of Alexandria has long been suspected of leanings toward Gnosticism, and they seem to be confirmed in a unique letter discovered by Morton Smith. In it Clement makes use of something like Papias on Mark but goes beyond Papias toward Gnosticism. Like Papias he holds that Mark did not write down all the actions of the Lord or his secret teachings but made a selection of those most useful to increase the faith of catechumens. He adds that after Peter's death, Mark went to Alexandria with his own notes and those of Peter, and enlarged his earlier work into a "more spiritual gospel," though he did not include "things not to be uttered" or "the hierophantic teaching of the Lord." Later the Gnostic Carpocrates got a copy of this spiritual gospel, kept secret in the church of Alexandria, from a presbyter there and proceeded to "defile it, mixing it" with statements of his own doctrine.[30] In other words, he inter-polated it. Just what Clement might have meant by "hierophantic teach-ing" and "more spiritual gospel" is unclear, though one can think of the prayer in John 17 and note that Clement elsewhere called John "the spiritual gospel," different from and later than the others.[31] Gnostics tended to believe they possessed special "keys" to scripture. The ortho-dox often shared such ideas, it must be confessed.

Elsewhere, however, Clement calls the Savior's words self-explana-tory, following the traditional Hellenistic idea of interpreting an author from himself. The phrase commonly used of this procedure, "explaining Homer from Homer," did not occur to an early critic like Aristarchus but was expressed later not only by Porphyry but before him by Aelian.[32]

From Serapion to Tertullian

Clement's contemporary, Serapion of Antioch, became involved with critical method when he found the *Gospel According to Peter* in nearby Rhossus and at first permitted it to be used without reading it. Docetic heretics seem to have claimed that the bishop was giving approval to them, and an investigation revealed that most of the book agreed with "the correct word of the Savior," but some of it had been interpolated. Serapion stated that he received "Peter and the other apostles as Christ" but rejected "writings falsely ascribed to them, knowing that we did not receive such books from tradition."[33] Presumably he has such writings in mind as the *Gospel*, *Apocalypse*, and *Preaching* of Peter, perhaps also 2 Peter. The fact of tradition comes first and apparently answers the question of authenticity.

We should mention the pleasure the Carthaginian Tertullian took in noting, a little later, that those who authorized women to teach and even baptize relied on the apocryphal *Acts of Paul*. He knew that the Asian presbyter who invented these acts claimed he had written "for love of Paul"[34] but was convicted and deposed all the same. He himself takes refuge in the traditional Pauline text restricting women's activities: "Let them be silent . . .[and] ask their husbands at home" (1 Cor. 14:34–35).[35]

Gaius of Rome, Controversialist and Critic

At Rome under Zephyrinus, however, a "very learned and orthodox" exegete named Gaius contended with the subtleties of second-generation Montanists by using radical criticism. Several fragments remain from his important discussion with a certain Proclus, who argued for the apostolic origins of the Montanists because of the apostolic tombs they venerated, those of John and Philip. Proclus claimed that after Philip "the four daughters of Philip who were prophetesses were at Hierapolis in Asia; their grave is there, as is their father's." Gaius argued against Proclus that he could point out the "trophies" (presumably tombs) of the two apostolic founders of the Roman church, on the Vatican hill and on the Via Ostiense.

It was more important that Gaius clearly attributed the ideas of the book of Revelation, used by Montanists, to a Jewish-Christian heretic. "Cerinthus, who through revelations attributed to the writing of a great apostle [John], falsely introduces portents to us as if shown him by angels, and says that after the resurrection will be on earth and that humanity will dwell in Jerusalem and again be enslaved to lusts and pleasures." In Gaius's view, the Montanists were composing "new scriptures," though his grounds for rejection were basically theological. He himself rejected the Epistle to the Hebrews[36] as well as the Apocalypse (and probably the Gospel) ascribed to John.

Presumably his arguments against the Apocalypse were those assigned by Epiphanius to people whom he calls *Alogi* because they lacked the Logos found in John's writings and (therefore?) lacked reason. They argued that Cerinthus wrote the books ascribed to John, claiming that these did not agree with the other apostles.[37] As for the Gospels, the other evangelists begin the story of Jesus differently from John—though in Epiphanius's opinion while they seem to disagree among themselves, they really supplement one another. Finally Epiphanius offers some direct quotations from the Alogi. We cite them with supplements from Gaius in the commentary on Revelation by Dionysius Bar Salibi.

Fragments of Gaius and the Alogi

The first of these fragments deals with the different ways in which the Synoptic Gospels and John begin:

> How did the other evangelists say that Jesus took flight from the face of Herod into Egypt and coming back after the flight he stayed in Nazareth, then after receiving baptism he went away into the wilderness and after that he returned and after returning he began to preach? The gospel written in John's name makes false statements, for after saying "the Logos became flesh and tabernacled among us" [John 1:14], and a few other matters, it immediately says, "There was a wedding in Cana of Galilee" [2:1].[38]

Second, they disagree on the length of Jesus' ministry: "John says that the Savior observed two Passovers in a period of two years [2:23, 6:4], while the other evangelists speak of one Passover."[39]

The third fragment seems to be based on contemporary information. "Again it says, 'Write to the angel of the church in Thyatira' [Rev. 2:18]; and there is no church of Christians at all there in Thyatira. How then did he write to a non-existent church?"[40]

Finally, a group of fragments contrasts the predictions of Revelation 8–9 with the true predictions reported by Matthew and made by Paul. "The things [described in Rev. 8:7–11] are not what will take place; for the coming of the Lord will take place as a thief by night."[41] The description is contradicted by Revelation itself (3:3, cf. 16:15), as well as by Paul in 1 Thessalonians 5:2 (cf. Matt. 24:43–44 = Luke 12:39–40). Again, "As in the flood the heavenly bodies were not taken away [against Rev. 8:12], so at the end it will happen, according to the scripture [Matt. 24:37] and the writing of Paul: 'When they say peace and security, then their destruction will be total'" [1 Thess. 5:3].[42] Both Matthew and Paul contradict the Apocalypse. Finally, "how can the lawless be tormented by locusts [Rev. 9:3–5] when the scripture says that sinners prosper and the righteous are persecuted in the world [Ps. 72(73):3, Job 21:9]? Paul says that believers will be persecuted and evil men will grow worse, deceiving and deceived [2 Tim. 3:12–13]."[43] David, Job, and Paul, therefore, contradict the eschatology of the Apocalypse. "It is not written that angels shall war nor that a quarter of mankind shall be destroyed [Rev. 9:14-15 (a third)], but that nation shall rise against nation [Matt. 24:7]."[44] Matthew is scripture; Revelation is not.

Several quotations show that Revelation is simply absurd. "Of what value to me is the Apocalypse of John, which tells about seven angels and seven trumpets [Rev. 8:2]?"[45] Such apocalyptic details are pointless. "'And I saw, and he said to the angel, Loose the four angels which are in the Euphrates. And I heard the number of the army, ten thousand times ten thousand, and a thousand times a thousand, and they were clad in breastplates of fire and brimstone and hyacinth' [Rev. 9:14-17]. This is ridiculous."[46]

Origen as Critic

Like Galen, Origen was concerned with textual criticism. He created a *Tetrapla* and *Hexapla*, presentations of his Septuagint text with other versions, including Hebrew, in four and six parallel columns with use of the critical signs developed by Hellenistic editors of Homer.[47] (He was not searching for the earliest form of the text, for any of the versions could illuminate the spiritual significance of a word or passage.) He did not provide a text of the New Testament, however, even though the Gospel manuscripts were in deplorable confusion. "The differences among the manuscripts have become great, either through the negligence of some copyists or through the perverse audacity of others; they either neglect to check over what they have transcribed or, in the process of checking, they make additions or deletions as they please."[48] Origen thus ascribes to negligence or even audacity what the opponent of the Adoptionists (chapter 5) had assigned to heresy.

Origen tried to avoid the problem about the Apocalypse and Gospel of John by simply stating that "John, who leaned back on Jesus' breast [John 13:25], has left one Gospel, confessing that he could write so many that the world could not contain them [John 21:25], and he also wrote the Apocalypse, ordered to keep silence and not write the voices of seven thunders [Rev. 10:3–4]."[49] This comes from Origen's fifth volume on John, though Neuschäfer notes that such discussions usually appear in the prologues to commentaries, in treatments of the titles of books.[50] Examples of the practice appear in Galen's prologues to his Hippocratic commentaries. Such a discussion should have appeared in Origen's first volume on John—though there he does compare the way John presents Jesus as saying "I am the light of the world," etc., "and in the Apocalypse, 'I am the Alpha and the Omega.'"[51] At Caesarea Origen changed his mind, perhaps under the influence of his own former disciple Dionysius. In his treatise *On the Pascha*, written about twenty-five years later, he referred to "the Apocalypse attributed to John," and in a list of apostolic works written around the same time, he ascribed only the Gospel and epistles to John.[52]

The first of Origen's homilies on Luke deals with the closely related question of the New Testament canon. Because Luke begins with the words, "Since many have undertaken to compile a narrative," Origen believes he is implicitly criticizing gospels other than the four the church accepts, for Matthew, Mark, and John, not to mention Luke himself, did not "undertake" but were inspired by the Holy Spirit. Those who "undertook" wrote the apocryphal Gospel of the Egyptians or the Gospel of the

Twelve, while the heretic Basilides, in Origen's opinion, wrote a gospel named after himself, and there are also the Gospels according to Thomas and Matthias. A Greek scholion, not certainly from Origen, ascribes to "a written account" the notion that the apostle John, "still alive under Nero, collected the written gospels and approved and recognized those which the plot of the devil had not touched but refused and rejected those which he knew did not contain the truth."[53]

Origen also inquired about the genuineness of the *Preaching of Peter*. Was it genuine, spurious, or interpolated?[54] He did not give the grounds for his judgment, presumably negative, though he must have relied on criteria of content, vocabulary, and style, and taken First Peter (or Mark?) as his model. (Peter, like John and Barnabas, wrote one "epistle general."[55]) He shared this critical approach with Galen and contemporary philosophers. He knew some of Galen's writings, including the treatise *On His Own Books*, which begins with a story about the rejection of a book ascribed to Galen himself because of its vocabulary and the peculiar form of its title.[56] His younger contemporary Plotinus attacked the Gnostic "apocalypses" of Zoroaster, Zostrianus, Nikotheos, Allogenes, and Messos, while his disciple Amelius wrote forty volumes against the book of Zostrianus, and Porphyry proved that the book of Zoroaster was "entirely spurious and recent, forged by the sectarians."[57] Naturally Origen criticized others for their criticism, notably the Jewish-Christian Elchasaites whose heresy "deletes items from every scripture and, while using texts from the whole Old Testament and the gospels, absolutely rejects the apostle [Paul]."[58] This rejection showed how wrong they were.

Origen recognized the existence of "interpolations" in scripture and viewed them as guides to exegesis. The Word of God inserted stumbling blocks into both law and history so that the reader would not be completely ensnared by the written word, and therefore there are historical and nonhistorical passages, laws to be obeyed and impossible commandments. In brief, in both Testaments the Spirit "wove in" to the history additions that do not correspond with real events and provided legislation and precepts that do not always express what is reasonable. While Origen shared the common Christian belief that "none of the evangelists made an error or spoke falsely," and held that "the gospels were accurately written with the cooperation of the Holy Spirit, and those who wrote them made no mistakes in their remembering," he maintained that their apparent disagreements were intentional and pointed to a deeper consistency.[59]

The creation story cannot be taken literally, and there are "myriads" of other examples. The Gospels too are "full" of such expressions, as when the devil takes Jesus to a high mountain to show him all the kingdoms of the world and their glory. Persians? Scythians? Indians? Parthians? And so on—"sometimes the letter taken literally is not true and is even irrational and impossible." Things were "woven in" to the history that took place and to the literally useful legislation.[60] In other words, interpolations had a theological function.

Elsewhere Origen used the method of confirmation when he defended books used by Christians from pagan criticism. When Celsus charged that Christians had interpolated the *Sibylline Oracles*, Origen asked for an example of an interpolation or else some proof "that the older copies were purer and did not contain the verses he supposes were interpolated."[61] Given the primitive state of textual criticism, no proof could have been provided.

Origen criticized the Gnostic Heracleon for his exegesis of the Gospel of John with refutation and confirmation[62] but applied the method himself when he discussed the differences between its introductory chapters and those of the Synoptic Gospels. In dealing with this problem, he is opposing the notion that gospel truth lies in the "bodily characters." Indeed, he insists, it would be wrong to say that God appeared to such a person at such a time in such a place, where he did these things to him, appearing to him in such a guise, and led him to such a place, where he did such things. The form of Origen's criticism is based precisely on discussions of the falsity of myth, as in the *Progymnasmata* by the rhetorician Theon.[63] He concludes theologically that scripture really uses a historical image to speak of a God who cannot be limited by history. The evangelists "wove in" to their "historical" stories items that were purely spiritual, and thus the spiritual is preserved in the corporeal "falsehood."[64] This is to say that on the literal level the method of refutation works. Taken literally, the stories are false because inconsistent, and Origen is free to move to allegory.

He deals in a similar psychological-historical manner with the story of Jesus' cleansing the Temple. How could the supposed son of a carpenter attack the merchants? Would one not accuse him of insolence? Would not someone struck by his whip strike back? How could the Son of God use a whip anyway?[65] Just so, Theon argues that Medea could not have killed her children because she was their mother, her husband's power was greater than hers, she would not have committed murder publicly, and the motivation for the story is inadequate.[66]

In addition, Origen made a distinction in Jesus' sayings that brought him close to the Valentinian Theodotus and even toward his Adoptionist namesake (chapter 5). Jesus says of the divinity within him, "I am the way, the truth, and the life," but he also indicates that he was in a human body by saying, "But now you seek to kill me, a man who told you the truth."[67] Origen was willing to speak of "the supposedly human Jesus" and to argue that "he had several aspects, and to those who saw him he did not appear alike to all."[68] He admitted with the Adoptionists that "he who suffered human sorrows was a man" (citing Isa. 53:2–3 with John 8:40), but he held that other passages from John showed that "the person and essence of the divine being in Jesus is quite a different matter from that of his human aspect . . . . It was the one who dwelt in the supposedly human Jesus who said that he was the resurrection." Even apart from "dialectical subtleties" (which Origen could obviously invoke), "none of us is so idiotic as to say that the life died or that the resurrection died."

The dialectical subtleties were to be found in the Stoic "syllogism of two conditionals." (1) If the first is true, the second is true; (2) if the first is true, the second is not true, (3) then the first is not true. This means that (1) if the prophets of God said that God would be crucified (or that life would die), they necessarily spoke the truth; (2) if they said this, since things by nature impossible are not true, what they say of God would not happen; (3) then they did *not* say that God would be crucified (or that life would die).[69] This is the formal logical foundation for Origen's claim. In turn it is based on the assumption that "God crucified" and "life dead" are contradictions.[70]

It is interesting, though perhaps not important, to note that Origen shared Galen's attitude toward his own importance. Galen calls himself renowned at Rome for his "predictions and cures, which were worthy of great praise." He reminds Epigenes that "in much glory among all, as you know, and great was the name of Galen." Unfortunately "envy grew with glory among those who thought they were somebody," and he suffered criticism for many years.[71] Just so, Origen explained his dealings with learned heretics and philosophers. "As I was devoted to teaching and the fame of our skill was in circulation, sometimes heretics approached me and sometimes those from Greek studies, especially philosophy, and it seemed right to investigate the doctrines of the heretics and the claim of the philosophers to speak about the truth." The envy came from his bishop.[72]

Julius Africanus and Biblical Criticism

Two studies that go beyond Julius Africanus's efforts on the *Odyssey* (see chapter 2) reflect his concern with the comparison of texts. In his *Letter to Origen*, he addresses him as "master and son" and criticizes the story of Susanna in the book of Daniel as "clever but recent and fictitious." Daniel sounds like a judge, not a prophet. The way in which the two old observers are defeated is more ridiculous than the comedies of Philistion, and includes plays on Greek words, not Hebrew.[73] Therefore the story is not part of the Old Testament. And how could the Jews, captives in Babylonia, impose a death sentence on the wife of their king? Finally, the Old Testament prophets never quote from one another, while the story of Susanna echoes Exodus 23:7, and the character of the style is different from that of Daniel. These "proofs" reflect the basic critical method for uncovering forgeries, a modest knowledge of Persian history, some acquaintance with the Hebrew language, and a concern for restricting the Old Testament to Hebrew books. (Susanna was "a spurious forgery," as Eusebius summarizes the case.[74]) Africanus ends by saying "I have struck my blow" and asking Origen to reply and give him instruction. "Greet all my masters. All the scholars [here] greet you."

Origen begins with an over-polite reference to his own modest attainments but insists on his Old Testament studies and provides some detailed arguments (not very convincing) for the authenticity of Susanna. He hopes to have set Africanus straight and simply denies the contrast in the styles of the two works. His argument about Susanna as Hebrew is strange since in writing *On Prayer* he discussed various kinds of prayer and found examples of the Greek "address" in Daniel (addition after 3:23: Song of the Three Children) and in Tobit (3:1–2). Since he knew that "they [Jewish scholars?] obelized" (marked as questionable) the expression in Daniel because it was found in Greek but not Hebrew, and rejected Tobit as not canonical, he went on to give examples from more authoritative Old Testament books. He is obviously on the defensive, for according to his *Commentary on Matthew* he himself had "obelized" such passages.[75] He must have recognized them as Greek, not Hebrew.

Africanus's *Letter to Aristides* opposes those who wrongly claim that the genealogies of Jesus in the Gospels of Matthew and Luke (both based on 1 Chronicles and Ruth) do not diverge because they combine priestly and royal. Such an interpretation would mean that the genealogies are forged and false since in fact only the tribe of Judah produced kings; only Levi, priests.[76] Africanus tries to solve the problem and "set forth the true history of the events" by positing that Jacob (Matt. 1:16) and Eli (Luke 3:23) were half-brothers, both sons of a woman named Estha by marriages with Matthan and Melchi. When Eli died without children, Jacob took his widow and begot Joseph, the natural son of Jacob but the legal son of Eli. This purely hypothetical construction explains why Matthew wrote "Jacob begat Joseph" as well as why Luke called Jesus "as was supposed, the son of Joseph, the son of Eli, . . . the son of Melchi."[77]

Dionysius of Alexandria on the Apocalypse

Dionysius of Alexandria had to criticize the Johannine literature after whole churches in Egypt had suffered schism and apostasy because of literalist exegesis of the Apocalypse. So he convoked village elders and teachers for a three-day colloquy on the subject. At the end, the literalist leader declared himself convinced by Dionysius's arguments. In excerpts from Dionysius's written record, Eusebius reports that "some of the rest of the brothers rejoiced over the colloquy and the accommodation and consideration toward all." Since he does not finish the sentence, we do not know how "others" than the "some" reacted.[78]

Dionysius began discussing the Apocalypse by referring back to Gaius's criticism as coming from "some of those before us" who "rejected and refuted the book." They "corrected each chapter, declaring that it was unintelligible and illogical (*asyllogiston*) and that its title was false." It was not by John, and it was not an apocalypse or unveiling, but a book veiled by a curtain of unintelligibility. The author was not an apostle or a churchman but the heretic Cerinthus.[79] Dionysius fully describes this view since he wants to show his own moderation. "I should not venture to reject the book, since many of the brothers take it seriously. Holding that the common understanding of it is greater than my perception, I hold that the interpretation of each passage is hidden and more marvelous. For though I do not understand it, I suspect that some deeper meaning lies within the expressions."

Perhaps he is influenced by Origen's early acceptance of the Apocalypse, but he wants either criticism or allegory to dispose of the idea of a kingdom of Christ on earth. He is replying to the *Refutation of Allegorists* composed by the literalist Nepos.[80] He was quite willing, however, to use the Apocalypse for an imperial eschatology of his own. He refers Revelation 13:5 ("to him there was given a mouth uttering haughty and blasphemous words, and it was allowed to exercise authority for forty-two months") to the emperor Valerian, persecutor from 257 to 260. Dionysius also carefully counted the seven years of his pro-Christian co-emperor Gallienus and his restoration in the ninth year, after a revolt. It was now time to celebrate the paschal feast without the leaven of malice and wickedness.[81] Gallienus's reign was more than double the time of persecution.

Dionysius held that the author of the Apocalypse was named John because the book says so, though he was not the author of the Gospel and the General Epistle (of John). The name John makes little difference, however, since "there have been many persons with the same name as John the apostle." (This too is a typical question raised by grammarians: how many authors were there with the same name? Diogenes Laertius frequently discusses the topic.) The books are quite different. Dionysius bases his conclusion on the character of each writer, the style of each, and what is called the "continuity" of the book. The Evangelist never names himself, while the Apocalyptist does so at the beginning and the end. (Here Dionysius carries on the tradition of Homeric criticism. Dio Chrysostom noted that Homer, unlike less noble writers, "never referred to himself anywhere in his poetry," and claimed he was like a prophet of the gods, speaking from their inmost shrine.[82]) Different conceptions and expressions and the whole arrangement prove the books were not written by one author, as does the difference in style. The Greek of the Gospel and Epistle are correct; so are the vocabulary, logical arguments, and style. No barbarous words or bad Greek are present. This is the way to "establish the dissimilarity of these writings," though for the present Dionysius does not give examples of the poor Greek of the Apocalypse.[83] This is the method already employed by Galen and other critics, by Christian heretics, and by Gaius of Rome. Indeed, Galen had differentiated the powerful author of the authentic aphorisms of Hippocrates from the different author of the *Prorrhetic*, who used bad Greek.[84]

Dionysius uses vocabulary studies to show that John and 1 John were written by the same person, first pointing to the way both begin and then listing twenty expressions to be found in both works. The list is not quite right, for it includes "turning from darkness," "forgiveness of sins," and "the devil," found in neither of them. He is more concerned with theology than philology, and some of the expressions he cites must be his own interpretations of clearly Johannine terms. Perhaps he may be excused because he relies on his memory as he records and interprets what went on at the conference. He goes on to claim that "the Apocalypse has hardly a syllable in common with these writings."[85] That is a rhetorical exaggeration not based on the evidence he cites. Presumably he agreed with Galen's criteria as set forth in his commentary on *Regimen in Acute Diseases*. Style and vocabulary were important and so was the thought of Hippocrates[86]—or, for that matter, of John.

In the work of this bishop of Alexandria the literary criticism that had entered the church through heretical initiatives had now become fully orthodox, or perhaps orthodoxy had changed so that the cultural weapon could be valued by bishops as well as philosophers. There was no reason for churchmen to fear critical method, for theologians had shown that it could effectively defend the Christian tradition.

Eusebius: Canon and Criticism

By the time of Eusebius, the method of "refutation" had proved to be just as useful as "confirmation," especially in the hands of scholars like Gaius, Origen, and Dionysius. It is reflected in Eusebius's attempts to reach conclusions on the canonicity of various books. He divides "recognized" books from those that were "disputed," and the latter group into two classes: those "known to many," including the epistles called James,

Jude, 2 Peter, 2 and 3 John, and perhaps also the book of Revelation, and "spurious" books such as the apocryphal gospels and acts, "the forgeries of heretics," which have an unapostolic "character" of expression.[87]

Eusebius reflects confusion between literary criteria, intended to prove authenticity or the lack of it, and theological criteria, intended to demonstrate orthodoxy or heresy. The problem was a difficult one, as some of Eusebius's own quotations show. For example, he cites Serapion of Antioch for the notion that though the *Gospel of Peter* was pseudepigraphical, i.e., had a false title, "most of it was in agreement with the real message of the Savior, but some things were added." As both false and interpolated, the book presented canonists with a difficult problem.[88] He also cites Origen's doubts about 2 Peter and his statement that not all regard 2 and 3 John as "genuine."[89]

The Epistle to the Hebrews also aroused critical suspicions, and Eusebius conveniently collected statements from Clement and Origen about it. He first discussed it in relation to 1 Clement, pointing out that this letter shares many ideas with Hebrews and has some explicit quotations from it. This proves that Hebrews is not late, and therefore it was natural for it to be included with the other writings of the apostle. Paul wrote to the Hebrews in their native language, and either the evangelist Luke or Clement of Rome translated his letter into Greek. The proof? Similarity of style and ideas.[90]

This seems to be Eusebius's own compilation out of Clement of Alexandria and Origen. Later he refers to Clement as supposing that Paul wrote for Hebrews in Hebrew and Luke translated it for Greeks, thus creating the same stylistic "complexion" as in Acts. Paul does not name himself in the letter, for Hebrews were prejudiced against him, nor does he call himself "apostle," for he was an apostle to the Gentiles, not the Jews. Clement refers to "the blessed elder" for this information.[91] With greater and more self-conscious rhetorical skill, Origen suggested in homilies on Hebrews that the character of the style of the Epistle was superior to Paul's. "Everyone who knows how to judge differences in style would acknowledge this," though the thoughts were not inferior to his. Therefore the thoughts were Paul's, but the style and composition came from some disciple who was "writing scholia on what his teacher said." Origen says that "if any church holds this epistle belonging to

Paul, it should be commended," and refers to his predecessor(s) who ascribed authorship to Clement or Luke—though "God knows who wrote the epistle."[92] Gaius of Rome had spoken more emphatically, denouncing "the recklessness and audacity of his opponents in composing new scriptures."[93]

Eusebius himself came back to the Johannine question, first citing Irenaeus to show that John wrote the Apocalypse under Domitian and then providing two witnesses, also orthodox, for his death under Trajan. These were Irenaeus and Clement.[94] The differences between John and the other evangelists can be explained from oral traditions or anonymous scholarship.

After the other Gospels were written, John supplemented them with his narrative about the beginning of Jesus' ministry. John gave "the first of the acts of Christ" and left out his genealogy according to the flesh.[95] These statements take Gaius's criticisms of the Gospel into account without naming him. Eusebius, no enthusiast for the eschatology of the Apocalypse, quotes at length from the criticisms by Dionysius of Alexandria, pupil and successor of Origen.

Galen is related to heresy in the *Church History* and, perhaps for this reason, there is no trace of him in the *Gospel Preparation*, for which Eusebius and his assistants ransacked the church library at Caesarea.[96] Presumably none of Galen's works was included in the collection, any more than works by Aristotle.

Jerome and Authorship

The famous scholar and heresy-hunter Jerome had been a pupil of the grammarian Donatus,[97] and he was therefore quite ready to use grammatical studies to serve his idea of orthodoxy. In 392–393 he produced his little book on *Famous Men*, primarily based on Eusebius's *Church History* but with independent comments often related to literary criticism.[98] He rejected the *Acts, Gospel, Preaching, Apocalypse,* and *Judgment* associated with Peter as among apocryphal writings. James wrote one epistle, which is said to have been edited by someone else under his name but gradually gained authority with the passage of time. The evangelist Matthew uses the Septuagint translation, not the Hebrew text of the Old Testament. The bishops of Asia asked John to write his

Gospel against such heretics as Cerinthus and the Ebionites. Another reason for writing was to confirm but supplement the accounts in Matthew, Mark, and Luke. Jude, the Lord's brother, left a brief letter, rejected by many because it uses a testimony from the apocryphal book of Enoch. It deserves authority, however, and is counted among holy scriptures because of its antiquity and long usage. On the Epistle to the Hebrews, Jerome sets forth the theories of authorship mentioned by Eusebius but adds that Tertullian ascribed it to Barnabas.[99]

His discussion of 2 Peter is inconclusive. He treated the letter as canonical and included it in his Latin Bible, but in *Famous Men* he stated that many regard 2 Peter as not apostolic because its style is not in harmony with the first letter. In the *Letter to Hedibia* he explained that though it differed in "style, character, and the structure of words," an interpreter of Peter could have composed it, just as Titus and Mark assisted Paul.[100] Why did he mention the controversy at all? Presumably he was torn between contemporary orthodoxy and his memories of what Eusebius, and behind him Origen, had said.[101]

Since his account of Theophilus of Antioch is entirely based on Eusebius, it is surprising to find him saying that "I read commentaries under his name on the gospel and the proverbs of Solomon, but they do not seem to me to be in accord with the elegance and style of the other volumes." His statement gives a false impression. In his *Letter 121*, he did quote allegorical exegesis of a Lucan parable from the commentary supposedly by Theophilus, but he had never seen the "other volumes," and the style of Theophilus's books *To Autolycus* is not elegant.[102] The question is not of great importance, but it shows that Jerome, like more modern critics, could nod.

As for the pseudepigrapha, he reports Tertullian's rejection of the *Acts of Paul and Thecla* with its myth about a baptized lion. Hermas, the author of the *Shepherd*, was known to Paul (because the name appears in Rom. 16:14); his "useful" book is still popular among the Greeks, though practically unknown among Latins.[103] The correspondence of Paul with Seneca is read by many, though Jerome does not vouch for it.[104] When he writes about later authors, he usually does not discuss authenticity, presumably because the debates reported by Eusebius had concerned the earlier writers.

Only a few years later he went beyond Eusebius to give a more complete account of the origin of John's Gospel. John

> was asked by practically all the bishops of Asia and embassies from many churches to write more deeply on the divinity of the Savior . . . as the *Church History* tells, when he was forced to write by the brothers, he replied that he would do so if after fasting all prayed together to God. After that, filled with revelation he burst forth with that preface that came from heaven: "In the beginning was the Word and the Word was with God and the Word was God; he was in the beginning with God."[105]

By *Church History* Jerome means Eusebius's work, which does not contain this story but does provide two "traditions" from Clement of Alexandria: that John appointed bishops in Asia, and that his disciples urged him to write his spiritual Gospel under divine inspiration.[106]

This seems to be the source of the account in the Muratorian Fragment. After naming the fourth of the Gospels as derived from the disciples of John, it launches at once into the "traditional" story. "When John's fellow-disciples and bishops urged him he said, 'Fast with me today for three days and whatever is revealed to each we will tell to one another.' In that night it was revealed to Andrew, one of the apostles, that with the recognition of all John should write down everything under his own name." Other aspects of this account of the canon clearly suggest a date late in the fourth century or early in the fifth.[107]

Jerome was disturbed by the attack that the Neoplatonist Porphyry made on the book of Daniel, the weak link in the Christian chain of prophecy and fulfillment—though not disturbed enough to read Porphyry's work.[108] Porphyry had noted that the book was not really composed by a prophet but written by some Judean who lived in the time of Antiochus Epiphanes. The book does not predict the future but describes the past.[109] Jerome did not agree with this view. On the other hand, as he went ahead with his commentary, he admitted that because the Song of the Three Children was not in the Hebrew text, he was not going to comment on it, and at the end of the commentary he noted that the story of Susanna was similarly absent though found in Theodotion's Greek. In place of a commentary, he simply translated notes on Susanna from the tenth book of Origen's *Miscellanies*. (We have seen that Origen regarded Susanna as authentic, but Jerome echoes the negative comments of Julius Africanus.[110])

More examples of literary criticism, both lower and higher, occur in other works, especially as Jerome struggled with Rufinus over the orthodoxy of Origen.[111] At the end of the fourth century, Rufinus translated the first book of the defense of Origen by the martyr Pamphilus and added a brief essay called *On the Falsification of Origen's Works*. He began by complaining that many Greek patristic writings had been interpolated and went on to discuss examples. First came the *Recognitions*, which Rufinus (and Jerome) thought had been written by Clement of Rome in the first century, a notion that does little credit to their sense of history or historical theology. The writings of Clement of Alexandria also suffered from interpolations stating that the Son of God was "created."[112] Athanasius had been compelled to write a *Defense* of Dionysius of Alexandria because of interpolated texts (editors note that this statement is false). More interestingly, Rufinus insisted that at Ephesus a heretic had attacked Origen in a discussion and later wrote it down with interpolations. The written version was brought to Antioch before Origen arrived and demanded to see the record, "so that my style would be recognized by the brothers, who know the way I regularly dispute and what doctrine I regularly use."[113] The heretic did not dare to show his report. In addition, Rufinus says, Hilary of Poitiers was attacked on the basis of a corrupt text, and Cyprian was condemned for his treatise *On the Trinity*, actually written by Tertullian.[114]

Jerome rather enjoyed dealing with these points since he could ask where, when, and why Hilary was attacked and also correctly point out that the author of the treatise *On the Trinity* was not Tertullian but Novatian.[115]

He derives some amusement from the ideas of those who refused to treat Philemon as a letter of Paul, claiming that it was not divinely inspired but dealt with mundane problems. They said that it was not by Paul or, if it was, it was not edifying; it had been repudiated by many ancient writers because written merely to exhort, not to teach. Jerome ridiculed their claim that inspiration excludes practicality and added that even Marcion accepted the whole little letter without emending it.[116] On the other hand, he ridiculed the legend about the inspired Septuagint translators. "A seer is one thing, a translator another. In the former case the Spirit predicts things to come; in the latter, erudition and verbal facility transposes what it understands." He suggested ironically that perhaps Cicero was inspired by "the spirit of rhetoric" when he translated works by Xenophon, Plato, and Demosthenes.[117]

Jerome also supplied two comments on readings he found in Origen's New Testament manuscripts. First, Matthew 24:36 in the manuscripts of Origen and Pierius did not contain the words "nor the Son" at "Of that day and hour no one knows, not even the angels of heaven nor the Son." (Presumably they were left out for a Christological reason, but Jerome retains them.) Second, Origen's manuscripts omitted "not to believe the truth" from "O foolish Galatians, who bewitched you not to believe the truth" (Gal. 3:1). Jerome deletes the words because they are not found in Origen's manuscripts.[118] Here he obviously does not follow any basic principles such as Galen espoused.

It is a pleasure, however, to find him citing medical writers in a letter, "especially Galen in his books entitled *On Health,*" even though not for literary criticism but for the importance of cold food and drink.[119]

By now the use of literary criticism for questions of authorship and interpolation had taken firm root in the Christian tradition and would flourish for millennia. Christians were no longer willing to accept documents uncritically just because they were said to be ancient or even orthodox. Indeed, such a period of simple acceptance, if it really existed, did not last long. We have seen that heretics were the first to raise critical questions, but the orthodox rapidly forged ahead (so to speak) into the Greco-Roman world of lower and higher criticism. Above all others Origen was responsible for this move, but later giants included such antagonists as Eusebius, Rufinus, and Jerome. By the fourth century Christian leaders had passed beyond the anonymous author against heretics once cited by Eusebius. This critic had been indignant over their use of the arts of godless unbelievers and their "correction" of scriptural texts. Others, especially biblical scholars, had come to recognize that literary criticism could supply some of the answers to literary problems.

Obviously it was not a universal solvent, and arguments about criticism have often masked more basic theological issues. At the same time, it can be a useful corrective to the almost universal human tendencies to forget, to distort, and to imagine past doings and sayings. It usually involves some kind of appeal to evidence and, indeed, to common human experiences, not least the experiences of authors as they struggle against lethargy, error, and some of their own prejudices. Origen in the East and Jerome in the West made sure that criticism was generally respected, but even in the second century Christian theologians had begun to find that criticism, though not all-sufficient, was indispensable.

Abbreviations

CAG	*Commentaria in Aristotelem Graeca*
CCL	*Corpus Christianorum, Series Latina*
CMG	*Corpus Medicorum Graecorum*
CSCO	*Corpus Scriptorum Christianorum Orientalium*
CSEL	*Corpus Scriptorum Ecclesiasticorum Latinorum*
FVS	*Die Fragmente der Vorsokratiker*
GCS	*Die griechischen christlichen Schriftsteller der ersten drei Jahrhunderte*
HTR	*Harvard Theological Review*
JBL	*Journal of Biblical Literature*
JTS	*Journal of Theological Studies*
LCL	Loeb Classical Library
PG	Migne, *Patrologia Graeca*
PL	Migne, *Patrologia Latina*
RAC	*Reallexikon für Antike und Christentum*
RE	Pauly-Wissowa, *Realencyclopädie der classischen Altertumswissenschaft*
SC	*Sources Chrétiennes*
Scr. min.	*Claudii Galeni Pergameni scripta minora*
SVF	*Stoicorum Veterum Fragmenta*, ed. H. von Arnim
TU	Texte und Untersuchungen
VC	*Vigiliae Christianae*

Notes

1. Authenticity and Heresy in Early Christianity

1. 1 Cor. 7:10–11 (contrast 7:12, 25, 40); 11:23–25; 15:3–8; 1 Thess. 4:15–17.

2. David E. Aune, *Prophecy in Early Christianity and the Mediterranean World* (Grand Rapids: Wm. B. Eerdmans Publishing Co., 1983), 242.

3. H. Windisch, *Der zweite Korintherbrief* (Göttingen: Vandenhoeck & Ruprecht, 1924), 327.

4. For John, see most recently, M. Hengel, *The Johannine Question* (London: SCM, 1989), 1–23.

5. 2 Peter 3:1, 16. On 1 and 2 Peter, see N. Brox, *Falsche Verfasserangaben. Zur Erklärung der frühchristlichen Pseudepigraphie* (Stuttgart: KBW, 1975), 17–19.

6. He urged his Galatian correspondents to "see with what large letters" he was personally writing to them (6:11). Second Thessalonians ends with a greeting in Paul's own hand, and he adds, "This is the mark in every letter of mine; it is the way I write" (3:17, RSV). Such is not really the case, but the author is concerned with the possibility of forgery (2:2).

7. H. von Staden, "Hairesis and Heresy: The Case of the haireseis iatrikai," in *Jewish and Christian Self-Definition*, vol. 3, *Self-Definition in the Greco-Roman World*, ed. B. F. Meyer and E. P. Sanders (Philadelphia: Fortress Press, 1983), 76–100, and M. Desjardins, "Bauer

and Beyond: On Recent Scholarly Discussion of *Hairesis* in the Early Christian Era," in *The Second Century* 8 (1991): 68–82.

8. W. F. Arndt and F. W. Gingrich, *A Greek-English Lexicon of the New Testament*, 2d ed. (Chicago: University of Chicago Press, 1979), cite Josephus and Acts for both Sadducees and Pharisees as sects.

9. Ignatius *Ephesians* 6.2; *Trallians* 6.1.

10. G. Bardy, "L'inspiration des pères de l'Église," *Recherches de science religieuse* 40 (1952): 7–26.

11. Hippolytus *Refutation* 6.42.2; Irenaeus *Heresies* 1.14.1; Epiphanius *Heresies* 49.1.3.

12. Clement *Miscellanies* 7.106.4; Hippolytus *Refutation* 5.7.1.

13. Clement *Miscellanies* 1.11.3; *Outlines* in Eusebius *Church History* 2.1.4. By "Barnabas," Clement means the author of the Epistle of Barnabas, just as by "Paul" he means the author of the Pauline epistles.

14. *Acts of Archelaus* 67, *GCS*, 96; Clement *Miscellanies* 4.81.1–83.1; Irenaeus *Heresies* 1.24.4; Eusebius *Church History* 4.7.7; Clement *Miscellanies* 6.53.2–5.

15. Epiphanius *Heresies* 42.1.7, 2.2. But is Epiphanius ever reliable in such matters?

16. Irenaeus *Heresies* 3.4.3; Hippolytus (*Refutation* 6.35.5–6) says that Italian Valentinians include Heracleon and Ptolemaeus; for the episcopate, see Tertullian *Valentinians* 4.1; Epiphanius *Heresies* 42.1.8.

17. Irenaeus *Heresies* 3.3.4.

18. Ibid. 1.25.6.

19. On heresy, see W. Bauer, *Orthodoxy and Heresy in Earliest Christianity* (Philadelphia: Fortress Press, 1970); A. Le Boulluec, *La notion d'hérésie dans la littérature grecque IIe–IIIe siècles*, 2 vols. (Paris: Études Augustiniennes, 1985).

20. Robert M. Grant, *The Formation of the New Testament* (London: Hutchinson, 1965), 32–51.

21. Irenaeus *Heresies* 2.28.2; 3.1.1; 3.12.11; 4.15.2 (cf. Ptolemaeus, chapter 4.

22. *Paschal Chronicle* preface; cf. O. Perler, *Méliton de Sardes Sur la Pâque et fragments* (Paris: Du Cerf, 1966), 244–247.

23. Eusebius *Church History* 3.39.3–4; 15. Cf. W. R. Schoedel, *Polycarp, Martyrdom of Polycarp, Fragments of Papias* (Camden, N.J.: Nelson, 1967), 6–102.

24. Irenaeus *Heresies* 5.33.3–4.

25. Eusebius (*Church History* 3.39.17) says Papias quoted 1 Peter.

26. Schoedel, *Polycarp*, 105–110.

27. L. O. Bröcker, "Die Methoden Galens in der literarischen Kritik," *Rheinisches Museum* 40 (1885): 429 (references to Galen 15.760 and 901, in C. G. Kühn, *Galeni opera omnia* [Leipzig: Cnoblochius, 1821–1833]).

28. Irenaeus *Heresies* 5.33.3–4; apparently from the Jewish *Apocalypse of Baruch* 29.5.

29. Justin *Apology* 1.26; 58.1.

30. Justin *Dialogue* 35.6.

31. Ibid. 80.5 (the word means "thinking straight" in Philo *Flight* 12, cf. 24).

32. Only in Justin *Apology* 1.66.3, 67.3 (liturgical), and *Dialogue* 100–107, a Christological commentary on Psalm 21(22).

33. Justin *Apology* 2.11.3–5 is a paraphrase of Xenophon *Memorabilia* 2.1.21–34); cf. 2.10.5 (*Memorabilia* 1.1.1). The second-century sophist Favorinus also wrote at least five books of *Memoirs*, used by Diogenes Laertius; cf. E. Mensching, *Favorinus von Arelate* 1 (Texte und Kommentare 3) (Berlin: De Gruyter, 1963), 50–64 (users), 65–99 (fragments).

34. Justin *Apology* 103.8. Proof that Justin knew John is provided by *Apology* 1.61.4–5 (John 3:3–5); *Dialogue* 105.1 (John 1:1–18); and note that "John, one of Christ's *apostles*," wrote the Apocalypse (*Dialogue* 81.4). Cf. Robert M. Grant, *Greek Apologists of the Second Century* (Philadelphia: Westminster Press, 1988), 58–59.

35. Justin *Dialogue* 106.3 (Mark 3:16–17).

36. H. Koester, "The Text of the Synoptic Gospels in the Second Century," in *Gospel Traditions in the Second Century*, ed. W. L. Petersen (Notre Dame, Ind.: Notre Dame Press, 1989), 28–33.

37. Le Boulluec, *La notion d'hérésie*, 67.

38. W. L. Petersen, "Tatian's Diatessaron," in H. Koester, ed., *Ancient Christian Gospels: Their History and Development* (London: SCM, 1990), 403–430; for another source, see J. Joosten, "West Aramaic Elements in the Old Syriac and Peshitta Gospels," *JBL* 110 (1991): 271–289.

39. Justin *Dialogue* 71–74; O. Skarsaune, *The Proof from Prophecy: A Study in Justin Martyr's Proof-Text Tradition*, Supplements to Novum Testamentum 56 (Leiden: Brill, 1987), 35–45.

40. Justin *Apology* 1.36–39.

41. Eusebius *Church History* 4.23.12.

42. Cf. W. C. Van Unnik, "De la règle *Méte prostheinai méte aphelein* dans l'histoire du canon," VC 3 (1949): 1–36; Le Boulluec, *La notion de hérésie*, 250–253.

43. See P. Nautin, *Lettres et écrivains chrétiens des IIe et IIIe siècles* (Paris: Du Cerf, 1961), 13–32.

2. Literary Criticism in Early Christian Times

1. On the whole question, see W. Speyer, *Die literarische Fälschung im heidnischen und christlichen Altertum. Ein Versuch ihrer Deutung* (München: Beck, 1971), 112–128 ("Die antike Echtheitskritik"). Literature still worth consulting includes A. Gudeman, "Literary Frauds Among the Greeks," in *Classical Studies in Honour of Henry Drisler* (New York: Macmillan, 1894), 52–74; A. Gudeman, "Literary Frauds Among the Romans," *Transactions of the American Philological Association* 25 (1894): 140–164; G. Bardy, "Faux et fraudes littéraires dans l'antiquité chrétienne," *Revue d'histoire ecclésiastique* 32 (1936): 5–23, 275–302; Robert Grant, "The Appeal to the Early Fathers," *JTS* 11 (1960): 13–24. The first Gudeman essay and the Bardy article are both found in N. Brox, ed., *Pseudepigraphie in der heidnischen und jüdisch-christlichen Antike* (Darmstadt: Wissenschaftliche Buchgesellschaft, 1977).

2. The absence of these words from most early Christian authors is partly due to chance since Irenaeus refers to Gnostic use of "an innumerable multitude of apocryphal and spurious scriptures" (*Heresies* 1.20.1, Greek in Epiphanius *Heresies* 34.18.7). Origen, writing in Alexandria before 231, stated that "not all say that 2–3 John are genuine"

(*Commentary on John* 5 frag., *GCS*, 101,33 = Eusebius *Church History* 6.25.10). At Caesarea after 231, he criticized the Gnostic Heracleon for using the *Preaching of Peter*, which must be classified as "genuine or spurious or mixed [interpolated]" (*Commentary on John* 13.17, *GCS*, 241,15).

3. Diogenes Laertius 7.34.

4. Ibid. 10.3; Athenaeus 611B; H. Usener, *Epicurea* (Leipzig: Teubner, 1887), 135.

5. G. B. Pecorella, *Dionisio Trace, Technē grammatikē* (Bologna: Capelli, 1962), 31 (c. 1), 71 (commentary); cf. W. G. Rutherford, *A Chapter in the History of Annotation = Scholia Aristophanica* 3 (London: Macmillan, 1905), 399–455; T. W. Allen and D. B. Monroe, *Homeri opera* (Oxford: Clarendon Press, 1912–1946), 154.

6. Dionysius *Lysias* 12; *Dinarchus* 2–13; on the problems in Dionysius's method, cf. S. Usher, *Dionysius of Halicarnassus Critical Essays*, LCL (Cambridge, Mass.: Harvard University Press, 1985), 2:248.

7. Xenon and Hellanicus, Proclus in Allen, *Homeri opera*, 102,3; dividers, J. W. Kohl, *De chorizontibus* (Darmstadt: Bender, 1917), Fragments and commentary; J. W. Kohl, "Die homerische Frage der Chorizonten," *Neue Jahrbücher* 47 (1921): 198–214.

8. *On the Sublime* 9.11–13.

9. Seneca *Dialogue* 10 (*On the Shortness of Life*) 13.2.

10. K. Lehrs, *De Aristarchi studiis Homericis* (Leipzig: 1882; reprint, Hildesheim: Olms, 1964), 26 and n. 9.

11. Texts in G. Kinkel, *Epicorum Graecorum Fragmenta* (Leipzig: Teubner, 1877); Allen, *Homeri opera*, 93–144; H. G. Evelyn-White, *Hesiod the Homeric Hymns and Homerica*, LCL (London: Heinemann, 1914), 480-533.

12. Pausanias 9.5.10; 9.9.5; Apollodorus 1.74; Athenaeus 465E. Fragment 1 of the *Thebais* with the expression "parched Argos," ascribed to Homer in the *Contest of Homer and Hesiod*, in Allen, *Homeri opera*, 235, lines 255–257, may be reflected in Favorinus *On Exile* 7, in A. Barigazzi, *Favorino di Arelate Opere* (Florence: Le Monnier, 1966), 382, line 25, and commentary, 434. Cf. R. A. Pack, *The Greek and Latin Papyri from Graeco-Roman Egypt*, 2d ed. (Ann Arbor, Mich.: University of Michigan Press, 1967), 44 (no. 455), though "parched Argos" also

appears in *Iliad* 4.171. Pack lists many other papyrus fragments of epic poetry, mostly Hellenistic or Alexandrian (100–102, with nos. 1772, 1807, 1831, 1836 possibly cyclic).

13. Herodotus 1.116–117; *Iliad* 6.289–292.

14. Aristotle *Poetics* 23, 1459 a 30.

15. Horace *Art of Poetry* 136–142.

16. For the authors' names, see A. Sadurska, *Les Tables Iliaques*, Centre d'archéologie de l'Académie polonaise des sciences (Warsaw: Panstwowe Wydawnictwo Naukowe, 1964).

17. Clement *Miscellanies* 1.131.6–8; 132.1; 6.25.2.

18. Seneca *Epistles* 88.40.

19. Text by U. von Wilamowitz, "Lesefrüchte CXCIII," *Hermes* 60 (1925): 281.

20. Photius *Library* Codex 239, in R. Henry, ed., *Photius Bibliothèque* (Paris: Belles Lettres, 1959–1977), 5:157 = *PG* 103, 1197A–B.

21. Plato *Alcibiades* 2.147C; Aristotle *Poetics* 4.12.

22. Dio Chrysostom *Oration* 53.4. The Stoics defended Zeno's own *Republic* in a similar way: "He wrote it when he was still young and foolish. . . . He was not always Zeno." See W. Crönert, "Kolotes und Menedemos," *Studien zur Paläographie und Papyruskunde* 6 (1906): 55.

23. Clement *Miscellanies* 1.25.1.

24. Plutarch *On the Malice of Herodotus* 873F.

25. [Plutarch] *Plutarch On Homer* 5,2, in J. F. Kindstrand, [Plutarchus] *De Homero* (Leipzig: Teubner, 1990), 4,85–87.

26. Josephus *Against Apion* 1.12

27. A. Gudeman, *Grundriss der Geschichte der klassischen Philologie*, 2d ed. Leipzig and Berlin: Teubner, 1909, 10–11.

28. Text and discussion in J.–R. Vieillefond, *Les "Cestes" de Julius Africanus* (Florence: Sansoni; Paris: Didier, 1970), 277–291; photograph of lines 44–55 in C. H. Roberts, *Greek Literary Hands 350 B.C.–A.D. 400* (Oxford: Clarendon Press, 1955), opposite 23.

29. On the library at Nysa, see Vieillefond, *Les "Cestes" de Julius Africanus*, 281–282.

30. Either the first thirteen lines of the incantation, *Odyssey* 3.15–17 plus additions, or—as would make more sense—*Odyssey* 11.34–43 + 48–50.

31. See E. Nash, *Pictorial Dictionary of Ancient Rome*, 2d ed. (New York: Praeger, 1962), 460–464; cf. W. L. MacDonald, *The Pantheon* (Cambridge, Mass.: Harvard University Press, 1976), 23, illustration 15 (from a model).

32. See M. T. Boatwright, *Hadrian and the City of Rome* (Princeton: Princeton University Press, 1987), 49.

33. Josephus *Against Apion* 1.12; Sextus Empiricus *Against Professors* 1.203–204.

34. Hippias (*FVS* 86 B6) in Clement *Miscellanies* 6.15.2; Plato *Apology* 41A, *Republic* 363B (Hesiod-Homer); *Protagoras* 316D, *Ion* 531A (Homer-Hesiod).

35. Seneca *Epistles* 88.6–7, 38–39.

36. Xenophanes *FVS* 21 B10–12; Plato *Republic* 2.337D–378A; Herodotus 2.53.

37. Quintilian 1.1.15; Aelian *Miscellanies* 12.36 (*Catalogue*) and Pausanias 2.26.7 (*Catalogue* interpolated; but by Hesiod himself, 1.43.1); Pausanias refrains from ascribing the *Great Eoiai* to Hesiod (seven instances).

38. Pausanias 8.18.1; 9.31.4.

39. Athenaeus 49B; 503D.

40. Notably in Philo *Eternity of the World* 17; cf. Justin *Apology* 1.59.6; Irenaeus *Heresies* 2.21.2. What looks like an allusion to *Theogony* 149 appears in the Wisdom of Solomon 14:6 with its reference to "haughty giants."

41. Athenagoras *Embassy* 29.2 (fragment 51, R. Merkelbach and M. L. West, *Fragmenta Hesiodea* (Oxford: Clarendon Press, 1967); Clement: fragments 273, 282, 306, 308, 310 (and 362, dubious). Clement used introductory material about him: *Miscellanies* 1.61.2, 117.4; 6.26.7. The conventional criticism of the *Theogony* by Theophilus of Antioch (*To Autolycus* 2.5–8, 12–13; cf. Sextus Empiricus *Against Professors* 10.18–19; Simplicius *On Aristotle On the Heaven* 3.1, *CAG*, 560,24) contrasts with his use of the *Theogony* in his own Christology; cf. C. Curry, "The Theogony of Theophilus," *VC* 42 (1988): 318–326.

42. Origen *Against Celsus* 4.79; Merkelbach and West, *Fragmenta Hesiodea*, fragment 1; *The Oxyrhynchus Papyri* 23.2354 (second century); Pandora, *Theogony* 53–82, 90–98; Origen *Against Celsus* 4.38.

43. Dionysius *On Nature* in Eusebius *Gospel Preparation* 14.26.13.

44. Plato *Republic* 363A–C (*father* of Musaeus?); Aristophanes *Frogs* 1031–1036; Chrysippus in O. Kern, *Orphicorum Fragmenta* (Berlin: Weidmann, 1922), F 30 = H. Diels, *Doxographi Graeci* (1879; reprint, Berlin: De Gruyter, 1929), 547b10.

45. Herodotus 7.6.

46. Aristotle *On Philosophy,* fragment 7, R. Walzer, *Aristotelis Dialogorum Fragmenta* (Firenze: Sansoni, 1934); W. D. Ross, *Aristotelis Fragmenta Selecta* (Oxford: Clarendon Press, 1955); cf. A. S. Pease, *M. Tulli Ciceronis De Natura Deorum*, 2 vols. (Cambridge, Mass.: Harvard University Press, 1955, 1958), 489–490 (on Cicero *Nature of the Gods* 1.107).

47. Pausanias 8.31.3, 37.5; 9.35.5; cf. 1.14.3, 22.7 (Kern, *Orphicorum Fragmenta*, F 51, T 192–195); Sextus Empiricus *Pyrrhonian Outlines* 3.30 (= *Against Professors* 9.361); Kern, *Orphicorum Fragmenta*, T 187, 191; otherwise "Orpheus" (*Against Professors* 2.31; 9.15).

48. Kern, *Orphicorum Fragmenta*, T 189–190.

49. Plutarch *On the Pythian Oracle* 407B.

50. Tatian *Oration* 41, M. Whittaker, *Tatian Oratio ad Graecos and Fragments*, Oxford Patristic Texts (Oxford: Clarendon Press, 1982), with pages and lines of Schwartz's edition, 42,5; *Oration* 8, Schwartz, 9,12 (in a mythological context); *Oration* 1, Schwartz, 1,9–10 (the inventor of poetry).

51. Clement *Miscellanies* 1.131.1–5, 134.3; 5.49.3–4; 6.5.3–8.

52. Athenagoras *Embassy* 17.1–2; 18.3–6; 20.1–4.

53. Gudeman, "Literary Frauds Among the Greeks," in *Classical Studies in Honour of Henry Drisler*, 54.

54. Hippolytus *Refutation* 5.4; 5.20.4–5.

55. Theophilus *To Autolycus* 3.2; full references in M. Marcovich, *Pseudo-Justinus Cohortatio ad Graecos, De monarchia, Oratio ad Graecos*, Patristische Texte und Studien, 32 (Berlin: De Gruyter, 1990), 43–44 (*Exhortation* 15.1); 88–89 (*On Monotheism* 2.4). Palinode in Theophilus *To Autolycus* 3.2; Clement *Exhortation* 74.3; Pseudo-Justin 36.4 (Marcovich, *Pseudo-Justinus*, 74).

56. S. G. Kapsomenos, "Der Papyrus von Derveni," *Gnomon* 35 (1963): 222–223; anonymous, "Der orphische Papyrus von Derveni,"

Zeitschrift für Papyrologie und Epigraphik 47 (1982): 1–12 (after p. 300).

57. Books, Galen *Doctrines of Hippocrates and Plato* 3.3 (*SVF*, 2:906; H. von Arnim, *Stoicorum Veterum Fragmenta*, 4 vols. [Leipzig: Teubner, 1905–1924], 255; cf. 907); drugs, Kern, *Orphicorum Fragmenta*, fragment 322; Galen *Antidotes* 14.144 in C. G. Kühn, *Galeni opera omnia*, 20 vols. (Leipzig: Cnoblochius, 1821-1833; reprint, Hildesheim: Olms, 1967).

58. Origen *Against Celsus* 7.53–54.

59. K. Ziegler, "Orphische Dichtung," *RE* 18 (1942): 1345.

60. A. D. Nock, *Essays on Religion and the Ancient World*, ed. Z. Stewart, 2 vols. (Oxford: Clarendon Press, 1972), 857 no. 17; Galen *Temperament and Force of Simple Drugs* 11.798 in Kühn, *Galeni opera omnia* (cf. 792).

61. Iamblichus *The Mysteries of Egypt* 8.4, E. Des Places, *Les mystères d'Égypte* (Paris: Belles Lettres, 1966), 198. Cf. W. Kroll in *RE* 8 (1912), 797–798. Iamblichus also gives the unlikely figures of 20,000 or 36,525 books (8.1).

62. On this question cf. G. Fowden, *The Egyptian Hermes* (Cambridge: Cambridge University Press, 1986).

63. Plutarch *The Fortune or Virtue of Alexander* 328A; Galen sensibly says that, like Socrates, he wrote nothing (*Hippocrates On the Nature of Man*, 15.68 in Kühn, *Galeni opera omnia=CMG* 5.9.1, p. 36,21; cited in Nock, *Essays on Religion and the Ancient World*, 623); Diogenes Laertius 1.16, 8.6 (rejecting the view); Porphyry *Life of Pythagoras* 57 in A. Nauck, *Porphyrii Philosophi Platonici opuscula selecta*, 2d ed. (Leipzig: Teubner, 1886; reprint, Hildesheim: Olms, 1963), 49,18–19; Iamblichus *Life of Pythagoras* 157, in L. Deubner, *Iamblichus De Vita Pythagorica liber* (Leipzig: Teubner, 1937), 88 ("written by the Pythagoreans"), 199, in Deubner, *Iamblichus*, 109 (Philolaus first to write).

64. Origen *Against Celsus* 5.57; Diogenes Laertius 8.6–10; cf. *FVS* 14, fragments 17–19.

65. N. Brox, *Fälsche Verfasserangaben. Zur Erklarung der frühchristlichen Pseudepigraphie* (Stuttgart: KBW, 1975), 66–67, 71–74; B. L. van der Waerden, "Pythagoras (Die Schriften und Fragmente), *RE*

Suppl. 10 (1965): 862–863; behind him, August Müller, *Die griechischen Philosophen in der arabischen Überlieferung* (Halle: Waisenhaus, 1873), 33–34 (the "badly corrupted" passage was "partly incomprehensible" to this learned Arabist).

66. Olympiodorus *Prolegomena and Commentary on the Categories*, *CAG*, 13–14; Elias *Commentaries on the Introduction of Aristotle and the Categories of Porphyry*, *CAG* 128. Cf. N. Brox, *Fälsche Verfasserangaben*, 72.

67. Galen *On the Passions of the Soul* 5.30 = *Scr. min.* 1:23,11–16; Nock, *Essays on Religion and the Ancient World*, 623.

68. Origen *Against Celsus* 7.53 (some Christians "Sibyllists," 5.61); cf. Henry Chadwick, *Origen Contra Celsum* (Cambridge: Cambridge University Press, 1953; reprint, 1965), 440 n.2.

69. Plato does mention the Sibyl but not written oracles, in *Phaedrus* 244B (B. McGinn).

70. Pseudo-Justin *Exhortation* 37, cf. Marcovich, *Pseudo-Justinus*, 75–76 (notes).

71. Lactantius (*Divine Institutions* 4.15.27) claims they were known to Cicero and Varro but misunderstood in pre-Christian times. Cf. Speyer, *Die literarische Fälschung*, 247–248.

72. Josephus *Against Apion* 1.39–42; cf. Deut. 4:2.

73. Cf. Robert M. Grant, *The Formation of the New Testament* (London: Hutchinson, 1965), 32–52; A. C. Sundberg, Jr., *The Old Testament of the Early Church*, Harvard Theological Studies 20 (Cambridge, Mass.: Harvard University Press, 1964).

74. E. Stein, "Alttestamentliche Bibelkritik in der späthellenistischen Literatur," *Collectanea Theologica Societatis Theologorum Polonorum* 16 (1935): 3–48.

75. Sundberg, *The Old Testament of the Early Church*, 171–176; cf. Philo *Life of Moses* 2.31–44; Josephus *Antiquities* 1.10–12; 12.11–16, 34–57, 89–118; *Against Apion* 2.45–46; Justin *Apology* 1.31.2–3; Irenaeus *Heresies* 3.21.1–3; Clement *Miscellanies* 1.148–149 (from Irenaeus); Tertullian *Apology* 18.5–8. Cf. R. Pfeiffer, *History of Classical Scholarship from the Beginnings to the End of the Hellenistic Age* (Oxford: Clarendon Press, 1968), 99–104 (critical).

76. Cf. Robert M. Grant, *The Letter and the Spirit* (London: SPCK, 1957), 97.

77. Pseudo-Justin *Exhortation* 13, in Marcovich, *Pseudo Justinus*, 40–41 (notes).

78. Diogenes Laertius 1.23, 34, 40–44, 48, 64–67.

79. Ibid. 2.39, 105, 124; 3.62, 66; 4.32. Metrocles supposedly burned his own works (6.95).

80. Ibid. 5.92–93; Gudeman, "Literary Frauds Among the Greeks," in *Classical Studies in Honour of Henry Drisler*, 58–59.

81. Ibid. 6.73, 80, 100.

82. Ibid. 2.64. Asclepius *On the Metaphysics of Aristotle* 991 b 3, *CAG*, 90, says that Panaetius rejected the *Phaedo* as spurious because he said the soul was mortal, but this notice may be confused.

83. Ibid. 2.48, 45; cf. 3.52: "Even when Socrates and Timaeus are the speakers, it is Plato's doctrines that are laid down"; 3.35.

84. Ibid. 3.34; Plato *Laws* 3.694C; Xenophon *Memorabilia* 3.6.1.

85. Diogenes Laertius 3.37; *Phaedo* 59B; *Apology* 34A; for a similar dossier, Athenaeus 504B–509E.

86. Diogenes Laertius 3.57. On editing and transmitting, H. Alline, *Histoire du texte de Platon*, Bibliothèque de l'École des Hautes Études, 218 (1915; reprint, Paris: Champion, 1984), 34–64.

87. M. Norsa, "Elenco di opere letterarie," *Aegyptus* 2 (1921): 17–20; J. V. Powell and E. A. Barber, *New Chapters in the History of Greek Literature*, 2d series (Oxford: Clarendon Press, 1929), 211–214. The list includes the *Anarcharis* of Lucian (see *Halcyon* mentioned above) and the early *Eudemus* of Aristotle.

88. Diogenes Laertius 3.66.

89. *Halcyon* also circulated among the writings of the satirist Lucian (see M. D. McLeod, *Lucian*, LCL, 8:303–317).

90. Aelian *Miscellanies* 8.2 (cf. U. von Wilamowitz, *Platon*, 2d ed. [Berlin: Weidmann, 1920], 325); Athenaeus 506C.

91. Clement *Miscellanies* 1.93.1 (*Demodocus*); 3.20.3 and 5.7.6 (*Epinomis*); 5.17.2 ("Socrates to Alcibiades"), 5.103.1 (*Epistle II*), 5.102.3–4 (*Epistle VI*), 5.77.1 (*Epistle VII*); allusions to the *Minos* in *Exhortation* 104.1 and *Miscellanies* 2.18.3.

92. Diogenes Laertius 3.62.

93. Anonymous *Prolegomena to the Philosophy of Plato* 25–26, C. F. Hermann, *Plantonis Dialogi*, 6 vols. (Leipzig: Teubner, 1874–1880), 218–219 = L. G. Westerink, *Prolégomènes à la philosophie de Platon* (Paris: Belles Lettres, 1990), 37–39 (cf. lxvii–lxviii). [Plato] *Epinomis* 987B is contrasted with, e.g., *Timaeus* 36C–D.

94. Pack, *Greek and Latin Papyri*, 81–83 (nos. 1386–1429).

95. Diogenes Laertius 5.22–27, 34.

96. Only one book is mentioned in Diogenes Laertius 5.26.

97. Ammonius *On the Categories*, preface, *CAG*, 13,20–30.

98. Pack, *Greek and Latin Papyri*, 26–27 (nos. 158–165).

99. Strabo 13.1.54, c. 608–609; Plutarch *Sulla* 26.1.

100. Athenaeus 3A–B. Alline, *Histoire du texte de Platon*, 57–58, notes that the library must have included the dialogues of Plato.

101. Werner Jaeger, *Aristotle* (Oxford: Clarendon Press, 1947), 11–101.

102. A. L. Peck, *Aristotle Historia Animalium*, 3 vols. (London: Heinemann, 1965, 1970), 1:lviii.

103. Philo *On the Eternity of the World* 10–11, 15–18.

104. E. A. Clark, *Clement's Use of Aristotle* (Lewiston, N.Y.: Mellen, 1977), 4 n.23; cf. Clement *Miscellanies* 2.60; Aristotle *Nicomachean Ethics* 3.2, 1111 a 3–15.

105. I think this was the way H. J. Cadbury later expressed the idea. In Cadbury, *The Making of Luke-Acts* (New York: Macmillan, 1927), 330, he had said that "no matter how closely [a Hellenistic author] followed either text or subject matter, he would not mention his source or indicate what he was doing."

106. W. D. Smith, *The Hippocratic Tradition* (Ithaca, N.Y.: Cornell University Press, 1979), 234; Erotian, in J. Klein, *Erotiani vocum Hippocraticarum conlectio* (Leipzig: Dyk, 1865), 36,7.

107. J. Ilberg, "Die Hippokratesausgaben des Artemidoros Kapiton und Dioskurides," *Rheinisches Museum* 45 (1890): 111–137; Smith, *The Hippocratic Tradition*, 234–240.

108. Ibid., 145–146; Galen *The Surgery* 18B.630–632 in Kühn, *Galeni opera omnia*.

109. Theon *Progymnasmata* 3, in L. Spengel, *Rhetores Graeci* (Leipzig: Teubner, 1854), 76,6–9 (to p. 78 on myth; also 6, pp. 93–96 on narrative; 13, p. 129, 7–10 on law).

110. Hermogenes *Progymnasmata* 5, in H. Rabe, *Hermogenes Opera* (Leipzig: Teubner, 1913), 11.

111. See the discussion in Robert M. Grant, *The Letter and the Spirit*, 98–102; on Dio's use of *anaskeue*, cf. W. Kroll, "Randbemerkungen XII," *Rheinisches Museum* 70 (1915): 607–610.

112. Origen *Against Celsus* 1.42.

113. A. Gudeman, *Grundriss der Geschichte der Klassischen Philologie*, 2d ed. (Leipzig: Teubner, 1909), 35; H. Rabe, "Die Liste griechischer Profanschriftsteller," *Rheinisches Museum* 65 (1910): 329–344; L. Radermacher, "Kanon," *RE* 10 (1919): 1873–1878; H. Oppel, "KANON. Zur Bedeutungsgeschichte des Wortes und seiner lateinischen Entsprechungen (regula-norma)," *Philologus* Suppl. 30 (1937): heft 4. See also Pfeiffer, *History of Classical Scholarship*, 203–208.

114. Theophilus *To Autolycus* 3.2; compare Sextus Empiricus *Against Professors* 1.58; even better, Dionysius of Halicarnassus *On Imitation* II epitome, 2–5, H. Usener, *Dionysii Halicarnassensis Librorum de imitatione reliquiae epistulaeque criticae duae* (Bonn: Cohen, 1889), 19–30.

115. W. H. Willis, "Greek Literary Papyri from Egypt and the Classical Canon," *Harvard Library Bulletin* 112 (1958): 5–34.

3. Marcion's Criticism of Gospel and Apostle

1. For chronology and almost everything else, see Adolf von Harnack, *Marcion: das Evangelium vom fremden Gott*, 2d ed. (Leipzig: Hinrichs, 1924), 18*–30*. Hereafter cited simply as "Harnack."

2. Marcion's exegesis can have arisen from Luke 23:42, the "penitent thief," or from the apocryphal Jeremiah cited by Justin *Dialogue* 72.4: "the Lord remembered his dead from Israel . . . and he descended to them to preach his salvation to them." It is significant that Jesus "in the spirit . . . went and preached to the spirits in prison, formerly disobedient," according to 1 Peter 3:18–20—a letter sent from Rome to Pontus.

3. It should be noted that we know less than might be imagined about

the early history of the "New Testament canon." E. Gutwenger, "The Anti-Marcionite Prologues," *Theological Studies* 7 (1946): 393–409, proved that the so-called anti-Marcionite prologues to the Gospels depend on Tertullian and thus come from the third century, not the second, while A. C. Sundberg, Jr., "Canon Muratori: A Fourth–Century List," *HTR* 66 (1973): 1–41, removed the Muratorian list from the second century.

4. Morton Smith, *Palestinian Parties and Politics That Shaped the Old Testament* (New York: Columbia University Press, 1971), 210 n.8, citing W. Bauer, *Das Leben Jesu im Zeitalter der neutestamentlichen Apokryphen* (Tübingen: Mohr, 1909), 494, who also viewed Marcion as an editor.

5. See R. Pfeiffer, *History of Classical Scholarship from the Beginnings to the End of the Hellenistic Age* (Oxford: Clarendon Press, 1968), 87–233; see also Robert M. Grant, "Marcion and the Critical Method," in P. Richardson and J. C. Hurd, *From Jesus to Paul: Studies in Honour of Francis Wright Beare* (Waterloo, Ont.: Wilfrid Laurier University Press, 1984), 207–215.

6. Diodorus 1.92.3, 93.3.

7. Cornutus 35.

8. Plutarch *On Isis* 352C; nothing irrational or mythical or from superstition, 353F; none of the tales happened in the way in which they are related, 355B.

9. Ibid. 358E.

10. Ibid. 360F. The same point is made in a fragment (157 Sandbach) preserved by Eusebius (*Gospel Preparation* 3.1.1, in K. Mras, *Eusebius Werke 8. Die Praeparatio Evangelica* (Berlin: Akademie, 1954–1956), 106,10–16.

11. Philo of Byblos in Eusebius *Gospel Preparation* 1.9.21, 26; 10.38–40.

12. O. Eissfeldt, *Ras Schamra und Sanchunjaton*, Beiträge zur Religionsgeschichtedes Altertums 4 (Halle: Niemeyer, 1939), 88–90; T. S. Brown, "Euhemerus and the Historians," *HTR* 39 (1946): 271–274; L. Troiani, *L'opera storiographica di Filone da Byblos* (Pisa: Libreria Goliardica, 1974), 42–51.

13. Strabo 16.2.35, c. 761.

14. Harnack 260*, 262*, 264*–266*, 268*–269*, 272*, 278*–280*.

15. A. Marmorstein, *The Old Rabbinic Doctrine of God* (London: Oxford University Press, 1927), 43, 46; H. A. Wolfson, *Philo*, 2 vols. (Cambridge, Mass.: Harvard University Press, 1947), 136.

16. Harnack 291*, 293*; Tertullian *Marcion* 3.21.3, 24.1, cited hereafter as "Tertullian."

17. Harnack 212*; Tertullian mentions neither verse.

18. Ibid. 231*.

19. Tertullian 4.25.1.

20. Harnack 212*, 219*.

21. Indeed, J. Knox, *Marcion and the New Testament* (Chicago: University of Chicago Press, 1942; reprint, New York: AMS, 1980), 103, notes that "of such interests of Luke-Acts as signs and wonders (especially punitive miracles), angels, visions, and the Holy Spirit [except in the Lord's Prayer], not one appeared conspicuously, if at all, in the Marcionite Gospel."

22. Harnack 207*; cf. Tertullian 4.26.3–4.

23. Tertullian 4.33.8. Kroymann bracketed *Christus ipse*, but cf. Origen *Commentary on Matthew* 14.7 (*GCS*, 209,27: Christ is kingdom).

24. Similarly Ptolemaeus (chapter 4) apparently read, "there is only one good God, my Father whom I revealed" (Epiphanius *Heresies* 33.7.5).

25. Tertullian 4.33.9; cf. Luke 24:25.

26. Harnack 239* = Tertullian 4.43.4; possibly "he" instead of "I."

27. Tertullian 4.3.5.

28. Ibid. 4.7.7.

29. Ibid. 4.42.1. The words about the law and the prophets seem to reflect Matt. 5:17; cf. also Harnack 249*-254*.

30. Harnack 197* claims that Luke 7:29–35 on the Baptist was lacking but cites no evidence.

31. Tertullian 4.33.7.

32. Knox, *Marcion and the New Testament*, 86 (table).

33. Tertullian 4.21.7 reads "after the third day."

34. Harnack 226*.

35. Ibid. 234*.

36. Ibid. 206*.

37. Ibid. 209*–210*.

38. Ibid. 219*.

39. Ibid. 189* and 227* = Tertullian 4.11.2; 37.1. Conceivably these alterations (or quotations from memory) are due to Tertullian rather than Marcion. The expression "Gentile and tax collector" occurs in Matt. 18:17, which Marcion did not accept.

40. Ibid. 231* = Tertullian 4.39.9.

41. Ibid. 237* = Epiphanius *Heresies* 42.9.1. Irenaeus 3.14.3 refers to no such passages (see chapter 7).

42. Ibid. 233*.

43. Ibid. 234*.

44. Ibid. 236*. The verse is omitted by Codex Vaticanus and the first hand of Codex Bezae, retained by the first hand of Sinaiticus.

45. Ibid. 236*; Knox, *Marcion and the New Testament*, includes only verses 39–43. On the other hand, the promise to the penitent thief recalls Marcion's picture of Jesus' preaching to sinners (see above).

46. So Harnack 238*.

47. Ibid. 239*; Tertullian 4.43.6–7.

48. Harnack relies primarily on Epiphanius and supplements his account from Tertullian. He rightly calls many passages in Luke "unattested" rather than "absent," noting how uncertain any reconstruction is. Knox, *Marcion and the New Testament*, 86, lists "non-Marcionite passages." See also R. J. Hoffman, *Marcion: On the Restitution of Christianity*, AAR Series 46 (Chico, Calif.: Scholars Press, 1984), 115–124.

49. D. S. Williams, "Reconsidering Marcion's Gospel," *JBL* 108 (1989): 477–496.

50. H. Koester, *Synoptische Überlieferung bei den apostolischen Vätern* (Berlin: Akademie, 1957), 45–56.

51. H. J. Cadbury, review of J. Knox, *Marcion and the New Testament*, *JBL* 62 (1943): 123–127.

52. Robert M. Grant, *The Letter and the Spirit* (London: SPCK, 1957), 115–119.

53. Harnack 21–22.

54. Ibid. 67*.

55. Rom. 2:16, where Marcion omits "my," and Rom. 16:25; but he left out chapters 15–16.

56. Gal. 1:6–9; 2 Cor. 11:4.

57. Origen *Commentary on John* 5.7, *GCS*, 10, p. 104,26. Adamantius (*Dialogue* 1.6, *GCS*, 4, p. 12,10) shows that they read "my gospel" in Gal. 1:7; cf. Harnack 68*–69*.

58. See Tertullian 1.19.2; Harnack 184*.

59. Origen *Commentary on Matthew* 15.3, *GCS*, 40, p. 356,28.

60. Harnack 76*.

61. Ibid. 259*–260*.

62. 2 Thess. 2:2 is not attested (Harnack 114*), but Marcion can hardly have omitted this valuable testimony.

63. Eusebius *Church History* 6.25.11; for Origen's methods, cf. B. Neuschäfer, *Origenes als Philologe*, 2 vols., Schweizerische Beiträge zur Altertumswissenschaft 18, 1–2 (Basel: Reinhardt, 1987), esp. nn. 748–752 on pp. 245–246.

64. Eusebius *Church History* 7.25.24–27; 7.25.1 (false title?). See chapter 7.

65. Justin *Apology* 1.58.2 (cf. 54.1).

66. Irenaeus *Heresies* 3.14.1; cf. Col. 4:14: "Luke the beloved physician . . . greets you."

67. G. Strecker, *Das Judenchristentum in den Pseudoklementinen*, TU 70 (Berlin: Akademie, 1958), 169–170; cf. H. J. Schoeps, *Theologie und Geschichte des Judenchristentums* (Tübingen: Mohr, 1949), 148–187.

68. *Clementine Homilies* 3.55.1–57.1. Harnack 278*–279* ascribed a similar list in *Clementine Homilies* 3.38–40 to Marcion's *Antitheses*, but they could come from general Hellenistic criticisms.

69. *Clementine Homilies* 3.47.1–4.

70. Ibid. 3.48–53.

71. The *Aphorisms* are printed in W. H. S. Jones, et al., *Hippocrates* (London: Heinemann, 1923–1988), 4:98–221.

72. Ibid. xxxv.

73. L. O. Bröcker, "Die Methoden Galens in der literarischen Kritik," *Rheinisches Museum* 40 (1885): 421–425.

74. Texts and discussion in Harnack 127*–134*.

75. Polycarp *Philippians* 3.2, 7.1; Irenaeus *Heresies* 3.3.4; for possible but not necessary combinations, see P. N. Harrison, *Polycarp's Two Epistles to the Philippians* (Cambridge: Cambridge University Press, 1936); H. von Campenhausen, *Polykarp von Smyrna und die Pastoralbriefe. Sitzungsberichte der Heidelberger Akademie der Wissenschaften, Philosophische-historische Klasse*, No. 2 (1951).

4. The Hidden Agenda of Ptolemaeus

1. Hippolytus *Refutation* 6.35.5.

2. Tertullian *Valentinians* 4.1–2.

3. Clement *Miscellanies* 7.106.4. Praise of his style and logic in E. Norden, *Die antike Kunstprosa* (Leipzig: Teubner, 1898), 2.920–922.

4. Epiphanius *Heresies* 33.4.4–9.

5. Lydus *On the Months* 4.73, R. Wuensche, *Ioannis Laurentii Lydi Liber de Mensibus* (Leipzig: Teubner, 1898), 125,7–10; for Amor as the secret name (*Roma* backwards), ibid., and J. H. Oliver, *The Ruling Power, Transactions of the American Philosophical* Society 43, no. 4 (1953): 883–884.

6. Epiphanius *Heresies* 33.3–7; G. Quispel, *Ptolémée: Lettre à Flora* (Paris: Du Cerf, 1949).

7. Cf. Quispel, *Ptolémée*, 7.

8. Epiphanius *Heresies* 33.3.6, 5.15, 6.6.

9. Quispel, *Ptolémée*, 84; Justin *Dialogue* 44.2.

10. Quispel, *Ptolémée*, 79, relying on Irenaeus *Heresies* 3.2.2.

11. See F. M. Sagnard, *Saint Irénée et la gnose valentinienne* (Paris: Vrin, 1947), 188–190.

12. Irenaeus *Heresies* 1.1.3.

13. Ibid. 1.3.2–3.

14. Ibid. 1.8.2–4.

15. Ibid. 1.3.6; 2.10.1; Robert M. Grant and David Tracy, *A Short History of the Interpretation of the Bible*, 3d ed. (Philadelphia: Fortress Press, 1984), 49–50.

16. Irenaeus *Heresies* 1.4.3.

17. For *pros* meaning "with" cf. F. Blass and A. Debrunner, *A Greek Grammar of the New Testament*, trans. R. W. Funk (Chicago: University of Chicago Press, 1961), paragraph 239.

18. Quispel, *Ptolémée*, 73–75.

19. Irenaeus *Heresies* 4.35.1.

20. Ibid. 1.7.3; Sagnard, *Saint Irénée et la gnose valentinienne*, 190–191.

21. Irenaeus *Heresies* 1.30.11; cf. Robert M. Grant, "Gnostics and the Inspiration of the Old Testament, in A. L. Merrill and T. W. Overholt, eds., *Scripture in History and Theology: Essays in Honor of J. Coert Rylaarsdam* (Pittsburgh: Pickwick, 1977), 269–277.

22. Irenaeus *Heresies* 1.8.51–9.3.

23. Ibid. 1.9.4.; cf. Tertullian *Prescription of Heretics* 39.5. J. Daniélou, *Message évangélique et culture hellénistique* (Louvain: Desclée, 1961), 84–86, argued that Irenaeus quotes from a work by Valentinus, but R. L. Wilken, "The Homeric Cento in Irenaeus' 'Adversus Haereses' I,9,4," *VC* 21 (1967): 25–33, followed by A. Rousseau and L. Doutreleau et al., *Irénée de Lyon contre les Hérésies*, 10 vols. (Paris: Du Cerf, 1965–1982), 1.1.222, showed that it was simply Hellenistic.

5. Galen's Literary and Logical Criticism

1. Athenaeus 1F; 57C; cf. Potter, *Hippocrates*, LCL, 6:259–260.

2. J. Mewaldt, "Galenos," *RE* 7 (1910): 578–581.

3. R. Walzer, *Galen on Jews and Christians* (London: Oxford University Press, 1949); Marcus Aurelius *Meditations* 11.3; Hippolytus *Refutation* 9.12.10–11.

4. Galen *Antidotes* 14.65 in C. G. Kühn, *Galeni opera omnia*, 20 vols. (Leipzig: Cnoblochius, 1821–1833; reprint, Hildesheim: Olms, 1967); Tertullian *To Scapula* 4.5–6.

5. Cf. the passages collected in Walzer, *Galen on Jews and Christians*, 11–15.

6. L. Edelstein, "Nachträge (Hippokrates)," *RE* Suppl. 6 (1935): 1290–1345; L. Edelstein, "Hippocrates (2)," *Oxford Classical Dictionary*, 2d ed. (Oxford: Clarendon Press, 1970), 518–519; G. E. R. Lloyd, "The Hippocratic Question," *Classical Quarterly* 69 (1975): 189; also the comments in G. E. R. Lloyd, *Methods and Problems in Greek Science* (Cambridge: Cambridge University Press, 1991), 194–198.

7. D. G. Meade, *Pseudonymity and Canon: An Investigation Into the Relation of Authorship and Authority in Jewish and Early Christian Tradition* (Tübingen: Mohr, 1986), 193.

8. W. D. Smith, *The Hippocratic Tradition* (Ithaca, N.Y.: Cornell University Press, 1979), 234. According to *Prognosis to Epigenes* (in Kühn, *Galeni opera omnia*, 14.622), some physicians say that *Prorrhetic II* is not genuine.

9. *CMG* 5.10.2.2, p. 55 = Kühn, *Galeni opera omnia*, 17A.888, and p. 283 = 18B.268.

10. Smith, *The Hippocratic Tradition*, 235–238.

11. *Faculties of Foods* 6.473 = *CMG* 5.4.2, p. 212,18–20. Galen's commentaries are cited hereafter without the word "commentaries" or mention that numbers refer to the Kühn edition.

12. *Critical Days* 9.859, 894; contemporary with *Abnormal Breathing* according to *On His Own Books* 19.34 = *Scr. min.* 2:111,18–20.

13. *Abnormal Breathing* 7.854–855, 890–891.

14. *Doctrines of Hippocrates and Plato* 5.527–529 = *CMG* 5.4.1.2, p. 378,36–380,24; fuller discussion in P. de Lacy, *De placitis Hippocratis et Platonis* (Berlin: Akademie, 1978–1984), notes, 663–664. Aristotle *History of Animals* 3.3, 512b12–513a7, ascribes the notion to Polybus.

15. *Epidemics III*, 17A.577–580 = *CMG* 5.10.2.1, pp. 60–63 (also *Aphorisms* and *Prognostics*).

16. *Joints* 18A.379.

17. Genuine, *Prognostic* 18B.18 = *CMG* 5.9.2, p. 206,13. "Not a few" think that Hippocrates did not write the part after the discussion of baths, but Galen will discuss that part anyway (*Regimen in Acute Diseases* 15.732–733 = *CMG* 5.9.1, p. 271; cf. *Abnormal Breathing* 7.913).

18. *Regimen in Acute Diseases* 15.455 = *CMG* 5.9.1, p. 135,2–10 (cf. Hippocrates *Regimen in Acute Diseases* [Appendix] 53, in Potter, *Hippocrates*, LCL, 314; examples in Athenaeus 127B–C.

19. *Epidemics III*, 17A.517, 579 = *CMG* 5.10.2.1., pp. 23,12–15, 62.

20. *Critical Days* 9.859; *Abnormal Breathing* 7.854, 890.

21. *Epidemics II* (*CMG* 5.10.1, pp. 155, 310–311, from Arabic).

22. Ibid., p. 402,17–25.

23. Ibid., p. 402,31–42; G. Strohmaier, "Übersehenes zur Biographie Lukians," *Philologus* 120 (1976): 117–122.

24. R. Walzer, "Galens Schrift 'Über die Siebenmonatskinder,'" *Rivista degli Studi orientali* 15 (1935): 345–346 (c. 2, from Arabic).

25. So also Clement of Alexandria *Miscellanies* 6.139.1; cf. H. Diels, *Doxographi Graeci* (1879; reprint, Berlin: De Gruyter, 1929), 429.

26. The same information recurs in *Nature of Man* 15.11–12 = *CMG* 5.9.1, p. 8,19–32.

27. *Prorrhetic* 16.625 = *CMG* 5.9.2, p. 68,1–8.

28. Ibid. 16.511 = *CMG* 5.9.2, pp. 13,27–14,1.

29. *Epidemics III* 17A.579 = *CMG* 5.10.2.1, p. 62,17.

30. *Epidemics VI* 17A.796 = *CMG* 5.10.2.2, p. 5,8; 922 = p. 76.2 (some say also *IV*); 17B.60–61 = p. 156,6; 17B.249 = p. 272,7.

31. Called spurious, *Nature of Man* 15.13 = *CMG* 5.9.1, p. 7,15.

32. Galen *On His Own Books* 19.35–37 = *Scr. min.* 2:112–114; cf. also J. Ilberg, "Über die Schriftstellerei des Klaudios Galenos," *Rheinisches Museum* 44 (1889): 229–237.

33. *Faculties of Foods* 6.473 = *CMG* 5.4.2, pp. 212,18–213,8; cf. Smith, *The Hippocratic Tradition*, 59.

34. *Aphorisms* 18A.8–9.

35. *Regimen in Health* 15.174–175 = *CMG* 5.9.1, p. 89,14. On Polybus, Hippocrates' son-in-law, H. Grensemann, "Der Arzt Polybos als Verfasser hippokratischer Schriften," *Abhandlungen der Geistes- und Sozialwissenschaftlichen Klasse der Akademie der Wissenschaften und der Literatur in Mainz*, 1968, 2, 53–95; H. Grensemann, "Polybos (8)," *RE* Suppl. 14 (1974): 428–436; J. Jouanna, "Le médicin Polybe est-il l'auteur de plusieurs ouvrages de la collection hippocratique?" *Revue des Études Grecques* 82 (1969): 552-562; cf. Smith, *The Hippocratic Tradition*, 218–221.

36. *Nature of Man* 15.11–12 = *CMG* 5.9.1, p. 8,25–27.

37. *Prognostic* 18B.17–18 = *CMG* 5.9.2, p. 206,13–16.

38. L. O. Bröcker, "Die Methoden Galens in der literarischen Kritik," *Rheinisches Museum* 40 (1885): 430.

39. Galen's term "acknowledged" will reappear in Eusebius's discussion of accepted and rejected New Testament books (chapter 7).

40. Lloyd, *Methods and Problems in Greek Science*, 416.

41. *Use of the Parts of the Body* 3.830 = 2:105,10, G. Helmreich.

42. *On His Own Books* 19.39–42 = *Scr. min.* 2:115–121.

43. *Doctrines of Hippocrates and Plato* 5.213 = *CMG* 5.4.1.2, p. 104,3–15.

44. For the passages, see Walzer, *Galen on Jews and Christians*, 11–15; similarly Celsus in Origen *Against Celsus* 1.9.

45. Galen may not have written the text. I. von Müller, "Über Galens Werk vom wissenschaftlichen Beweis," *Abhandlungen der philosophischen Classe der königlich bayerischen Akademie der Wissenschaften* 20 (1897): 403–478, tried to reconstruct.

46. Galen *Instruction in Logic* in C. Kalbfleisch, *Galeni Institutio Logica* (Leipzig: Teubner, 1896), 32,13–17; 8,7–9,16; translation, B. Mates, *Stoic Logic* (Berkeley and Los Angeles: University of California Press, 1961), 117–118, 120, 123. See also Aulus Gellius 16.8.9–14.

47. Diogenes Laertius 7.71–73.

48. Cf. D. A. Bertrand, "L'argumentation scripturaire de Théodote le Corroyeur (Epiphane, Pararion 54)," *Lectures anciennes de la Bible: Cahiers de Biblia patristica* (Strasbourg: Centre d'Analyse et de Documentation Patristiques, 1987), 1:153–168, for more emphasis on exegesis of the Bible as such.

49. Hippolytus *Refutation* 9.11.1.

50. Ibid. 9.11.3.

51. Galen *On His Own Books* 19.39 = *Scr. min.* 2:116,9.

52. Eusebius *Church History* 5.28.3–6, 13–19.

53. These were Justin (e.g., *Apology* 1.63.15), Miltiades (writings lost), Tatian (*Oration* 13.3, in M. Whittaker, *Tatian Oratio ad Graecos and Fragments*, Oxford Patristic Texts [Oxford: Clarendon Press, 1982], with pages and lines from Schwartz's edition, 15,5), and Clement of Alexandria (e.g., *Tutor* 1.55.2).

54. These were Irenaeus (e.g., *Heresies* 5.14.4) and Melito of Sardis (S. G. Hall, *Melito of Sardis On Pascha and Fragments*, Oxford Patristic Texts [Oxford: Clarendon Press, 1979], fragment 6, probably inauthentic, xxx–xxxi).

55. Apelles cited the apocryphal saying, "Become approved money-changers," in reference to sayings of Jesus and the Demiurge (Epiphanius *Heresies* 44.2.6).

56. Galen *On the Natural Faculties*, A. J. Brock, *Galen On the Natural Faculties*, LCL (London: Heinemann, 1916), 140.

57. Eusebius *Church History* 5.28.13–14; for the terms, cf. J. W. Stakelum, *Galen and the Logic of Propositions* (Rome: Angelicum, 1940), 26–30, 43–45.

58. For syllogistic arguments in Homer, see H. Erbse, *Scholia Graeca in Homeri Iliadem (scholia vertera)*, 7 vols. (Berlin: De Gruyter, 1969–1988), 1:7, 11, 12.

59. H. Schöne, "Ein Einbruch der antiken Logik und Textkritik in die altchristliche Theologie," *Pisciculi . . . Franz Josef Doelger*, ed. T. Klauser and A. Rücker (Münster: Aschendorff, 1939); Walzer, *Galen on Jews and Christians*, 75–79.

60. Harnack claimed that the Valentinian Alexander also wrote a book of syllogisms (Texte und Untersuchungen 6 [1890]: 114 n.1), but Tertullian's language (*Incarnation* 17.1) seems imprecise.

61. Eusebius *Church History* 5.28.17. The textual critic K. Lake comments ironically, "Apparently these Roman heretics added textual criticism to the sin of using Aristotle's logic, and were unable to resist the temptations of conjectural emendation" (Lake, *Eusebius The Ecclesiastical History* [London: Heinemann, 1926], 1:523 n.3).

62. Galen *The Surgery* 18B.630–632, cited in Smith, *The Hippocratic Tradition*, 145–146; cf. also Bröcker, "Die Methoden Galens in der literarischen Kritik," 415–421; Walzer, *Galen on Jews and Christians*, 80–85. On Origen, see chapter 7.

63. Epiphanius *Heresies* 54.1.9, 4.1, 5.1, 5.9, 6.1.

64. Irenaeus *Heresies* 3.12.2; 3.18.3, 7; 3.19.2; 4.33.1, 11–12; 5.17.1.

65. Epiphanius *Heresies* 54.2.3.

66. Clement *Miscellanies* 4.71.

67. Epiphanius *Heresies* 54.3.1; on Theodotus's text and exegesis, cf. Walzer, *Galen on Jews and Christians*, 84–85.

68. Julian *Against the Galilaeans* 253C–D.

69. Epiphanius *Heresies* 54.3.5. On the deletion of "therefore," cf. Adolf von Harnack, *Lehrbuch der Dogmengeschichte*, 5th ed. (Tübingen: Mohr, 1931), 1:710 n.1.

70. Hippolytus *Refutation* 7.35.2.

71. Clement *Excerpts from Theodotus* 60–61.4; F. M. Sagnard, *Clément d'Alexandrie: Extraits de Théodote* (Paris: Du Cerf, 1949), 181 n.3.

6. The Syllogistic Exegesis of Apelles

1. Philo *Special Laws* 1.260; cf. J. Weiss, *Der erste Korintherbrief* (Göttingen: Vandenhoeck & Ruprecht, 1910), 236.

2. Philo *Virtues* 145–146 (125–160).

3. Josephus *Antiquities* 4.233.

4. *SVF* 3.367–376.

5. Origen *First Principles* 4.3.1; cf. Philo *Planting* 32–36.

6. H. Crouzel and M. Simonetti, *Origenes: Traité des principes: Commentaire et Fragments* (Paris: Du Cerf, 1977), 4:194. In his *Commentary on John* 6.48, Origen could ask, "What sort of corporeal dragon was ever described as seen in the corporeal river of Egypt?"

7. B. A. Pearson, *Gnosticism, Judaism, and Egyptian Christianity* (Minneapolis: Fortress Press, 1990), 21–22, 39–51, has pointed to Nag Hammadi Codex IX 3, where God kept Adam away from the tree of knowledge, had to ask where Adam was, and grudgingly kept him from the tree of life; cf. J. M. Robinson, ed., *The Nag Hammadi Library in English*, 3d ed. (San Francisco: Harper & Row, 1988), 455.

8. Tertullian *Prescription of Heretics* 30.6.

9. Eusebius *Church History* 5.13.2.

10. Epiphanius *Heresies* 44.1.4–6.

11. Tertullian *Dress of Women* 1.2.

12. Adolph von Harnack, *Marcion: das Evangelium vom fremden Gott*, 2d ed. (Leipzig: Hinrichs, 1924), 408*–409* (hereafter cited simply as "Harnack") = Augustine *Heresies* 24 (*CCL* 46.301 = *PL* 42.30 n.1), from a ninth-century manuscript.

13. Origen *Commentary on Titus*, fragment in Pamphilus (*PG* 17.559A–B); Harnack 417*: *non omnibus modis Dei esse deneget legem vel prophetas.*

14. E. Junod, "Les attitudes d'Apelles, disciple de Marcion, à l'égard de l'Ancien Testament," *Augustinianum* 22 (1982): 113–133.

15. Pseudo-Tertullian *Against All Heresies* 6.6, in A. Kroymann, *Adversus omnes haereses* (Turnhout: Brepols, 1954), 1409.

16. Texts in Harnack 413*–416*; translation revised from Robert M. Grant, *Second-Century Christianity* (London: SPCK, 1946), 84–88.

17. Aristotle *Rhetoric* 1.2.13; cf. 14: "Few of the propositions of the rhetorical syllogism are necessary."

18. Tatian, like Apelles, claimed that Adam could not be saved (Irenaeus *Heresies* 1.28.1). In addition, he claimed that "Let there be" (Gen. 1:3) was optative, the prayer of the creator to the God above him. Clement used theology (*Prophetic Selections* 38.1), Origen grammar (*On Prayer* 24.5; *Against Celsus* 6.51) against his claim.

19. Eusebius *Church History* 5.13.8.

20. This is an important testimony to the method of the *Syllogisms*; cf. B. Neuschäfer, *Origenes als Philologe*, 2 vols. (Basel: Reinhardt, 1987), 242–263, and Dionysius of Alexandria in Eusebius *Church History* 7.25.1, 17, 22.

21. Rhodo was not a Stoic, able to speak of "appetition" (*hormē*) as "the first movement of the soul" (*SVF* 2.459, p. 150,22; cf. Clement *Miscellanies* 2.110.4–111.1).

22. Eusebius *Church History* 5.13.5–7.

23. Clement *Miscellanies* 2.8.4; also followers of Basilides, 2.27.2; cf. S. R. C. Lilla, *Clement of Alexandria* (London: Oxford University Press, 1971), 118–142; R. M. Berchman, *From Philo to Origen*, Brown Judaic Studies 69 (Providence: Brown University Press, 1984), 177.

24. Cf. I. Mueller, "An Introduction to Stoic Logic," in J. M. Rist, ed., *The Stoics* (Berkeley and Los Angeles: University of California Press, 1978), 11; Berchman *From Philo to Origen*, 207–208.

25. Clement *Miscellanies* 8.7.1–2.

26. Galen *Doctrines of Hippocrates and Plato* 5.213 = *CMG* 5.4.1.2, p. 104,3–15.

27. R. Walzer, *Galen on Jews and Christians* (London: Oxford University Press, 1949), 11–14 (texts 1–3); Galen *Differences of Pulses* 8.579; *Use of the Parts of the Body* 3.904 = *Scr. min.* 2:158,2–159,19. Men out of stone: Matt. 3:9 = Luke 3:8.

28. Cf. Robinson, *The Nag Hammadi Library in English*, 112, 117, 118, 121.

29. Ambrose *Paradise* 5.28 (hereafter "Ambrose").

30. Ibid.; cf. Philo *Questions on Genesis* 1.51: "If he [Adam] had been desirous of virtue, which makes the soul immortal, he would certainly

have obtained heaven as his lot," and Irenaeus *Heresies* 4.38.1:
"Someone may say, Could not God have made man perfect from the
beginning?"

31. Theophilus *To Autolycus* 2.24 (hereafter "Theophilus"); cf.
M. Alexandre, *Le commencement du livre Génèse I–IV*, Christianisme
Antique 3 (Paris: Beauchesne, 1988), 249; *Clementine Recognitions*
2.53.1, cf. G. Strecker, *Das Judenchristentum in den Pseudoklementinen*,
TU 70 (Berlin: Akademie, 1958), 168.

32. Theophilus 2.27.

33. Ambrose 6.30; cf. *Clementine Recognitions* 2.53.5.

34. Aulus Gellius 2.7; cf. B. Mates, *Stoic Logic* (Berkeley and Los
Angeles: University of California Press, 1961), 122.

35. Ambrose 6.31, Theophilus 2.25 agrees that Adam was an infant,
but "when the child does not obey his father's command, he is beaten and
receives chastisement because of his disobedience."

36. Theophilus 2.25; Irenaeus *Heresies* 4.38.1.

37. Junod, "Les attitudes d'Apelles," 124–125.

38. *Clementine Homilies* 3.17.1; 3.21.2; H. J. W. Drijvers, "Adam and
the True Prophet in the Pseudo-Clementines," *Loyalitatskonflikte in der
Religionsgeschichte: Festschrift für Carsten Colpe* (Würzburg:
Königshausen & Neumann, 1990), 315.

39. Ambrose 6.32.

40. Julian *Against the Galileans* 89A, 94A.

41. Ambrose 5.28; obviously a syllogism; Junod, "Les attitudes
d'Apelles," 121.

42. Ambrose 7.35; cf. Theophilus 2.25: The tree of knowledge was
good and its fruit was good; the tree did not contain death, as some suppose, but disobedience brought death.

43. Sextus Empiricus *Pyrrhonean Outlines* 3.10–12; Lactantius *Wrath
of God* 13.19–21; H. Usener, *Epicurea* (Leipzig: Teubner, 1887), 253,
Frag. 374; A. S. Pease, *M. Tulli Ciceronis De Natura Deorum*
(Cambridge, Mass.: Harvard University Press, 1958), 2:1232–1233; cf.
R. Philippson, "Die Quelle der epikureischen Götterlehre in Ciceros
erstem Buch de Natura Deorum," *Symbolae Osloenses* 19 (1939): 21–22.

44. Harnack 269*–270*.

45. Ambrose 8.38; cf. Theophilus 2.25: God wanted to test him, to see

if he would be obedient to his command; also 2.26: "As for God's calling and saying, Where are you, Adam? (Gen. 3:9), God did this not as if he were ignorant. . . ."

46. Jerome *Dialogue against the Pelagians* 3.6 (*CCL* 80,19–25 = *PL* 23.602B); Harnack 274* refers it to Marcion's *Antitheses*.

47. Robinson, *The Nag Hammadi Library in English*, 455.

48. Ambrose 8.40.

49. Ibid. 8.41. For Marcion's examples of the weakness of the Demiurge, see Harnack 270*.

50. Theophilus 2.28.

51. Justin *Dialogue* 102.3–4.

52. Harnack 414* n.1.

53. Eusebius *Church History*, 5.13.9.

54. According to Philo (*Questions on Genesis* 1.32), all animals spoke and still speak, but at the beginning human beings were very large and had more accurate senses.

55. Similarly the emperor Julian asks whether the serpent spoke "the language of human beings" (Julian *Against the Galilaeans* 86A).

56. This was the view of Philo (*Questions on Genesis* 1.33).

57. Ambrose 12.56 (*CSEL*, 325,23).

58. Some rabbis supposed that what the serpent saw was the intercourse of Adam and Eve; consequently it "conceived a passion for her" (*Bereshith Rabbah* 18.6 = H. Freedman, *Midrash Rabbah, Genesis*, 3d ed. (1939; London: Soncino, 1983), 1:146–147.

59. This statement is absent from Luke and therefore from Marcion's gospel; it may have stood in the *Antitheses*, however (cf. Harnack 80, 251*–252*).

60. "Simon Magus" describes Adam as "blind" in the Jewish-Christian *Clementine Homilies* 3.39.1; cf. Harnack 279*; Drijvers, "Adam and the True Prophet in the Pseudo–Clementines," 317. Some rabbis asked if the pair were blind (*Bereshith Rabbah*, Freedman, *Midrash Rabbah*, 152). According to Augustine (*City of God* 14.17), most people thought they were originally blind (cf. his *Marriage and Concupiscence* 1.5.6).

61. Philo *On the Creation* 156–157.

62. Theophilus 2.28 calls Eve the "pioneer of sin," but, like Irenaeus and Clement, does not cite the verse from 1 Timothy (cf. Sirach

25:24–25). Cf. Alexandre, *Le commencement du livre Génèse I–IV*, 310–311.

63. Erwin R. Goodenough, "A Jewish-Gnostic Amulet of the Roman Period," *Greek and Byzantine Studies* 1 (1958): 71–80, refers to the Naassene heretics discussed by Hippolytus.

64. Justin *Dialogue* 102.3.

65. Theophilus 2.23; Philo *Questions on Genesis* 1.48–49.

66. Origen *Homilies on Genesis* 2.2, *GCS* 6, pp. 27–30; cf. *Against Celsus* 4.41. Celsus calls the ark "monstrous" (*allokotos*) and says the story was told artlessly (*atechnos*) for infants. In other words, it was mythical.

67. W. Richter, "Zoologie," *Der Kleine Pauly* 5 (1975): 1556–1557.

68. Gen. 6:15: length 300 cubits, beam 50, height 30 = 450,000 cubic cubits, but Origen *Homilies on Genesis* 2.1, *GCS* 6, pp. 23–24, claims that the ark resembled a raft with a superstructure (or a Union ironclad of the Civil War) that narrowed to one cubit square at the thirty-cubit top. If so, it held 150,000 cubic cubits ($V=1/3$ Bh). Similarly W. G. Williams calls it "a floating house," though he gives its content as 1,500,000 cubic feet (roughly equivalent to 450,000 cubic cubits), evidently rejecting a pyramidal shape (*Interpreter's Dictionary of the Bible*, s.v. "Ark").

69. Origen, *Homilies on Genesis*, 2.2, *GCS* 6, pp. 27–30. Procopius of Gaza (cited *GCS* 6, p. 28,28) adds "and their food for a year."

70. Pliny *Natural History* 8.1 and 35.

71. *Apocryphon of John*, in Robinson, *The Nag Hammadi Library in English*, 121. Irenaeus supposes that they took the ark literally but refers to the cloud of light that saved Noah and his family (*Heresies* 1.30.10).

72. *Hypostasis of the Archons* in Robinson, *The Nag Hammadi Library in English*, 166. Norea is the sister of Seth in Irenaeus *Heresies* 1.30.9 (fires not mentioned), but according to Gnostics in Epiphanius *Heresies* 26.1.8, she was Noah's wife and set fires three times. On her, cf. A. McGuire, "Virginity and Subversion: Norea against the Powers in the HA," 239–258; and B. A. Pearson, "Revisiting Norea," 265–275, both in *Images of the Feminine in Gnosticism*, ed. K. L. King (Philadelphia: Fortress Press, 1988).

73. My thanks to W. R. Schoedel for this important point.

74. Apollodorus *Epitome* 5.14, R. Wagner *Apollodori Bibliotheca*, 2d ed. (Leipzig: Teubner, 1926), 208,15–19 (*Ilias parva*, fragment 22 in

T. W. Allen and D. B. Monroe, *Homeri opera* [Oxford: Clarendon Press, 1912–1946]). Eustathius on the *Odyssey* cites "a hundred according to Stesichorus, twelve according to others": J. M. Edmonds, *Lyra Graeca*, LCL (London: Heinemann, 1924), 2:50–51 (frag. 30 = frag. 24 Bergk).

75. Dio Chrysostom *Oration* 11.123, 125, 128.

76. Palaephatus *Incredible Stories* 16; N. Festa, *Palaephati Peri Apiston*, Mythographi Graeci 3.2 (Leipzig: Teubner, 1902), 23–24.

77. Pausanias 1.23.8; cf. Pliny *Natural History* 7.202: "among siege engines the horse, now called the ram"; H. J. Rose, *A Handbook of Greek Mythology* (New York: Dutton, 1929), 252 n.50.

78. Clement *Miscellanies* 2.113.2, based on Plato *Theaetetus* 184D.

79. Augustine *Confessions* 1.13.

80. Origen *Against Celsus* 4.41; N. de Lange, *Origen and the Jews* (Cambridge: Cambridge University Press, 1976), 127; cf. Philo *Questions on Genesis* 2.2 (quadrangle, not square).

81. Philo *Questions on Genesis* 2.5; Clement *Miscellanies* 6.87.1.

82. *Bereshith Rabbah* 31.10, Freedman, *Midrash Rabbah*, 243–244; on dimensions 31.11, Freedman, 244–245.

83. Origen *Homilies on Genesis* 2.2, *GCS* 6, 29,6–9.

84. Ibid., p. 28,20; cf. I. Thomas, *Selections Illustrating the History of Greek Mathematics*, 2 vols., LCL (Cambridge, Mass.: Harvard University Press, 1951), 520–523 (Diophantus).

85. Augustine *City of God* 15.27; *Questions on the Heptateuch* 1.4 (cf. 1.5) (*PL* 34.549); Henry Chadwick, *Origen Contra Celsum* (Cambridge: Cambridge University Press, 1953; reprint 1965), 217 n.3.

86. Augustine *City of God* 20.7.

87. Ibid. 15.27.

88. Philo *The Worse Attacks the Better* 170–173; seven, *On the Creation* 117. Naturally the Valentinian Marcosians found their thirty aeons in the height of the ark (Irenaeus *Heresies* 1.18.4).

89. Ambrose *Noah* 6.13; Philo *Questions on Genesis* 2.1–6 (cf. Augustine *City of God* 15.26).

90. See E. Lucchesi, *L'Usage de Philon dans l'oeuvre exégétique de saint Ambroise* (Leiden: Brill, 1977), 3–4. Aucher called Ambrose "Philo Christianus"; cf. C. Siegfried, *Philo von Alexandria* (Jena: Dufft, 1875), 371–391.

91. Ambrose *On the Faith* 1.5.42 (*PL* 16.559B); cf. 1.13.84 (571A).

92. H. Savon, *Saint Ambroise devant l'exégèse de Philon le Juif* (Paris: Études Augustiniennes, 1977), 1:26–27 (thanks to J. Patout Burns for this reference); see also Lucchesi, *L'Usage de Philon dans l'oeuvre exégétique de saint Ambroise*, esp. 53–88.

93. Junod, "Les attitudes d'Apelles," 124.

7. The Orthodox Counterattack

1. W. L. Petersen, "Tatian's Diatessaron," in H. Koester, *Ancient Christian Gospels: Their History and Development* (London: SCM, 1990), 427–428.

2. Jerome *Commentary on Titus* preface (*PL* 26.590B = Tatian fragment 10, in M. Whittaker, *Tatian Oratio ad Graecos and Fragments*, Oxford Patristics Texts [Oxford: Clarendon Press, 1982], with pages and lines of Schwartz's edition). When Eusebius (*Church History* 4.29.6) says he paraphrased some of Paul's words as though correcting their syntax, he may be referring to a fragment on 1 Corinthians 7:5, criticized by Clement (*Miscellanies* 3.81–82).

3. Clement *Miscellanies* 1.131.1. For grammar in Tatian's theology, see Robert M. Grant, *Greek Apologists of the Second Century* (Philadelphia: Westminster Press, 1988), 127.

4. Clement *Miscellanies* 2.52.5–6; Origen *Series Commentary on Matthew* 117, *GCS*, 250,6–10.

5. Theophilus *To Autolycus* 3.9–10.

6. Ibid. 2.22.

7. For blasphemy, cf. Mark 14:64; Sabbath, Matt. 12:1–4, etc.; transformed, not abolished, according to H. Weiss, "The Sabbath in the Fourth Gospel," *JBL* 110 (1991): 311–321.

8. R. H. Connolly, *Didascalia Apostolorum* (Oxford: Clarendon Press, 1929).

9. Theophilus *To Autolycus* 2.35; 3.13.

10. Irenaeus *Heresies* 5.30.1; 3.7.1–2.

11. Eusebius *Church History* 5.20.2–3.

12. Irenaeus *Heresies* 1.20.1.

13. Ibid. 2.10.1; cf. Clement and Porphyry as cited below.

14. Ibid. 3.2.1.

15. Ibid. 3.4.1–2; Papias in Eusebius *Church History* 3.39.4.

16. Robert M. Grant, *The Formation of the New Testament* (London: Hutchinson, 1965), 151–152; cf. M. Hengel, *The Johannine Question* (London: SCM, 1989), 3.

17. Irenaeus *Heresies* 1.20.1.

18. Ibid. 3.11.8; 3.1.1; 3.14.1.

19. Gobarus in Photius *Library*, Codex 232, in R. Henry, *Photius Bibliothèque* (Paris: Belles Lettres, 1959–1977), 5:79,12–14 = *PG* 103.1104D. At Codex 121, Henry, 2:95–96 = *PG* 103.404A, Photius says he read a little book against heresies by Hippolytus, based on Irenaeus's lectures; this explains the correlation of Hippolytus with Irenaeus.

20. Irenaeus *Heresies* 5.30.2 (Revelation); 3.3.3 (Clement); 3.3.4 (Polycarp); 4.20.2 (Hermas); 5.28.4 (Ignatius).

21. Ibid. 3.1.1–2; 3.14.1.

22. Ibid. 3.14.3–4.

23. Luke 1–2; 3:23; 3:1; 6:24–26.

24. Luke 5:1–11; 13:10–17; 14:1–6.

25. These two passages (Luke 14:7–14 and 11:5–8) also refer to John the Baptist.

26. Luke 7:36–50; 12:16–20; 16:19–31; 17:5–6; 19:1–10; 18:9–14. He may have altered Luke 19:9b to show that Zacchaeus was a Gentile; see chapter 3.

27. Luke 17:11–19; 14:21–24; 18:1–8; 13:6–9; 24:13–32.

28. References in Adolf von Harnack, *Marcion: das Evangelium vom fremden Gott*, 2d ed. (Leipzig: Hinrichs, 1924), 184*–185* (hereafter cited simply as Harnack). Epiphanius says Marcion omitted Luke 13:6–9 (Harnack 217*).

29. A. Le Boulluec, *La notion d'hérésie dans la littérature grecque IIe–IIIe siècles* (Paris: Études Augustiniennes, 1985), 1:119–120 n.18.

30. M. Smith, *Clement of Alexandria and a Secret Gospel of Mark* (Cambridge, Mass.: Harvard University Press, 1973), 22–23, on Papias.

31. Clement *Outlines*, in Eusebius *Church History* 6.14.7.

32. R. Pfeiffer, *History of Classical Scholarship from the Beginnings to the End of the Hellenistic Age* (Oxford: Clarendon Press, 1968), 225–227; N. C. Wilson, "An Aristarchean Maxim," *Classical Review* 21 (1971): 172;

Clement *Who Is the Rich Man?* 4.2; see also J. Pépin, "Hermeneutik," *RAC* 14 (1988): 457–458, with a reference to Galen *Coma According to Hippocrates* 7.646 = *CMG* 5.9.2, p. 182,23. See also Irenaeus as cited above.

33. Eusebius *Church History* 6.12.3–6. He echoes Paul's words in Gal. 4:14: "You received me as a messenger of God, as Christ Jesus."

34. A disciple's love of his master is one of the reasons for forgery, according to the Neoplatonists Olympiodorus and Elias (see chapter 2).

35. Tertullian *Baptism* 17.5.

36. Eusebius *Church History* 3.31.4; 2.25.6–7; 3.28.1–2; 6.20.3.

37. Epiphanius *Heresies* 51.3.1–2, 5.

38. Ibid. 51.17.11–18:1 (cf. 51.4.5–10).

39. Ibid. 51.22.1.

40. Ibid. 51.33.1. Epiphanius, as interpreted by K. Holl, *Epiphanius (Ancoratus und Panarion)* (Leipzig: Hinrichs, 1915–1933), explained that Montanists controlled the church only in the years 171 to 264; unfortunately he unreliably dated Revelation under Claudius (51.33.35, 9).

41. Dionysius Bar Salibi *On the Apocalypse*, trans. I. Sedlacek, *CSCO*, Scriptores Syri, vol. 101 (Rome: de Luigi, 1910), 8.

42. Ibid. 9.

43. Ibid. 10.

44. Ibid.

45. Epiphanius 51.32.2.

46. Ibid. 51.34.2.

47. On Origen's editions, see Eusebius *Church History* 6.16–17.

48. Origen *Commentary on Matthew* 15.14, *GCS* 40, pp. 387–388; Bruce M. Metzger, "Explicit References in the Works of Origen to Variant Readings in New Testament Manuscripts," in *Biblical and Patristic Studies in Memory of R. P. Casey*, ed. J. N. Birdsall and R. W. Thomson (Freiburg: Herder, 1963), 78–80.

49. Eusebius *Church History* 6.25.9–10.

50. B. Neuschäfer, *Origenes als Philologe* (Basel: Reinhardt, 1987), 70–71 (cf. 62, citing Donatus' *Life of Vergil*).

51. Origen *Commentary on John* 1.4, *GCS* 10, p. 8.

52. O. Guéraud and P. Nautin, *Origène Sur la Pâque* (Paris: Beauchesne, 1979), 172 (p. 10,16–17); 119 n.23, with a reference to *Homilies on Joshua* 7.1, *GCS* 7, p. 328.

53. Origen *Homilies on Luke* 1, *GCS* 35, pp. 4–6. Perhaps Jerome preferred not to translate this story about John, though it was told by Eusebius, who insisted that it was "true" (*Church History* 3.24.7–8).

54. Origen *Commentary on John* 13.17, *GCS* 10, p. 241,15; cf. 5.3, *GCS* 10, p. 101,33.

55. Ibid. 6.18; 19.1; cf. Eusebius *Church History* 6.25.8, 10; Origen *Commentary on Matthew* 17.19; *Against Celsus* 1.63. (He was hesitant about Jude: *Commentary on Matthew* 17.30, *GCS* 40, p. 672,9.)

56. See Robert M. Grant, "Paul, Galen, and Origen," *JTS* 34 (1983): 533–536; Galen *On His Own Books* 19.9 = *Scr. min.* 2:91.

57. Porphyry *Life of Plotinus* 16. *Zostrianus* and *Allogenes* were found in Coptic translations at Nag Hammadi; see J. M. Robinson, ed, *The Nag Hammadi Library in English*, 3d ed. (San Francisco: Harper & Row, 1988), 402–430, 490–500.

58. Eusebius *Church History* 6.38.

59. Origen *Commentary on John* 6.34, *GCS* 10, p. 143,25; *Commentary on Matthew* 16.12, *GCS* 40 p. 510,15; Robert M. Grant, *The Letter and the Spirit* (London: SPCK, 1957), 98.

60. Origen *First Principles* 4.2.9–3.4. Origen's model is a spider weaving its web; ibid. 3.1.2.

61. Origen *Against Celsus* 7.53–54; 1.16; 7.56.

62. Origen *Commentary on John* 6.60.

63. Theon, in L. Spengel, *Rhetores Graeci* (Leipzig: Teubner, 1854), 2:76–77.

64. Origen *Commentary on John* 10.3–5; "falsehood," 10.5, *GCS* 10, p. 175,20; "weaving," *First Principles* 4.2.9.

65. Origen *Commentary on John* 10.25.

66. Theon in Spengel, *Rhetores Graeci*, 2:94.

67. Origen *Against Celsus* 1.66; 2.9, 25.

68. Ibid. 2.25, 64; references for "supposedly human," H. Chadwick, "Origen, Celsus and the Resurrection of the Body," *HTR* 41 (1948): 100 n.30.

69. Origen *Against Celsus* 7.14–16; B. Mates, *Stoic Logic* (Berkeley and Los Angeles: University of California Press, 1961), 80–81.

70. Origen *Against Celsus* 7.16, *GCS*, 168,1–4.

71. Galen *Prognosis to Epigenes* 4 (14.625). Cf. his claim that his

diagnosis made people think he worked miracles (*Examinations by Which the Best Physicians Are Recognized*, A. Z. Iskandar, *CMG* Suppl. Orientale [Berlin: Akademie, 1988], 4:61,15; cf. 63,14).

72. Origen in Eusebius *Church History* 6.19.12. Envy is the "human weakness" of the bishop Demetrius (6.8.4).

73. Susanna 54–59: *prinos* (oak tree)—*priō* (cut in pieces); *schinos* (mastich tree)—*schizō* (cut in two).

74. Eusebius *Church History* 6.31.1.

75. Origen *On Prayer* 14.4, *GCS*, 331,27; Origen *Commentary on Matthew* 15.14, *GCS*, 387–388.

76. W. Reichardt, *Die Briefe des Sextus Julius Africanus an Aristides und Origenes* (Leipzig: Hinrichs, 1909), 55,31–56,1.

77. Eusebius *Church History* 1.7.2–16.

78. Ibid. 7.24.6–9.

79. Ibid. 7.25.1–2.

80. Ibid. 7.24.2.

81. Ibid. 7.10.2; 7.23.

82. Ibid. 7.25.6–11, 14; Dio Chrysostom *Oration* 53.9–10; 55.8. Plato referred to himself only twice (see chapter 2).

83. Eusebius *Church History* 7.25.17–27.

84. Galen *Predictions* 1 (16.511); L. O. Bröcker, "Die Methoden Galens in der literarischen Kritik," *Rheinisches Museum* 40 (1885): 426–427.

85. Eusebius *Church History* 7.25.17–22.

86. Galen *Regimen in Acute Diseases* 15.734 = *CMG* 5.9.1, p. 271,23–272,1.

87. Eusebius *Church History* 3.25. For "character" as a criterion for authenticity (e.g., "Homeric"), cf. A. Ludwich, *Aristarchs homerische Textkritik* (Leipzig: Teubner, 1884), 42–47.

88. Eusebius *Church History* 6.12.3–6.

89. Ibid. 6.25.5 (1 Peter, "the catholic epistle"); 8 (one acknowledged, second doubted); 10 ("not all say these are genuine").

90. Ibid. 3.28.1–3.

91. Ibid. 6.14.2–4.

92. Ibid. 6.25.8–14, though in the late *Homilies on Joshua* (7.1) Origen ascribes fourteen epistles to Paul.

93. Ibid. 6.20.3.

94. Ibid. 3.18.1–3 (Irenaeus *Heresies* 5.30.3); 3.23.

95. Ibid. 3.24.6–13.

96. K. Mras, *Eusebius Werke* 8. *Die Praeparatio Evangelica* (Berlin: Akademie, 1954–1956), thought Galen's *Exhortation* was related to a quotation in *Gospel Preparation* 5.27.8, 33.8, but the quotation (from Oenomaus of Gadara) is not what Galen quoted.

97. See F. Lammert, *De Hieronymo Donati discipulo*, Commentationes philologae Ienenses 9.2 (1912).

98. T. D. Barnes, *Tertullian* (Oxford: Clarendon Press, 1971), 235–239.

99. Jerome *Famous Men* 1–5, 9.

100. Jerome *Epistle* 120.11 (*CSEL* 55, pp. 507–508 = *PL* 22.1002).

101. Eusebius *Church History* 3.1.4, 25.3; Origen in 6.25.8.

102. Jerome *Famous Men* 25; *Epistle* 121.6 (*CSEL* 56, pp. 24–26 = *PL* 22.1020–1021).

103. Jerome does not comment on Tertullian's claim that the *Shepherd* had been "judged among the apocrypha and false writings by every council of the churches—even your [probably African] churches" (*On Chastity* 10.12).

104. Jerome *Famous Men* 7, 10, 12.

105. Jerome *Commentary on Matthew* preface (*CCL* 77, pp. 3, 50 = *PL* 26.19).

106. Eusebius *Church History* 3.23.6; 6.14.7.

107. Cf. A. C. Sundberg, Jr., "Canon Muratori: A Fourth–Century List," *HTR* 66 (1973): 1–41; M. Hahneman, *The Muratorian Fragment and the Development of the Canon* (D. Phil. diss., Oxford University, 1987).

108. J. N. D. Kelly, *Jerome: His Life, Writings, and Controversies* (New York: Harper & Row, 1975), 300–301.

109. Jerome *Commentary on Daniel*, preface (*CCL* 75A, pp. 771–773 = *PL* 25.491–492).

110. Ibid. (*CCL* 75A, pp. 803, 945–950 = *PL* 25.509A, 580A–B).

111. K. K. Hulley, "Principles of Textual Criticism Known to St. Jerome," *Harvard Studies in Classical Philology* 55 (1944): 105–109.

112. Compare Clement Fragment 23 (*GCS* 3, p. 202,12) = Photius

Library, Codex 109, R. Henry, *Photius Bibliothèque* (Paris: Belles Lettres, 1959–1977), 2:80,15 = *PG* 103.384A.

113. At the beginning of Galen's work *On His Own Books*, which I believe Origen read (see Robert M. Grant, "Paul, Galen, and Origen"), he uses the same kind of argument.

114. Rufinus *Falsification of Origen's Works*, CCL 20, pp. 9–15 = *PG* 17.620A–629B.

115. Jerome *Against Rufinus* 2.19 (*CCL* 79, pp.55–56 = *PL* 23.464A–B).

116. Jerome *Commentary on Philemon* (*PL* 26.635D, 637C, 638B).

117. Jerome *Preface on the Pentateuch* (*PL* 28.181–182).

118. Jerome *Commentary on Matthew* (*CCL* 77, p. 231 = *PL* 26.188B); *Commentary on Galatians* (373C); Metzger, "Explicit References in the Works of Origen," 79–80.

119. Jerome *Epistle* 121 preface (*CSEL* 56, p. 4 = *PL* 22.1007); cf. 54.9.4 (*CSEL* 54, p. 475 = *PL* 22.554); Galen *Helath* 6.34,59 = *CMG* 5.4.2, pp. 17.1; 28,3. For Jerome's use of other works by Galen, see A. S. Pease, "Medical Allusions in the Works of St. Jerome," *Harvard Studies in Classical Philology* 25 (1914): 82; P. Courcelle, *Les lettres grecques en occident de Macrobe à Cassiodore*, 2d ed. (Paris: Boccard, 1948), 74–75.

Bibliography

1. Ancient Authors

Adamantius. W. H. van de Sande Bakhuyzen. *Der Dialog Peri tēs eis theon orthēs pisteos. GCS 4.* Leipzig: Hinrichs, 1901.

Aelian. *Miscellanies.* M. R. Dilts. *Claudii Aeliani Varia historia.* Leipzig: Teubner, 1974.

———. A. F. Scholfield. *Aelian On the Characteristics of Animals.* LCL. 3 vols. London: Heinemann, 1958–1959.

Africanus, Julius. M. J. Routh. *Reliquiae Sacrae.* 5 vols. Oxford: Typographeum Academicum, 1846.

———. J.-R. Vieillefond. *Les "Cestes" de Julius Africanus.* Florence: Sansoni; Paris: Didier, 1970.

Albinus. *Introduction;* in *Platonis Dialogi.* Edited by C. F. Hermann. Leipzig: Teubner, 1877, 6: 147–189.

Ambrose. *On the Faith. PL* 16.

———. C. Schenkl. *On Noah, On Paradise. CSEL* 32.1. Vienna: Tempsky, 1907.

Ammonius. A. Busse. *In Aristotelis Categorias commentarius. CAG* 4.4. Berlin: Reimer, 1895.

Anastasius of Sinai. *Hexaemeros. PG* 89.

Anonymous. *Prolegomena to Platonic Philosophy.* C. F. Hermann. *Platonis opera.* Leipzig: Teubner, 1880, 6: 196–222.

———. L. G. Westerink with P. Trouillard and A. Ph. Segonds. *Prolégomènes à la philosophie de Platon.* Paris: Belles Lettres, 1990.

Anonymus Londinensis. H. Diels. *Anonymus Londinensis.* Supplementum Aristotelicum 3. Berlin: Reimer, 1893.

——. W. H. S. Jones. *The Medical Writings of Anonymous Londinensis.* Cambridge: Cambridge University Press, 1947.

Apollodorus. *Library.* R. Wagner. *Apollodori Bibiotheca.* Mythographi Graeci 1. 2d ed. Leipzig: Teubner, 1926.

Aristotle. *Fragments.* R. Walzer. *Aristotelis Dialogorum Fragmenta.* Firenze: Sansoni, 1934. W. D. Ross. *Aristotelis Fragmenta Selecta.* Oxford: Clarendon Press, 1955.

——. *Categories.* H. B. Cooke and H. Tredennick. *Aristotle: The Organon I. The Categories of Interpretation—Prior Analytics.* LCL, Aristotle 1. London: Heinemann, 1938.

——. *On the Heavens.* W. K. C. Guthrie. *Aristotle On the Heavens.* LCL 6. London: Heinemann, 1939.

——. *History of Animals.* A. L. Peck. *Aristotle Historia Animalium.* LCL 9–11. 3 vols. London: Heinemann, 1965, 1970.

——. *Generation of Animals.* A. L. Peck. *Aristotle Generation of Animals.* LCL 13. London: Heinemann, 1943.

——. *Nicomachean Ethics.* H. Rackham. *Aristotle The Nicomachean Ethics.* LCL 19. London: Heinemann, 1926.

Asclepius. M. Hayduck. *Asclepii In Aristotelis Metaphysicorum Libros A–Z commentaria.* CAG 6.2. Berlin: Reimer, 1888.

Athenaeus. C. B. Gulick. *Athenaeus The Deipnosophists.* LCL. 7 vols. London: Heinemann, 1927–1941.

Athenagoras. W. R. Schoedel. *Athenagoras.* Oxford Patristic Texts. Oxford: Clarendon Press, 1972.

——. M. Marcovich. *Athenagoras: Legatio pro Christianis.* Patristische Texte und Studien, 32. Berlin and New York: De Gruyter, 1990.

Atticus. E. Des Places. *Atticus Fragments.* Paris: Belles Lettres, 1977.

Augustine. G. E. McCracken et al. *Saint Augustine The City of God, Against the Pagans.* LCL. 7 vols. London: Heinemann, 1957–1972.

——. *Confessions.* P. Knöll. *Confessiones.* Leipzig: Teubner, 1909.

——. *Heresies.* R. Vander Plaetse, with C. Beukers. *De haeresibus.* CCL 46: 283–351. Turnhout: Brepols, 1969. Also in *PL* 42.

——. *On Marriage and Concupiscence. PL* 44.

——. *Questions on the Heptateuch. PL* 34.

Barnabas. P. Prigent and R. Kraft. *Épître de Barnabé. SC* 172. Paris: Du Cerf, 1971.

1 Clement. K. Bihlmeyer, revised by W. Schneemelcher. *Die Apostolischen Väter.* Erster Teil. Tübingen: Mohr, 1956.

Clement. O. Stählin. *Clemens Alexandrinus. GCS* 12, 15, 17, 39. Leipzig: Hinrichs, 1905–1936.

———. F. Sagnard. *Clément d'Alexandrie: Extraits de Théodote. SC* 23. Paris: Du Cerf, 1949.

Clementine Homilies and Recognitions. B. Rehm. *Die Pseudoklementinen I–II. GCS* 42, 51. Berlin: Akademie, 1953, 1965.

Cornutus. C. Lang. *Cornuti Theologiae Graecae Compendium.* Leipzig: Teubner, 1881.

Dio Chrysostom. J. W. Cohoon. *Dio Chrysostom.* LCL. 5 vols. London: Heinemann, 1932–1951.

Diodorus Siculus. C. H. Oldfather et al. *Diodorus of Sicily.* LCL. 12 vols. London: Heinemann, 1933–1967.

Diogenes Laertius. H. S. Long. *Diogenis Laertii Vitae Philosophorum.* 2 vols. Oxford: Clarendon Press, 1964.

Dionysius of Alexandria. C. L. Feltoe. *The Letters and Other Remains of Dionysius of Alexandria.* Cambridge: Cambridge University Press, 1904.

Dionysius Bar Salibi. *On the Apocalypse.* Versio by I. Sedlacek. CSCO, Scriptores Syri, vol. 101. Rome: De Luigi, 1910.

Dionysius of Halicarnassus. H. Usener. *Dionysii Halicarnassensis Librorum de imitatione reliquiae epistulaeque criticae duae.* Bonn: Cohen, 1889.

Elias. A. Busse. *Eliae In Porphyrii Isagogen et Aristotelis Categorias commentaria. CAG* 18.1. Berlin: Reimer, 1900.

Epictetus. W. A. Oldfather. *Epictetus: The Discourses as Reported by Arrian, The Manual, and Fragments.* LCL. 2 vols. London: Heinemann, 1926, 1928.

Epiphanius. K. Holl. *Epiphanius (Ancoratus und Panarion). GCS* 25, 31, 37. Leipzig: Hinrichs, 1915–1933.

Erotian. J. Klein. *Erotiani vocum Hippocraticarum conlectio.* Leipzig: Dyk, 1865.

Eusebius. *Church History*. E. Schwartz. *Eusebius Werke* 2. *Die Kirchengeschichte*. *GCS* 9. Leipzig: Hinrichs, 1903–1909.

———. *Gospel Preparation*. K. Mras. *Eusebius Werke* 8. *Die Praeparatio Evangelica*. *GCS* 43, 1–2. Berlin: Akademie, 1954–1956.

Galen. C. G. Kühn. *Galeni opera omnia*. 20 vols. Leipzig: Cnoblochius, 1821–1833. Reprint. Hildesheim: Olms, 1967. Volume and page numbers of Kühn are in the margins of *CMG*; cited below without editor's name.

———. *Abnormal Breathing*. 7.753–960.

———. *Coma According to Hippocrates*. 7.643–665. G. Helmreich. *De coma*. *CMG* 5.9.2, pp. 179–194.

———. *Critical Days*. 9.769–941.

———. *Examinations by Which the Best Physicians Are Recognized*. A. Z. Iskandar. *CMG* Supplementum Orientale 4. Berlin: Akademie, 1988.

———. *Exhortation*. G. Kaibel. *Claudii Galeni Protreptici quae supersunt*. Berlin: Weidmann, 1894. Reprint 1963.

———. *Faculties of Foods*. 6.453–748. G. Helmreich. *Galeni De alimentorum facultatibus*. *CMG* 5.4.2, pp. 199–386. Leipzig and Berlin: Teubner, 1923.

———. *On His Own Books*. I. Müller. *Claudii Galeni Pergameni scripta minora*. Vol. 2. Leipzig: Teubner, 1891. Reprint. Amsterdam: Hakkert, 1967.

———. *Hygiene*. 6.1–452. K. Koch. *Galeni De sanitate tuenda*. *CMG* 5.4.2, pp.1–198. Leipzig and Berlin: Teubner, 1923.

———. *Instruction in Logic*. C. Kalbfleisch. *Galeni Institutio Logica*. Leipzig: Teubner, 1896. English translation: J. S. Kieffer. *Galen's Institutio Logica*. Baltimore: Johns Hopkins Press, 1964.

———. *Natural Faculties*. A. J. Brock. *Galen On the Natural Faculties*. LCL. London: Heinemann, 1916.

———. *The Doctrines of Hippocrates and Plato*. P. De Lacy. *De placitis Hippocratis et Platonis*. *CMG* 5.4.1.2. Berlin: Akademie, 1978–1984.

———. *Prognosis to Epigenes*. 14.597–673.

———. *The Timaeus*. H. O. Schröder. *Galeni In Platonis Timaeum commentarii fragmenta*. *CMG* Suppl. 1. Leipzig and Berlin: Teubner, 1934.

Use of the Parts of the Body. G. Helmreich. *Galen De usu partium Libri XVII*. 2 vols. Leipzig: Teubner, 1907–1909.

——. Commentaries on Hippocratic works (chronologically after W. D. Smith. *The Hippocratic Tradition*. Ithaca, New York: Cornell University Press, 1979, 123–124):

Fractures. 18B.318–628.

Joints. 18A.300–767.

Aphorisms. 17B.345–887; 18A.1–195.

Epidemics. I 17A.1-302. E.Wenkebach. *CMG* 5.10.1, pp. 6–151.

Prognostic. 18B.1–317. J. Heeg. *CMG* 5.9.2, pp. 195–378.

Regimen in Acute Diseases. 15.418–919. G. Helmreich. *CMG* 5.9.1, pp. 117–366; not genuine.

Regimen in Acute Diseases according to Hippocrates. M. Lyons. *CMG* Supplementum Orientale 2, pp. 74–111.

The Surgery. 18B.629–925.

Epidemics II. F. Pfaff. *CMG* 5.10.1, pp. 155–410.

Prorrhetic I. 16.489–840. H. Diels. *CMG* 5.9.2, pp. 1–178.

Epidemics III. 17A.480–792. E. Wenkebach. *CMG* 5.10.2.1, pp. 1–187.

Epidemics VI. 17A.793–1009. E. Wenkebach. *CMG* 5.10.2.2, pp. 3–351.

Nature of Man. 15.1–173. J. Mewaldt. *CMG* 5.9.1, pp. 3–88.

Regimen in Health. 15.174–223. J. Mewaldt. *CMG* 5.9.1, pp. 89–113.

Regimen in Acute Diseases. 15.418–919. J. Mewaldt. *CMG* 5.9.1, pp. 117–366.

Gellius, Aulus. M. Hertz. *A. Gellii Noctium Atticarum Libri XX*. 2 vols. Berlin: Hertz, 1883, 1885.

Heraclitus. F. Buffière. *Héraclite. Allégories d'Homère*. Paris: Belles Lettres, 1962.

Hermetic Writings. A. D. Nock and A.-J. Festugière. *Corpus Hermeticum*. 4 vols. Paris: Budé, 1945–1954.

Hermogenes. H. Rabe. *Hermogenes Opera*. Leipzig: Teubner, 1913.

Hesiod. H. G. Evelyn-White. *Hesiod: The Homeric Hymns and Homerica*. LCL. London: Heinemann, 1914.

——. F. Solmsen. *Theogonia Opera et dies Scutum*. Oxford: Clarendon Press, 1970.

——. R. Merkelbach and M. L. West. *Fragmenta Hesiodea*. Oxford: Clarendon Press, 1967.

Hippocrates. W. H. S. Jones et al. LCL. 6 vols. London: Heinemann, 1923–1988.

——. W. D. Smith. *Pseudepigraphic Writings*. Studies in Ancient Medicine 2. Leiden: Brill, 1990.

Hippolytus. H. Achelis. *Hippolyts kleinere exegetische und homiletische Schriften. GCS* 1.2. Leipzig: Hinrichs, 1897.

——. *Refutation*. P. Wendland. *Hippolytus Werke* 3: *Refutatio omnium haeresium. GCS* 26. Leipzig: Hinrichs, 1916. M. Marcovich. Hippolytus *Refutatio omnium haeresium*. Patristische Texte und Studien 25. Berlin and New York: De Gruyter, 1988. English translation. F. Legge. *Philosophumena or Refutation of All Heresies*. 2 vols. London: SPCK, 1921.

Homer. T. W. Allen and D. B. Monroe. *Homeri opera*. Oxford: Clarendon Press, 1912–1946. (Vol. 5 contains Pseudo-Homerica.)

Iamblichus. *Life of Pythagoras*. L. Deubner. *Iamblichus De Vita Pythagorica liber*. Leipzig: Teubner, 1937.

——. *Mysteries of Egypt*. E. Des Places. *Les mystères d'Égypte*. Paris: Belles Lettres, 1966.

Irenaeus. A. Rousseau, L. Doutreleau et al. *Irénée de Lyon Contre les Hérésies. SC* 100–101, 152–153, 210–211, 263–264, 294–295. 10 vols. Paris: Du Cerf, 1965–1982.

——. B. Reynders. *Lexique comparé du texte grec et des versions latine, arménienne et syriaque de l'"Adversus haereses" de Saint Irénée*. Louvain: Durbecq, 1954.

——. *Fragments*. W. W. Harvey. *Sancti Irenaei libros quinque adversus Haereses*. 2 vols. Cambridge: Typis Academicis, 1857.

Jerome. *Against Rufinus*. P. Lardet. *CCL* 79. Turnhout: Brepols, 1982. Also in *PL* 23.

——. *Commentary on Daniel*. F. Glorie. *CCL* 75A. Turnhout: Brepols, 1964. Also in *PL* 25.

——. *Commentary on Matthew*. D. Hurst and M. Adriaen. *CCL* 77. Turnhout: Brepols, 1969. Also in *PL* 26.

——. *Commentary on Galatians. PL* 26.

——. *Commentary on Philemon. PL* 26.

——. *Dialogue Against the Pelagians*. C. Moreschini. *CCL* 80. Turnhout: Brepols, 1990. Also in *PL* 23.

——. *Preface on the Pentateuch. PL* 28.

——. *Epistle 54*. I. Hilberg. *CSEL* 54 (1910).

——. *Epistle 120 to Hedibia.* I. Hilberg. *CSEL* 55 (1912).

——. *Epistle 121 to Algasia.* I. Hilberg. *CSEL* 56 (1918).

——. *Famous Men.* C. A. Bernoulli. *Hieronymus und Gennadius. De Viris Inlustribus.* Freiburg and Leipzig: Mohr, 1895.

Julian. W. C. Wright. *The Works of the Emperor Julian.* LCL. 3 vols. New York: Macmillan, Putnam, 1913–1923.

Justin. E. J. Goodspeed. *Die ältesten Apologeten.* Göttingen: Vandenhoeck & Ruprecht, 1914. Reprint. 1984.

Lactantius. S. Brandt. *Divinae Institutiones. CSEL* 19 (1890).

——. H. Kraft and A. Wlosok. *De Ira Dei: Vom Zorne Gottes.* Darmstadt: Gentner, 1957.

Lucian. A. M. Harmon et al. LCL. 8 vols. London: Heinemann, 1913–1967.

Lydus, Iohannes. R. Wünsch. *Ioannis Laurentii Lydi Liber de Mensibus.* Leipzig: Teubner, 1898.

Marcus Aurelius. A. S. L. Farquharson. *The Meditations of the Emperor Marcus Aurelius Antoninus.* 2 vols. Oxford: Clarendon Press, 1944.

Melito. O. Perler. *Méliton de Sardes Sur la Pâque et fragments. SC* 123. Paris: Du Cerf, 1966.

——. S. G. Hall. *Melito of Sardis On Pascha and Fragments.* Oxford Patristic Texts. Oxford: Clarendon Press, 1979.

Olympiodorus. A. Busse. *Olympiodori Prolegomena et In Categorias commentaria. CAG* 12.1. Berlin: Reimer, 1902.

Origen. *Against Celsus.* E. Preuschen. *Origenes Werke* 1–2. *Gegen Celsus, Vom Gebet.* Leipzig: Hinrichs, 1899. *GCS* 2–3. English translation: H. Chadwick. *Origen Contra Celsum.* Cambridge: Cambridge University Press, 1953. Reprint. 1965.

——. *First Principles.* P. Koetschau. *De principiis. GCS* 22. Leipzig: Hinrichs, 1913. H. Crouzel and M. Simonetti. *Origenes: Traité des principes: Commentaire et Fragments.* 5 vols. Paris: Du Cerf, 1978–1984.

——. *Commentary on Matthew* and *Series Commentary on Matthew.* E. Klostermann. *Origenes Matthäuserklärung. GCS* 38, 40. Leipzig: Hinrichs 1933, 1935.

——. *Homilies on Luke.* M. Rauer. *Die Homilien zu Lucas. GCS* 35. Leipzig: Hinrichs, 1930.

——. *Commentary on John.* E. Preuschen. *Der Johanneskommentar.* *GCS* 10. Leipzig: Hinrichs, 1903.

——. *Commentary on Titus. PG* 17.

——. *Homilies on Genesis and Joshua.* W. A. Baehrens. *Origenes Werke* 6: *Homilien zum Hexateuch in Rufins Übersetzung. GCS* 29, 30. 2 vols. Leipzig: Hinrichs, 1920, 1921.

——. *On the Pascha.* O. Guéraud and P. Nautin. *Origène Sur la Pâque.* Paris: Beauchesne, 1979.

——. *Philocalia.* J. A. Robinson. *The Philocalia of Origen.* Cambridge: Cambridge University Press, 1893.

Palaephatus. *Incredible Stories.* N. Festa. *Palaephati Peri Apiston.* Mythographi Graeci 3.2. Leipzig: Teubner, 1902.

Paschal Chronicle. PG 92.

Pausanias. W. H. S. Jones. *Pausanias Description of Greece;* and R. E. Wycherly, Companion Volume. LCL. 5 vols. London: Heinemann, 1918–1935.

Photius. *Library.* R. Henry. *Photius Bibliothèque.* 8 vols. Paris: Belles Lettres, 1959–1977. Also in *PG* 103.

Plato. C. F. Hermann. *Platonis Dialogi.* 6 vols. Leipzig: Teubner, 1874–1880.

Pliny. H. Rackham et al. *Pliny Natural History.* LCL. 10 vols. London: Heinemann, 1938–1962.

Plutarch. B. Perrin. *Plutarch's Lives.* LCL. 11 vols. London: Heinemann, 1914–1926. F. C. Babbitt et al. *Plutarch's Moralia.* LCL. 15 vols. London: Heinemann, 1927–1969.

Porphyry. *Life of Pythagoras.* A. Nauck. *Porphyrii Philosophi Platonici opuscula selecta.* 2d ed. Leipzig: Teubner, 1886. Reprint. Hildesheim: Olms, 1963.

Proclus. E. Diehl. *Procli Diadochi in Platonis Timaeum commentaria.* 3 vols. Leipzig: Teubner, 1903–1906.

Pseudo-Aristeas. L. Mendelssohn and P. Wendland. *Aristeae ad Philocratem epistula.* Leipzig: Teubner, 1900.

Pseudo-Justin. M. Marcovich. *Pseudo-Justinus Cohortatio ad Graecos, De monarchia, Oratio ad Grecos.* Patristische Texte und Studien 32. Berlin and New York: De Gruyter, 1990.

Pseudo-Plutarch. J. F. Kindstrand. [*Plutarchus*] *De Homero*. Leipzig: Teubner, 1990.

Pseudo-Tertullian. A. Kroymann. *Adversus omnes haereses*. *CC* 2.2. Turnhout: Brepols, 1954, 1399–1410.

Ptolemaeus. G. Quispel. *Ptolémée: Lettre à Flora*. *SC* 24. Paris: Du Cerf, 1949.

Rufinus. M. Simonetti. *Tyrannii Rufini opera*. *CCL* 20. Turnhout: Brepols, 1961. Also in *PG* 17.

Seneca. *Epistles*. R. M. Gummere. *Seneca ad Lucilium Epistulae Morales*. LCL. 3 vols. London: Heinemann, 1917–1925.

Sextus Empiricus. R. G. Bury. LCL. 4 vols. (sequence 1, 4, 2, 3). London: Heinemann, 1933–1936, 1949. K. Janáchek. *Indices*. Leipzig: Teubner, 1962.

Simplicius. I. L. Heiberg. *Simplicii in Aristotelis De Caelo commentaria*. *CAG* 7. Berlin: Reimer, 1893.

———. C. Kalbfleisch. *Simplicii in Aristotelis Categorias commentaria*. *CAG* 8. Berlin: Reimer, 1907.

Soranus. J. Ilberg. *Soranus*. *CMG* 4. Leipzig and Berlin: Teubner, 1927.

Strabo. H. L. Jones. LCL. 8 vols. London: Heinemann, 1917–1932.

Strato. F. Wehrli. *Die Schule des Aristoteles*. Vol. 5. 8 vols. Basel: Schwabe, 1944–1959. New ed., 1967ff.

Tatian. M. Whittaker. *Tatian Oratio ad Graecos and Fragments*. Oxford Patristic Texts. Oxford: Clarendon Press, 1982 (with pages and lines of Schwartz's edition).

Tertullian. E. Dekkers et al. *Tertulliani opera*. *CCL* 1. 2 vols. Turnhout: Brepols, 1954.

———. J. H. Waszink. *Tertullian De Anima*. Amsterdam: Meulenhoff, 1947.

Theodoret. *Heresies*. *PG* 83.

———. *Questions on Genesis*. *PG* 90.

Theon. L. Spengel. *Rhetores Graeci*, 2. Leipzig: Teubner, 1854.

Theophilus of Antioch. R. M. Grant. *Theophilus of Antioch Ad Autolycum*. Oxford Patristic Texts. Oxford: Clarendon Press, 1970.

2. Modern Authors

Alexandre, M. *Le commencement du livre Génèse I–IV.* Christianisme Antique 3. Paris: Beauchesne, 1988.

Alline, H. *Histoire du texte de Platon.* Bibliothèque de l'École des Hautes Études 218. 1915. Reprint. Paris: Champion, 1984.

Anonymous. "Der orphische Papyrus von Derveni." *Zeitschrift für Papyrologie und Epigraphik* 47 (1982): 1–12 (after p. 300).

Arndt, W. F., and F. W. Gingrich, after W. Bauer. *A Greek-English Lexicon of the New Testament.* 2d ed. Chicago: University of Chicago Press, 1979.

Arnim, H. von. *Stoicorum Veterum Fragmenta.* 4 vols. Leipzig: Teubner, 1905–1924.

Aune, D. E. *Prophecy in Early Christianity and the Mediterranean World.* Grand Rapids: Eerdmans, 1983.

Bardy, G. "Faux et fraudes littéraires dans l'antiquité chrétienne." *Revue d'histoire ecclésiastique* 32 (1936): 5–23, 275–302. Included in N. Brox, ed. *Pseudepigraphie in der heidnischen und jüdisch-christlichen Antike.* Darmstadt: Wissenschaftliche Buchgesellschaft, 1977.

——. "L'inspiration des pères de l'Église." *Recherches de science religieuse* 40 (1952): 7–26.

Barigazzi, A. *Favorino di Arelate Opere.* Florence: Le Monnier, 1966.

Barnes, T. D. *Tertullian.* Oxford: Clarendon Press, 1971.

Bauer, W. *Das Leben Jesu im Zeitalter der neutestamentlichen Apokryphen.* Tübingen: Mohr, 1909.

——. *Orthodoxy and Heresy in Earliest Christianity.* (1934.) English translation: Philadelphia: Fortress, 1970.

Berchman, R. M. *From Philo to Origen.* Brown Judaic Studies 69. Providence, R.I.: Brown University Press, 1984.

Bertrand, D. A. "L'argumentation scripturaire de Théodote le Corroyeur (Epiphane, Panarion 54)." In *Lectures anciennes de la Bible,* 153–168. Cahiers de Biblia Patristica 1. Strasbourg: Centre d'Analyse et de Documentation Patristiques, 1987.

Beutler, R. "Porphyrius." *RE* 22 (1953): 275–313.

Bickerman, E. J. *Chronology of the Ancient World.* Rev. ed. London: Thames & Hudson, 1980.

Blass, F., and A. Debrunner. *A Greek Grammar of the New Testament.* Translated by R. W. Funk. Chicago: University of Chicago Press, 1961.

Boatwright, M. T. *Hadrian and the City of Rome.* Princeton: Princeton University Press, 1987.

Bröcker, L. O. "Die Methoden Galens in der literarischen Kritik." *Rheinisches Museum* 40 (1885): 415–438.

Brown, T. S. "Euhemerus and the Historians." *HTR* 39 (1946): 259–274.

Brox, N. "Zum Problemstand in der Erforschung der altchristlichen Pseudepigraphie." *Kairos* 15 (1973): 10–23.

——. *Falsche Verfasserangaben. Zur Erklärung der frühchristlichen Pseudepigraphie.* Stuttgart: KBW. 1975.

——, ed. *Pseudepigraphie in der heidnischen und jüdisch-christlichen Antike.* Darmstadt: Wissenschaftliche Buchgesellschaft, 1977.

Cadbury, H. J. *The Making of Luke-Acts.* New York: Macmillan, 1927.

——. Review of J. Knox. *Marcion and the New Testament. JBL* 62 (1943): 123–127.

Campenhausen, H. von. *Polykarp von Smyrna und die Pastoralbriefe. Sitzungsberichte der Heidelberger Akademie der Wissenschaften, Philosophisch-historische Klasse,* no. 2, 1951.

Chadwick, H. "Origen, Celsus and the Resurrection of the Body." *HTR* 41 (1948): 83–102.

Clark, E. A. *Clement's Use of Aristotle.* Lewiston, N.Y.: Mellen, 1977.

Colson, F. H. "Two Examples of Literary and Historical Criticism in the Fathers." *JTS* 25 (1923–1924): 364–377.

Connolly, R. H. *Didascalia Apostolorum.* Oxford: Clarendon Press, 1929.

Courcelle, P. *Les lettres grecques en occident de Macrobe à Cassiodore.* 2d ed. Paris: Boccard, 1948.

Crönert, W. *Kolotes und Menedemos.* Studien zur Paläographie und Papyruskunde 6, ed. C. Wessely. Leipzig: Avenarius, 1906.

Curry, C. "The Theogony of Theophilus." *VC* 42 (1988): 318–326.

Daniélou, J. *Origène.* Paris: Table Ronde, 1948.

——. *Sacramentum Futuri.* Paris: Beauchesne, 1950.

——. *Théologie du Judéo-Christianisme.* Tournai: Desclée, 1958.

———. *Message évangélique et culture hellénistique.* Louvain: Desclée, 1961.

Desjardins, M. "Bauer and Beyond: On Recent Scholarly Discussions of *Hairesis* in the Early Christian Era." *The Second Century* 8 (1991): 68–82.

Diehl, E. "Thessalos (5)." *RE* 6A (1936): 165–168.

Diels, H. *Doxographi Graeci.* 1879. Reprint. Berlin: De Gruyter, 1929.

———. "Über die Excerpte von Menons Iatrika in dem Londoner Papyrus 137." *Hermes* 28 (1893): 407–435.

——— and W. Kranz. *Die Fragmente der Vorsokratiker.* 3 vols. 6th ed. Berlin: Weidmann, 1952.

Diller, H. "Zur Hippokratesauffassung des Galen." *Hermes* 68 (1933): 167–181.

Drijvers, H. J. W. "Adam and the True Prophet in the Pseudo-Clementines." In *Loyalitätskonflikte in der Religionsgeschichte. Festschrift für Carsten Colpe,* 314–323. Würzburg: Königshausen & Neumann, 1990.

Edelstein, L. "Nachträge (Hippokrates)." *RE* Suppl. 6 (1935): 1290–1345.

———. "Hippocrates (2)." *Oxford Classical Dictionary.* 2d ed. Oxford: Clarendon Press, 1970.

Eissfeldt, O. *Ras Schamra und Sanchunjaton.* Beiträge zur Religionsgeschichte des Altertums 4. Halle: Niemeyer, 1939.

Erbse, H. *Scholia Graeca in Homeri Iliadem (scholia vetera).* 7 vols. Berlin: De Gruyter, 1969–1988. Vol. 1, 1969.

Fowden, G. *The Egyptian Hermes.* Cambridge: Cambridge University Press, 1986.

Franco, R. "Filosofía griega y Cristianismo antigue: opiniones recientes." In *Plēroma ... Salus carnis ... Antonio Orbe, S.J.,* edited by E. Romero-Pose, 257–280. Santiago de Compostela, 1990.

Freedman, H. *Midrash Rabbah, Genesis* 1. 1939. London: Soncino 3d ed., 1983.

Goodenough, E. R. "A Jewish-Gnostic Amulet of the Roman Period." *Greek and Byzantine Studies* 1 (1958): 71–80.

Grafton, A. *Forgers and Critics: Creativity and Duplicity in Western Scholarship.* Princeton: Princeton University Press, 1990.

Grant, R. M. "Historical Criticism in the Ancient Church." *Journal of Religion* 25 (1946): 183–196.

———. *Second-Century Christianity.* London: SPCK, 1946.

———. *The Letter and the Spirit.* London: SPCK, 1957.

———. "The Appeal to the Early Fathers." *JTS* 11 (1960): 13–24 = *After the New Testament.* Philadelphia: Fortress Press, 1967, 20–34.

———. *The Earliest Lives of Jesus.* London: SPCK, 1961.

———. *The Formation of the New Testament.* London: Hutchinson, 1965.

———. "Gnostics and the Inspiration of the Old Testament." In *Scripture in History and Theology: Essays in Honor of J. Coert Rylaarsdam,* edited by A. L. Merrill and T. W. Overholt, 269–277. Pittsburgh: Pickwick, 1977.

———. "Paul, Galen, and Origen." *JTS* 34 (1983): 533–536.

———. "Marcion and the Critical Method." In *From Jesus to Paul: Studies in Honour of Francis Wright Beare,* edited by P. Richardson and J. C. Hurd, 207–215. Waterloo, Ontario: Wilfrid Laurier University Press, 1984.

———. *Greek Apologists of the Second Century.* Philadelphia: Westminster Press, 1988.

——— and D. Tracy. *A Short History of the Interpretation of the Bible.* 2d (3d) ed. Philadelphia: Fortress Press, 1985.

Grensemann, H. "Der Arzt Polybos als Verfasser hippokratischer Schriften." *Abhandlungen der Geistes- und Sozialwissenschaftlichen Klasse der Akademie der Wissenschaften und der Literatur in Mainz,* 1968, 2, 53–95.

———. "Polybos 8." *RE* Suppl. 14 (1974): 428-436.

Gudeman, A. "Literary Frauds Among the Greeks." In *Classical Studies in Honour of Henry Drisler,* 52–74. New York: Macmillan, 1894. Included in *Pseudepigraphie in der heidnischen und jüdisch-christlichen Antike,* edited by N. Brox. Darmstadt: Wissenschaftliche Buchgesellschaft, 1977.

———. "Literary Frauds Among the Romans." *Transactions of the American Philological Association* 25 (1894): 140–164.

———. *Grundriss der Geschichte der klassischen Philologie.* 2d ed. Leipzig and Berlin: Teubner, 1909.

Gutwenger, E. "The Anti-Marcionite Prologues." *Theological Studies* 7 (1946): 393–409.

Hahneman, M. "The Muratorian Fragment and the Development of the Canon." D. Phil. dissertation, Oxford University, 1987.

Harl, M., and N. de Lange. *Origène Philocalie, 1–20 Sur les Écritures. La Lettre à Africanus sur l'histoire de Suzanne. SC* 302. Paris: Du Cerf, 1983.

Harnack, A. von. *Der kirchengeschichtliche Ertrag der exegetischen Arbeiten des Origenes.* TU 42,3–4. Leipzig: Hinrichs, 1918–1919.

———. *Marcion: das Evangelium vom fremden Gott.* 2d ed., TU 45. Leipzig: Hinrichs, 1924.

Harrison, P. N. *Polycarp's Two Epistles to the Philippians.* Cambridge: Cambridge University Press, 1936.

Hengel, M. The Johannine Question. London: SCM, 1989.

Hoffman, R. J. *Marcion: On the Restitution of Christianity.* AAR Series 46. Chico, Calif.: Scholars Press, 1984.

Hulley, K. K. "Principles of Textual Criticism Known to St. Jerome." *Harvard Studies in Classical Philology* 55 (1944): 87–109.

Ilberg, J. "Die Hippokratesausgaben des Artemidoros Kapiton und Dioskurides." *Rheinisches Museum* 45 (1890): 111–137.

———. "Über die Schriftstellerei des Klaudios Galenos." *Rheinisches Museum* 44 (1889): 307–339; 47 (1892): 489–514; 51 (1896): 165–196; Nachtrag, 466.

Immisch, O. *Philologische Studien zu Plato.* 1: *Axiochus.* 2: *De recensionibus Platonicae praesidiis atque rationibus.* Leipzig: Teubner, 1896, 1903.

Jaeger, Werner. *Aristotle.* English translation. Oxford: Clarendon Press, 1947.

Joosten, J. "West Aramaic Elements in the Old Syriac and Peshitta Gospels." *JBL* 110 (1991): 271–289.

Jouanna, J. "Le médicin Polybe est-il l'auteur de plusieurs ouvrages de la collection hippocratique?" *Revue des Études Grecques* 82 (1969): 552–562.

Junod, E. "Les attitudes d'Apelles, disciple de Marcion, à l'égard de l'Ancien Testament." *Augustinianum* 22 (1982): 113–133.

Kapsomenos, S. G. "Der Papyrus von Derveni." *Gnomon* 35 (1963): 222–223.

Kelly, J. N. D. *Jerome: His Life, Writings, and Controversies.* New York: Harper & Row, 1975.

Kern, O. *Orphicorum Fragmenta.* Berlin: Weidmann, 1922.

Kettler, F.-H. "Funktion und Tragweite der historischen Kritik des Origenes an den Evangelien." *Kairos* 15 (1973): 36–49.

Kinkel, G. *Epicorum Graecorum Fragmenta.* Leipzig: Teubner, 1877.

Knox, J. *Marcion and the New Testament.* Chicago: University of Chicago Press, 1942. Reprint. New York: AMS, 1980.

Koester, H. *Synoptische Überlieferungen bei den apostolischen Vätern.* TU 65. Berlin: Akademie, 1957.

———. "The Text of the Synoptic Gospels in the Second Century." In *Gospel Traditions in the Second Century,* edited by W. L. Petersen, 26–35. Notre Dame, Ind.: Notre Dame University Press, 1989.

———. *Ancient Christian Gospels: Their History and Development.* London: SCM, 1990.

Kohl, J. W. *De chorizontibus.* Darmstadt: Bender, 1917. Fragments and commentary.

———. "Die homerische Frage der Chorizonten." *Neue Jahrbücher* 47 (1921): 198–214.

Kroll, W. "Randbemerkungen XII." *Rheinisches Museum* 70 (1915): 607–610.

Lammert, F. *De Hieronymo Donati discipulo.* Commentationes philologae Ienenses 9.2, 1912.

Lange, N. de. *Origen and the Jews.* Cambridge: Cambridge University Press, 1976.

Lawlor, H. J., and J. E. L. Oulton. *Eusebius.* 2 vols. London: SPCK, 1928.

Lazatti, G. *L'Aristotele perduto e gli scrittori cristiani.* Milan: Vita e Pensiero, 1938.

Le Boulluec, A. *La notion d'hérésie dans la littérature grecque IIe–IIIe siècles.* 2 vols. Paris: Études Augustiniennes, 1985.

Lehrs, K. *De Aristarchi studiis Homericis.* Leipzig: Teubner, 1882. Reprint. Hildesheim: Olms, 1964.

Lilla, S. R. C. *Clement of Alexandria*. London: Oxford University Press, 1971.

Lloyd, G. E. R. *Greek Science After Aristotle*. New York: Norton, 1973.

———. "The Hippocratic Question." *Classical Quarterly* 69, n.s. 25 (1975): 171-192 = G. E. R. Lloyd. *Methods and Problems in Greek Science*, 199–223; introduction, 194–198. Cambridge: Cambridge University Press, 1991.

———. *The Revolutions of Wisdom: Studies in the Claims and Practice of Ancient Greek Science*. Berkeley and Los Angeles: University of California Press, 1987.

———. *Methods and Problems in Greek Science*. Cambridge: Cambridge University Press, 1991.

Lucchesi, E. *L'Usage de Philon dans l'oeuvre exégétique de saint Ambroise*. Leiden: Brill, 1977.

Ludwich, A. *Aristarchs homerische Textkritik*. Leipzig: Teubner, 1884.

MacDonald, W. L. *The Pantheon*. Cambridge, Mass.: Harvard University Press, 1976.

Marmorstein, A. *The Old Rabbinic Doctrine of God*, 1. London: Oxford University Press, 1927.

Mates, B. *Stoic Logic*. Berkeley: University of California Press, 1961.

Mau, J. *Galen: Einführung in die Logik*. Berlin: Akademie, 1960.

McGuire, A. "Virginity and Subversion: Norea Against the Powers in the HA," In *Images of the Feminine in Gnosticism*, edited by K. L. King, 239–258. Philadelphia: Fortress Press, 1988.

Meade, D. G. *Pseudonymity and Canon: An Investigation Into the Relation of Authorship and Authority in Jewish and Earliest Christian Tradition*. Tübingen: Mohr, 1986.

Mensching, E. *Favorinus von Arelate* 1. Texte und Kommentare 3. Berlin: De Gruyter, 1963.

Merkelbach, R., and M. L. West. *Fragmenta Hesiodea*. Oxford: Clarendon Press, 1967.

Metzger, B. M. "Explicit References in the Works of Origen to Variant Readings in New Testament Manuscripts." In *Biblical and Patristic Studies in Memory of R. P. Casey*, edited by J. N. Birdsall and R. W. Thomson, 78–95. Freiburg: Herder, 1963.

———. "Literary Forgeries and Canonical Pseudepigrapha." *JBL* 91 (1972): 3–24.

Mewaldt, J. "Galenos über echte und unechte Hippocratica." *Hermes* 44 (1909): 111–134.

———. "Galenos," *RE* 7 (1910): 578–591.

Moraux, P. *Galien de Pergame: Souvenirs d'un médecin.* Paris: Belles Lettres, 1985.

Mueller, I. "An Introduction to Stoic Logic." In *The Stoics*, edited by J. M. Rist, 1–26. Berkeley and Los Angeles: University of California Press, 1978.

Müller, August. *Die griechischen Philosophen in der arabischen Überlieferung.* Halle: Waisenhaus, 1873.

Müller, I. von. "Galen als Philologe." *Verhandlungen der 41. Versammlung deutscher Philologen und Schulmänner in München*, 80–91. Leipzig: Teubner, 1892.

———. "Über Galens Werk vom wissenschaftlichen Beweis." *Abhandlungen der philosophischen Classe der königlich bayerischen Akademie der Wissenschaften* 20 (1897): 403–478.

Nash, E. *Pictorial Dictionary of Ancient Rome.* 2d ed. New York and Washington: Praeger, 1962.

Nautin, P. *Lettres et écrivains chrétiens des IIe et IIIe siècles.* Paris: Du Cerf, 1961.

———. *Origène, Sa vie et son oeuvre.* Paris: Beauchesne, 1977.

Neuschäfer, B. *Origenes als Philologe.* 2 vols. Schweizerische Beiträge zur Altertumswissenschaft 18, 1–2. Basel: Reinhardt, 1987.

Nock, A. D. *Essays on Religion and the Ancient World.* Edited by Z. Stewart. 2 vols. Oxford: Clarendon Press, 1972.

Norden, E. *Die antike Kunstprosa.* Leipzig: Teubner, 1898.

Norsa, M. "Elenco di opere letterarie." *Aegyptus* 2 (1921): 17–20.

Oliver, J. H. *The Ruling Power. Transactions of the American Philosophical Society* 43, 4, 1953.

Oppel, H. 1937. *KANON. Zur Bedeutungsgeschichte des Wortes und seiner lateinischen Entsprechungen regula-norma. Philologus* Suppl. 30, Heft 4 (1937).

Osborn, E. "Logique et exégèse chez Clément d'Alexandrie." In *Lectures anciennes de la Bible*, 169–190. Cahiers de Biblia Patristica 1. Strasbourg: Centre d'Analyse et de Documentation Patristiques, 1987.

Pack, R. A. *The Greek and Latin Papyri from Graeco-Roman Egypt*. 2d ed. Ann Arbor, Mich.: University of Michigan Press, 1967.

Pearson, B. A. "Revisiting Norea." In *Images of the Feminine in Gnosticism*, edited by K. L. King, 265–275. Philadelphia: Fortress Press, 1988.

———. *Gnosticism, Judaism, and Egyptian Christianity*. Minneapolis: Fortress Press, 1990.

Pease, A. S. "Medical Allusions in the Works of St. Jerome." *Harvard Studies in Classical Philology* 25 (1914): 73–86.

———. *M. Tulli Ciceronis De Natura Deorum*. 2 vols. Cambridge, Mass.: Harvard University Press, 1955, 1958.

Pecorella, G. B. *Dionisio Trace, Technē grammatikē*. Bologna: Capelli, 1962.

Pépin, J. "Hermeneutik." *RAC* 14 (1988): 757–758.

Petersen, W. L., ed. *Gospel Traditions in the Second Century*. Notre Dame, Ind.: University of Notre Dame Press, 1989.

———. "Tatian's Diatessaron." In H. Koester, *Ancient Christian Gospels: Their History and Development*, 403–430. London: SCM, 1990.

Pfeiffer, R. *History of Classical Scholarship from the Beginnings to the End of the Hellenistic Age*. Oxford: Clarendon Press, 1968.

Philippson, R. "Die Quelle der epikureischen Götterlehre in Ciceros erstem Buch de Natura Deorum." *Symbolae Osloenses* 19 (1939): 15–40.

Potter. *See* Galen.

Powell, J. U., and E. A. Barber. *New Chapters in the History of Greek Literature*. Second Series. Oxford: Clarendon Press, 1929.

Rabe, H. "Die Liste griechischer Profanschriftsteller." *Rheinisches Museum* 65 (1910): 329–344.

Radermacher, L. "Kanon." *RE* 10 (1919): 1873–1878.

Reichardt, W. *Die Briefe des Sextus Julius Africanus an Aristides und Origenes*. TU 34,3. Leipzig: Hinrichs, 1909.

Reid, J. S. *M. Tulli Ciceronis Academica*. London: Macmillan 1885.

Reynders, B. "La polémique de saint Irénée" *Recherches de théologie ancienne et médiévale* 7 (1935): 5–27.

Richter, W. "Zoologie." *Der Kleine Pauly* 5 (1975): 1556–1557.

Rist, J. M. "The Importance of Stoic Logic in the *Contra Celsum*." In *Neoplatonism and Early Christian Thought, Essays in Honour of A. H. Armstrong*, edited by H. J. Blumenthal and R. A. Markus, 64–78. London: Variorum, 1981.

Roberts, C. H. *Greek Literary Hands 350 B.C.–A D. 400.* Oxford: Clarendon Press, 1955.

Robinson, J. M., ed. *The Nag Hammadi Library in English.* 3d ed. San Francisco: Harper & Row, 1988.

Rose, H. J. *A Handbook of Greek Mythology.* New York: Dutton, 1929.

Ross, W. D. *Aristotelis Fragmenta Selecta.* Oxford: Clarendon Press, 1955.

Rutherford, W. G. *A Chapter in the History of Annotation = Scholia Aristophanica* 3. London: Macmillan, 1905.

Sadurska, A. *Les Tables Iliaques.* Centre d'archéologie de l'Académie polonaise des sciences. Warsaw: Panstwowe Wydawnictwo Naukowe, 1964.

Sagnard, F. M. *Saint Irénée et la gnose valentinienne.* Paris: Vrin 1947.

———. *Clément d'Alexandrie: Extraits de Théodote.* Paris: Du Cerf, 1949.

Savon, H. *Saint Ambroise devant l'exégèse de Philon le Juif.* Paris: Études Augustiniennes, 1977.

Schoedel, W. R. *Polycarp, Martyrdom of Polycarp, Fragments of Papias.* Camden, N. J.: Nelson, 1967.

Schöne, H. "Ein Einbruch der antiken Logik und Textkritik in die altchristliche Theologie." In *Pisciculi . . . Franz Josef Doelger*, edited by T. Klauser and A. Rücker, 252–265. Münster: Aschendorff, 1939.

Schoeps, H. J. *Theologie und Geschichte des Judenchristentums.* Tübingen: Mohr, 1949.

Schwartz, J. *Pseudo-Hesiodea: Recherches sur la composition, la diffusion et la disparition ancienne d'oeuvres attribuées à Hésiode.* Leiden: Brill, 1960.

Siegfried, C. *Philo von Alexandria.* Jena: Dufft, 1875.

Skarsaune, O. *The Proof from Prophecy. A Study in Justin Martyr's Proof-Text Tradition.* Supplements to Novum Testamentum 56. Leiden: Brill, 1987.

Smith, M. *Palestinian Parties and Politics That Shaped the Old Testament.* New York: Columbia University Press, 1971.

———. *Clement of Alexandria and a Secret Gospel of Mark.* Cambridge, Mass.: Harvard University Press, 1973.

Smith, W. D. *The Hippocratic Tradition.* Ithaca, New York: Cornell University Press, 1979.

Solmsen, F. "Early Christian Interest in the Theory of Demonstration." In *Romanitas et Christianitas . . . J. H. Waszink,* edited by W. den Boer et al., 281-291. Amsterdam and London: North-Holland, 1973.

Speyer, W. *Die literarische Fälschung im heidnischen und christlichen Altertum. Ein Versuch ihrer Deutung.* Munich: Beck, 1971.

Staden, H. von. "Hairesis and Heresy: The Case of the *haireseis iatrikai.*" In *Jewish and Christian Self-Definition,* vol. 3: *Self-Definition in the Greco-Roman World,* edited by B. F. Meyer and E. P. Sanders, 76–100. Philadelphia: Fortress Press, 1983.

Stakelum, J. W. *Galen and the Logic of Propositions.* Rome: Angelicum, 1940.

Stein, E. "Alttestamentliche Bibelkritik in der späthellenistischen Literatur." *Collectanea Theologica Societatis Theologorum Polonorum* 16 (1935): 3–48.

Strecker, G. *Das Judenchristentum in den Pseudoklementinen.* TU 70. Berlin: Akademie, 1958.

Strohmaier, G. "Übersehenes zur Biographie Lukians." *Philologus* 120 (1976): 117–122.

Sundberg, A. C., Jr. *The Old Testament of the Early Church.* Harvard Theological Studies 20. Cambridge, Mass.: Harvard University Press, 1964.

———. "Canon Muratori: A Fourth-Century List." *HTR* 66 (1973): 1–41.

Thee, F. C. R. *Julius Africanus and the Early Christian View of Magic.* Hermeneutische Untersuchungen zur Theologie 19. Tübingen: Mohr, 1984.

Thomas, I. *Selections Illustrating the History of Greek Mathematics.* 2 vols. LCL. Cambridge, Mass.: Harvard University Press, 1951

Troiani, L. *L'opera storiografica di Filone da Byblos*. Pisa: Libreria Goliardica, 1974.

Usener, H. *Epicurea*. Leipzig: Teubner, 1887.

Usher, S. *Dionysius of Halicarnassus Critical Essays*, LCL 2. Cambridge, Mass.: Harvard University Press, 1985.

Van den Hoek, A. *Clement of Alexandria and His Use of Philo in the Stromateis*. Leiden: Brill, 1988.

——. "How Alexandrian Was Clement of Alexandria?" *Heythrop Journal* 31 (1990): 179–194.

Van der Waerden, B. L. "Pythagoras (Die Schriften und Fragmente)." *RE* Suppl. 10 (1965): 843–864.

Van Unnik, W. C. "De la règle *Méte prostheinai méte aphelein* dans l'histoire du canon." *VC* 3 (1949): 1–36.

Van Winden, J. C. M. *An Early Christian Philosopher*. Leiden: Brill, 1971.

Walzer, R. *Aristotelis Dialogorum Fragmenta*. Florence: Sansoni, 1934.

——. "Galens Schrift 'Über die Siebenmonatskinder.'" *Rivista degli Studi orientali* 15 (1935): 323–357.

——. *Galen on Jews and Christians*. London: Oxford University Press, 1949.

Wehrli, F. *Die Schule des Aristoteles* 4. *Demetrius von Phaleron*. 2d ed. Basel and Stuttgart: Schwabe, 1968.

Weiss, H. "The Sabbath in the Fourth Gospel." *JBL* 110 (1991): 311–321.

Weiss, J. *Der erste Korintherbrief*. Göttingen: Vandenhoek & Ruprecht, 1910.

Wilamowitz, U. von. *Platon* 2. 2d ed. Berlin: Weidmann, 1920.

——. "Lesefrüchte CXCIII." *Hermes* 60 (1925): 281.

Wilken, R. L. "The Homeric Cento in Irenaeus 'Adversus Haereses' I,9,4." *VC* 21 (1967): 25–33.

Williams, D. S. "Reconsidering Marcion's Gospel." *JBL* 108 (1989): 477–496.

Willis, W. H. "Greek Literary Papyri from Egypt and the Classical Canon." *Harvard Library Bulletin* 112 (1958): 5–34.

Wilson, N. C. "An Aristarchean Maxim." *Classical Review* 21 (1971): 172.

Windisch, H. *Der zweite Korintherbrief*. Göttingen: Vandenhoeck & Ruprecht, 1924.

Wolfson, H. A. *Philo*. 2 vols. Cambridge, Mass.: Harvard University Press, 1947.

Ziegler, K. "Orphische Dichtung." *RE* 18 (1942): 1321–1417.

Index of Biblical Passages

Index of Authors, Books, and Subjects